Outdoor Play
"Fun 4 Seniors"
Volume III

By

Stephen L. Priest

Also by Stephen L. Priest

- *Outdoor Play "Fun 4 4 Seasons" Volume II*
  978-0-9850384-3-4

- *Outdoor Play "Fun 4 4 Seasons" Volume I*
  978-0-985-03840-3

- *Outdoor Enthusiast: Never Say, "I Wish I Had ..."*
  ISBN – 1440438404

- *Outdoor Enthusiast: Never Say, "I wish I had ..." e-book*
  ISBN – 13: 9780615225050

- *Avoiding Injuries: Tips from Master Outdoorsman Steve Priest*
  ISBN 9781440438455

Cover Design by LoonsNest.biz

Outdoor Play
"Fun 4 Seniors"
Volume III

© 2020 by Stephen L. Priest

www.outdoorsteve.com

ISBN-13: 978-0-9850384-5-8

Preface

Outdoor Play "Fun 4 Seniors" Volume III

By

Stephen L. Priest

The title, **Outdoor Play Fun 4 Seniors,** comes because I qualify as a "senior" in any sense of the word. I respond to Grampa, Papa, Dad, Steve, Outdoor Steve, and super senior. Recently, I have become immersed in an organization called **Outdoor Recreation for Seniors (ORFS)**.

Outdoor Play Fun 4 Seniors is compiled from my blog posts in **https://outdooradventurers.blogspot.com**.

Indeed, the people of each story cover the spectrum of teenagers through super seniors. Each outdoor enthusiast contributed significantly to my **Never to say, "I wish I had ..."** story.

This mission of **Outdoor Play "Fun 4 Seniors,"** is a continuation of my prior books to inspire and encourage families and individuals to make the outdoors a key component of their daily life. **Outdoor Play "Fun 4 4 Seasons" Volume's i & ii** and **Outdoor Enthusiast: Never Say, "I wish I had ....",** all focus on the insights and healthy lifestyle of outdoor activities. Their stories and lessons make you want to put on your backpack, find your running shoes, borrow a canoe or kayak from the neighbor, tune-up the bike, and get ready for cross country skiing!

Each outdoor story in **Outdoor Play "Fun 4 Seniors,"** is a full short read with tips, details on preparation, pictures, maps, and references. The videos make the stories "come alive."

Some folks call outdoor experiences "play." If "play" is defined as the choice made to take a course of action based on the rewards of participation and getting a perspective that can only come from 'doing,' then indeed outdoor adventures are play. Many seniors and children do not play enough.

Outdoor exercise has proven to make you healthier both physically and mentally. Your mind gets relieved of personal and business stress, and the result is a positive outlook on life. Your body gets stronger with movement and presence and the breathing of fresh air.

Challenge friends and family to discover new places to visit. Work together as a team sharing trip planning, preparation and camp duties. The camaraderie of these outdoor experiences is most inspiring … and bonds family and friends. Family outdoor adventures bring people together for unforgettable outdoor adventures. Make your outdoor exploration a lifetime commitment.

With each outing, I brought my camera, and when the time came to select pictures for the book, the memories they conveyed made it difficult to limit myself to only a few.

The beginning of **Outdoor Play "Fun 4 Seniors Volume III** offers a process to be an outdoor enthusiast for those who hesitate because of age, limited time, family commitments, or knowledge of an activity. We start with **Bucket List Accomplishments** to give the reader a sense of "I can do that."

I follow this section with **Warning Signs, Survival, Rescue and First Aid**. I place this section here to prepare you for what it takes to have a safe and fun outdoor adventure. I share with my readers my experience with avoiding dangerous situations as well as various outdoors/sports injuries and treatment I have experienced.

Next follows **Outdoor Recreation for Seniors (ORFS)**. This ORFS group meets every Tuesday year-round at 10 am. In the summer we kayak/canoe, swim and hike. In the fall and spring we hike, and in the winter, we snowshoe and cross-country ski. Membership is limited "to the young of ages between 50 and 90". The stories in this section are culled from my blog posts

The middle sections divide into the seasons of the year, **Spring, Summer, Fall** and **Winter** with glimpses of Steve's outdoor undertakings. These sections are from the last three years of Steve's blog – **Outdoor Adventurers**. Steve provides a peek into outdoor places and Internet sites to assist you in your research, expectations, and preparation.

The next to last section, **Places to Play in Northern New England**, provides web references to local activities and clubs to join as incentives to learn and participate – if indeed you need these supports.

The last section, **The Beginning**, is my story of how I went from a couch potato to an outdoor enthusiast.

"Everyone must do something. I believe I will go outdoors with family and friends" S. Priest

Dedication

"The best way to love your children, is to love their Mother."
- Harold L. Priest

Acknowledgments

My wife Cathy has been steadfast in her encouragement of my daily outdoor commitment. Amongst many of our outdoor activities, Cathy and I have swum, hiked, camped, paddled, walked, golfed, and run together. She has been my support team throughout my life. Some call her Nana, others Cathy, and I call her "My Love."

My sons Tim and Shaun, and friends John Kerrigan, Dundee Nestler, Paul Nestler, Nichols Nestler, Joe Ryan, Lennie Carroll, Steve Cullinane, Dave Masison, Dick Satter, George Potter, Betty Parsons, and Michael Dionian have been my consistent outdoor enthusiast partners. Shaun, Tim, Stephen Liu, Kathryn Coombs, James Harris, and my cousin Linwood Parsons have been my confidants and proofreaders throughout the preparation of this book.

My faithful advocate, Jefferson Nunn, and my web designer, Benee Garcia, have always been behind the scenes supporters for all my outdoor books.

My outdoor enthusiast friends encouraged me to go to the woods, lakes, and rivers of northern New Hampshire, and before we realized it, we had regular outdoor excursions. My cousin Linwood took us to the Allagash Wilderness Waterway in Maine – three times in fact! Other friends heard our wilderness stories and read my Outdoor Enthusiast blog, and soon we had yearly outdoor commitments.

Adventures with my wife and our two adult sons and their family are central to this book.

Get outdoors and be excited for your health, friendship, and a lifetime of exploration and learning.

Contents

Bucket List

Keep close to Nature's heart... and break clear away, once in a while, and climb a mountain or spend a week in the woods. Wash your spirit clean. – John Muir

Why place **Bucket List** at the beginning of this book? Because this book is to motivate individuals and families never to *say, "I wish I had spent more time in the outdoors"*. What better way to stimulate than to start with the excitement learned from accomplishing an outdoor trip you have heard about but cannot visualize how to do it.

Read these bucket list stories, then consider **"How to be an Outdoor Enthusiast"**.

Knife Edge Trail to Baxter Peak at Northern Terminus of Appalachian Trail

Six friends planned a long day of hiking, only to find a day and evening of climbing. The plan seemed relatively simple:

1. **Hike to Baxter Peak, the northern terminus of the 2,162 mile Appalachian Trail (AT)** [1].
2. **Cross the fabled 1.1 mile Knife Edge Trail.**
3. **Hike five miles on the AT starting at its northern terminus, Baxter Peak.**

The challenges of the Knife Edge and Mt Katahdin were achieved through endurance and teamwork. Below are comments, maps, pictures, and videos of our climb. Our accomplishments were both physically and mentally demanding. I am incredibly proud of my fellow adventurers, and how we worked together for this triumph.

---

[1] The precise length of the Appalachian Trail changes over time as sections are modified or rerouted.

Mount Katahdin is the highest mountain in Maine at 5,269 feet. Named Katahdin by the Penobscot Indians, the term means "The Greatest Mountain." It is part of the Appalachian Mountain range in Baxter State Park. Baxter State Park is a wilderness area permanently preserved as a state park, located in Piscataquis County in north-central Maine. It covers 327 square miles.

The Knife Edge was the highlight of our trip, but the descent from Pamola Peak was nearly as challenging as we had to use technical rock-climbing skills.

Figure 1 - Baxter Peak – Northern Terminus of AT

Our trip started at Roaring Brook campground on the Chimney Pond Trail at 6:45 am. We arrived at Chimney Pond Campground after a 2 hr 45-minute hike. From the Chimney Pond, we took Dudley Trail to Pamola Peak. We had to do a 40 foot straight down descent grabbing cracks in the granite rocks while seeking spots for footholds.

That was immediately followed by climbing straight up 40-feet to Chimney Peak. Admittedly, this 80-foot traverse was the most challenging section for this author. Once atop Chimney Peak we climbed and scooted the 1.1-mile Knife Edge Trail. This brought us to South Peak, then to the summit, Baxter Peak.

Figure 2 - The Knife Edge Trail

Our 15-hour trip was an extremely challenging 11.5 miles. We finished the last two hours of the decent in darkness with only our headlamps illuminating the strewn boulder trail.

Enjoy the below videos of our Mount Katahdin hike.

Detail Videos of Knife Edge, Google Route, and Overview on Our Katahdin Trek

- Sit back, **Click Here for our Knife Edge half-hour video**, and enjoy - **and cringe** - as we cross the fabled Knife Edge Trail. http://tiny.cc/2q401y

- Bedford Community Television (BCTV) is now showing the **Knife Edge to Baxter Peak at the Northern Terminus of the Appalachian Trail** http://tiny.cc/fs401y produced by OutdoorSteve.com
- **A narrated Map of our Katahdin Trail Route using Google Earth.** http://tiny.cc/6t401y
- A Little Stroll Along Katahdin with Dundee and LoonsNest.biz http://tiny.cc/gv401y

Figure 3 - Map - Roaring Brook to Katahdin Stream via Knife Edge Trail and Baxter Peak and AT

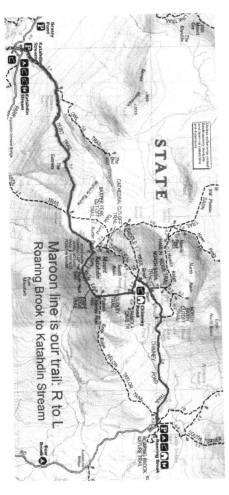

Page 1 of 2 Trails	Start	End	Hours and Miles	Comments
Roaring Brook Campground to Chimney Pond Campground	Start 6:45 am	9:30 am	2 ¾ hrs 3.3 miles	Chimney Pond Trail an easy hike. Four of us used trekking poles. Some nice side trail views.
Chimney Pond Campground to Pamola Peak via Dudley Trail	10 am	1 pm	3 hrs 1.4 miles	After a snack and rest at Chimney Pond Campground, we tied our trekking poles to our packs. The Dudley Trail is a 2,000 foot elevation gain and a relentless massive granite boulder laden trail nearly straight up. The Dudley Trail required our hands for pulling, grabbing rocks and hand holds, our legs for pushing, our arms for lifting our bodies, our feet for pushing and toe holds, and our butts to slide down granite formations. We were exhausted when we reached Pamola Peak. Indeed it was a very trying physical test of our mettle.
Pamola Peak to Chimney Peak/Knife Edge	1:20 pm	2:12 pm	¾ hrs	Our descent down the 40 foot drop from Pamola Peak was technical "rock climbing". We held indentations in the rocks while reaching for footholds. Indeed for this descent we used hands, arms, body and butt.
Knife Edge to South Peak	2:12	3:00 pm	3/4 hrs .8 miles	A .8 mile balancing act along the ridge of the Knife Edge Trail. Prior to this trip I had visions of panicking because of the elevation and the 2 to 3 thousand foot drop offs and extremely narrow trail. Truthfully, I had no fear as I crossed the Knife Edge trail.

Continue to Trails Page 2 of 2

Figure 4 - Mt Katahdin Hike: Trail Miles and Times Table

Page 2 of 2 Trails	Start	End	Hours and Miles	Comments
South Peak to Baxter Peak	3:00	3:50 pm	3/4 hrs .3 miles	This ridge trail went up and down. Just when we got to the top of the trail, it would drop and we would start another descent. Then an ascent followed by another descent. We were close to 7 hours since we left Roaring Brook campground and were tired. At each high ledge we could see Baxter Peak, but could not differentiate the cols in the undulating ridge.
From Baxter Peak via the Hunt Trail across the Katahdin Tablelands	4:00 pm	5:15 pm	1 ¼ hrs 1.0 miles	The Tablelands were like a country hike. It was flat and a welcome respite. We passed the famous Henry David Thoreau Spring. We had been hiking for nearly ten hours at this point.
Hunt Trail after the Tablelands to Katahdin Stream Campground	5:15 pm	10:00 pm	4 3/4 hrs 4.2 miles	We were now headed down and homeward bound, BUT still had 4.2 miles according to the trail sign. The first two miles were a steep descent over rough granite terrain. We did have some technical areas. One section had steel handles embedded in the granite pluton to make the descent from huge ledges a bit easier.

It took us two hours just to get below the tree line.

At 8:30 pm we put on our headlamps. We used our trekking poles to give us stability in navigating the descending rock strewn path.

At 10 pm we reached the ranger check-in station where we "signed-out" in the register that the six of us were safely down off the mountain. We also met the Park Ranger who had been told by two people with headlamps whom had passed us earlier in the dark that we were fine and on our way. |
| TOTAL HOURS and TOTAL MILES | 6:45 am | 10:00 pm | 15 hours 11.5 miles | What a Journey!!! Definitely a Bucket List accomplishment |

Knife Edge Trail

The Knife Edge Trail is perhaps the most spectacular trail in New England – and also the most dangerous. It would take us two hours to cross from Chimney Peak to South Peak.

To get to the start of the Knife Edge Trail, we had hiked 6 ½ hours from our Roaring Brook campsite. Three of these hours were on rock strewed Chimney Pond Trail; then three hours on a very rugged and prolonged steep Dudley Trail to reach Pamola Peak. The last half hour was a very technical Pamola descent, and then we ascended Chimney Peak. We were now at the start of the almost mile high 1.1 miles long Knife Edge Trail. Whew!

We were advised to avoid the Knife Edge in stormy weather. The exposure to high winds, rain, and lightning are extreme. We are warned that once we decided to cross the Knife Edge, we MUST STAY on that trail. There is no safe way to descend off either side of this mountain ridge. The drop is 2,000 feet off one side and 3,000 feet off the other.

The mile-long path stretches across the South Basin's headwall between Pamola and South Peak. I believe you will get a sense of what these six outdoor enthusiasts experienced crossing this unique narrow mile-high ridge with multi 1,000-foot drops on both sides. At one point for about 20 feet, the width of the ridge was close to 18 inches. The views, when we dared a birds-eye glimpse, were magnificent and undoubtedly breathtaking.

References

- **Blog and video: Knife Edge Trail to Baxter Peak at Northern Terminus of Appalachian Trail** http://tiny.cc/trcm1y
- www.baxterstateparkauthority.com/
- The Wilderness Map Company, Franconia, NH 03580 (I could find no website on the map I used titled, **Katahdin: Baxter State Park, Maine**)
- **Blog and Video: The Southern Terminus of the Appalachian Trail** http://tiny.cc/3tcm1y
- **Appalachian Trail Conservancy** http://www.appalachiantrail.org/

Figure 5 - Three Mt Katahdin Goals Accomplished

Four Days in Northern New Hampshire
Hiking, Paddling, Tenting, and Moose Sighting.

Figure 6 - Welcome to New Hampshire "Live Free or Die"

Grab a cup of coffee or another favorite beverage, kick up your feet, and enjoy how a family bonds in the great north woods of New Hampshire. My 18-year-old nephew Austin graduated from his southern California high school. For Austin achieving this educational milestone, my wife, Cathy, and I arranged for him to fly to New Hampshire in July to experience our "Live Free or Die" outdoors.

The four-day trip describes:
(1) Hiking Tuckerman Ravine Trail from the Appalachian Mountain Club's (AMC) Pinkham Notch hut to the AMC Lake of the Cloud (LOC) hut for a one night stay.
(2) Hiking from LOC hut to the peak of Mt Washington, the highest mountain in the northeast at 6,288 feet and "Home of the World's Worse Weather".

(3) Tenting for two days at Lake Francis State Park in the Connecticut Lakes area of Pittsburg, NH.

- Hike to and around the 4ᵗʰ Connecticut Lake located on the border of Canada and the United States. The 4ᵗʰ Connecticut Lake is the headwaters of the 410 miles long Connecticut River

- Paddle the Third Connecticut Lake

- Paddle Lake Francis

- Moose sightings on 18 mile Moose Alley

In addition to Austin and me, our fellow trekkers were his father (my brother Dennis), my sons Timothy and Shaun, my two grandchildren 15-year-old Madison and 12-year-old Carson, Ron, my brother-in-law, and invited friends Justin and his 17-year-old daughter Sarah. Ten would hike to the Lake of the Clouds (LOC) hut and Mt Washington, and seven of us would continue to the Great North Woods Lake Francis State Park campground.

Preparing the Hike to Lake of the Clouds Hut (LOC) and Mount Washington

As the hiking trek leader I had responsibility for the safety of my fellow outdoor enthusiasts:
- Which trail should we take?
  I had hiked Tuckerman's many times, and although Tuckerman's Ravine Trail is one of the most dangerous trails to LOC and Mt Washington, I wanted my group to safely experience the scenery, excitement, and knowledge of hiking this unique trail.

Figure 7 - View Overlooking Lake of the Cloud Hut

- What time in the morning do we start our hike to LOC?
  LOC serves their family style meals at 6 pm sharp (breakfast at LOC is 7 am sharp). I expected the hike from Pinkham to LOC to be between 4 and 5 hours.

- What kind of clothing, supplies, and food do we need for a one-day overnight hike in the White Mountains?
  Hiking Tuckerman Ravine Trail is not to be taken lightly. Snow, high winds, rain, lightning, and fog can be expected year round – this means ALWAYS prepare to spend the night on the trail in the mountains.

- What emergency supplies do we need in case of an unanticipated overnight while hiking?

  o AMC's Ten Essentials for a Safe Hike are mandatory. I enforced this by giving each person their own whistle and flashlight.

- For each person, I provided a three mil 30-gallon contractor bag (aka trash bag) in case we had to immediately camp on the trail (or daresay get lost for an overnight). To use this bag, we would make holes in the corner of the bag for our eyes and mouth, slip the bag over the head, and have some level of protection.

- Duct tape. You never know when this can come in handy e.g. broken eye glass frame, sling, strap, etc.

You need to be in good physical shape for a five-plus hour hike up Tuckerman's Ravine with sections nearly straight up (no need for climbing ropes), but there are places where you use your hands to assist crawling up rocks. My training schedule included two hikes up Uncanoonuc Mt in Goffstown, NH. Uncanoonuc, combined with two months of four times a week speed walking four miles in my hiking boots, prepared me for Mt Washington, and in particular climbing the headwall of Tuckerman Ravine.

An Educational Dinner

Hmm, how do I emphasize the importance of hiking safety to teenagers? The night before our trip my wife Cathy made a great spaghetti dinner for Austin, Madison, and Carson. This dinner was my opportunity to stress safety and necessary items for the hike. Unannounced, I demonstrated my hiking whistle (One toot for, "Where are you?" Two toots, "Come to me," and three toots, "Emergency.") I gifted to each a whistle and asked them to demonstrate a signal. Yes, they thought I was "loony", but indeed they practiced a lifesaving skill.

We spoke about hiking in groups. My son, Tim, has hiked with me many times and has my confidence in tight situations. He would lead one group up the mountain. Ron was also experienced, and he would lead another group. The sweep group (the slow hikers) would be led by me. Other than the aforementioned, no one was to get ahead of their leader – no matter what. We did not want to experience a lost hiker.

We cautioned about the importance of stopping every 10 to 15 minutes to drink water. An earlier hiking involvement, followed by a wilderness first aid course, made me realize dehydration can cause nausea and headaches and is easily avoided by frequent drinking of water. Mt Washington is a steep, long hike, and hydration is critical for our troop to completing a safe and enjoyable hike.

I emphasized **NO COTTON CLOTHING** – including underwear. I underscored this "strange request" by asking, "How long does it take the cotton to dry out after getting wet?" In survival situations, cotton is known as "DEATH CLOTH." Cotton holds moisture instead of wicking it away from the skin, and when wet, cotton has zero insulating properties.

Pinkham Notch to Lake of the Clouds (LOC)

I had a concern in guiding my group safely up to Lake of the Clouds. Years before when Tim and I took the Tuckerman Ravine Trail to Lake of the Clouds hut, we faced thick fog and could see only a few feet ahead. On that trek, we used cairns, the rock piles used to designate the trail when above the tree line, as the means to insure we kept on the trail. On this trip, I needed to watch closely the expected Mt Washington area weather to be sure I did not put my party in danger if the weather report indicated severe conditions.

They say a picture is worth a thousand words. Enjoy the short **Video Reference** below of our hike up Tuckerman Ravine Trail to Lake of the Clouds Hut followed by a next day hike to Mt Washington.

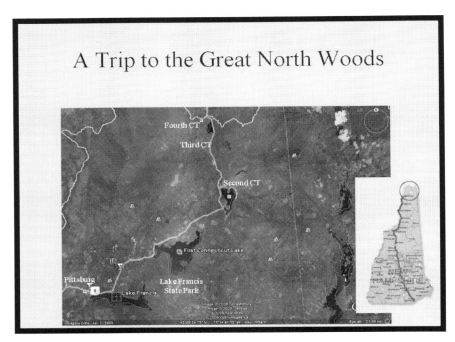

Figure 8 - The Connecticut Lakes of New Hampshire

The northern tip of New Hampshire has a pristine area known as the Great North Woods. I wanted Austin and my grandchildren to enjoy and appreciate this treasure of New Hampshire. Its many summer outdoor opportunities include paddling and fishing the Connecticut (CT) Lakes (Forth CT, Third CT, Second CT, First CT, and Lake Francis), hiking around the Fourth CT, and Moose sighting.

Moose Sighting.

Figure 9 - Brake for Moose!

The moose is the biggest and most mysterious and majestic four-legged inhabitant of northern New Hampshire. Seeing a moose is always a thrill for me. Certainly, for Austin and my grandkids, the thought of seeing these huge six to seven-foot-tall and 700 to 1200 pound animals was an expectation like waiting to get a glimpse of Santa Claus! There are 6,000 or so moose in New Hampshire, mostly in northern New Hampshire's Great North Woods, so this area enhances the opportunity to see a moose. The last 18 or so miles on route 3 in Pittsburg is designated, Moose Alley. Driving slowly on Moose Alley at 5 am also enhances your chance to see a moose. And, dusk is another good time.

What is the best way to find moose? My answer is always simple – look for cars pulled off alongside the road. For two days at dawn and dusk, we drove very slowly up Route 3. See our moose sighting success in the below **Video Reference**.

The Republic of Indian Stream (http://tiny.cc/ds5y1y

Figure 10 - Group Hug at the USA - Canada Boundary Marker

As we hiked to the Fourth Connecticut Lake, I shared a history lesson not readily known. For a few years in the 1830s, an area of today's Pittsburg, NH was an independent republic, not part of New Hampshire and not part of the United States. The US attempted to tax the 360 inhabitants, and Canada tried to make them serve in its military, so the people decided to establish their sovereign nation called, **The Republic of Indian Stream.** The existence of the Republic was ended by New Hampshire in 1835. Later, the Webster -Ashburton Treaty of 1842 established the border between Canada and the United States – the border markers that we would crisscross as we hiked to the Fourth Connecticut

Lake.

Hiking the Fourth Connecticut Lake

The 78 acre Fourth Connecticut Lake is located on the USA/Canada border. It is called a "Lake," but in my mind is similar to a small bog or marsh. The narrow swampy walk around the lake took us a half hour. We stopped to take pictures at the outlet stream - the Fourth CT is the headwaters of the 410 miles long Connecticut River that ends in Long Island Sound. The trail to the lake starts at the United States-Canada customs border crossing station in Pittsburg, NH on the international border between the United States and Canada. The whole hike from custom station to lake, walk around the lake, a brief ten-minute break, and the hike back, was less than two hours.

Paddle Third Connecticut Lake

Figure 11 - A Canoer on the 3rd Connecticut Lake

The 235 acres Lake is located about a half mile downhill from Fourth Connecticut. During our paddle on this pristine lake, we saw beaver lodges and dams, loons, and the outlet to Second Connecticut Lake. Carson went for a swim. As we paddled around the northern end of the lake, we stopped to see the inlet from Fourth Connecticut Lake.

Video References Hiking, Paddling, Tenting and Moose Sighting in Great North Woods of NH

- **Blog: Four Days in Northern New Hampshire with Family and Friends Hiking, Tenting, Paddling, and Moose Sighting** http://outdooradventurers.blogspot.com/2012/07/four-days-in-new-hampshire-of-family.html
- **Hiking Tuckerman Ravine** http://www.youtube.com/watch?feature=player_embedded&v=AkoJXIqB0kU
- **Moose Sightings** http://www.youtube.com/watch?feature=player_embedded&v=O-P__VJveeo
- **Crossing Headwaters of 460 mile long Connecticut River at 4th Connecticut Lake** http://www.youtube.com/watch?feature=player_embedded&v=dXM42H5KjuA

The Locks of the Trent-Severn Waterway

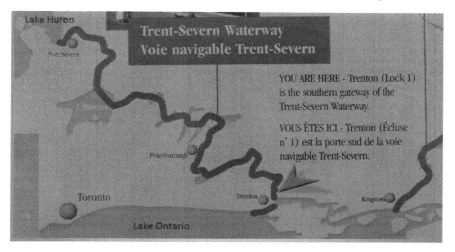

Figure 12 - Trent-Severn Map – Lake Ontario to Lake Huron

I found our Trent-Severn Waterway trip very difficult to make concise. Our Trent-Severn Waterway trek is so unique - such as our experience going through fourteen locks and living for eight days in a houseboat moving each day along the Waterway. With so much content, how do I describe all this and keep the discussion and videos under a few minutes?

The Trent-Severn Waterway is one of Canada's most spectacular waterways. The Waterway stretches 240 miles from Lake Ontario's Bay of Quinte to Lake Huron's Georgian Bay. My wife and I readily accepted an invitation to join our friends Linda and Dundee for a week on a houseboat on the Trent-Severn Waterway.

Friends have asked many questions such as, "What and where is the Trent-Severn Waterway?", "What was the houseboat like?", "What did it feel like going through a lock?", "How did you navigate?", and "Did you spend all your time on the houseboat?" I finally concluded I could only do this by breaking the trip into small videos and letting you choose for yourself which ones to view.

The waterway is an impressive chain of lakes and rivers linked by more than 40 locks and some 33 miles of excavated channels. All of the locks are situated in beautiful park-like settings, and most are integrated within small and inviting villages. Indeed, the Waterway is a unique gem of Canada.

Figure 13 - Houseboat Waiting to Enter a Lock

Given the extensive length of the Waterway, our timeframe of eight days, and the need to return our rented houseboat to where we picked it up at **Happy Days Houseboats** in Bobcaygeon, Ontario, our trip would take us through only seven of the locks as we headed from Lake Ontario and turned around after we locked through Kirkfield Lift Lock. On our return, we would repeat each of these seven locks.

Figure 14 - Our Houseboat Kitchen

The Waterway is home to two of the world's highest hydraulic lift locks, located in Peterborough and Kirkfield. Indeed, we locked the Kirkfield lift twice.

Also, we visited via car four locks (Trenton, Glen Miller, Sydney and Peterborough Lift Lock). These visits gave us another perspective of the locks because at two of these locks the lock master allowed me into their lock houses to be an "associate" to work the controls to "lock in" and "lock out" the boats. I was even told by one lock operator, "*You are the oldest kid whoever assisted us!*" Indeed all the lockmasters and operators were terrific.

The Lock Operators – Ontario Ambassadors

The lockmasters and operators, who guide and oversee the locks as your boat passes through, offer excellent assistance and indeed are ambassadors to Trent-Severn, Ontario, and certainly Canada. The warm welcome and support we received from them in going through the locks were exceptional.

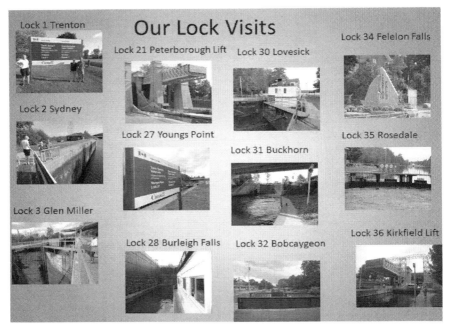

Figure 15 - Twelve Trent-Severn Waterway Locks

Each night we slept on the houseboat at designated areas outside the locks. One night we tied to trees on Wolf Island in Lower Buckhorn Lake with the back of the boat anchored in the lake.

The Trent-Severn includes fixed chamber locks and hydraulic lift locks. A lock is a device for raising and lowering boats between stretches of water of different levels on lake, river and canal waterways. The distinguishing feature of a conventional lock is it has a fixed chamber in which the water level is lowered or raised (as is the Bobcaygeon Lock); whereas in a boat lift lock, it is the chamber itself that rises and falls (such as the Kirkfield Lift Lock).

First, be sure to read the below **Seven Easy Steps for Locking Through**. Then, click on the two videos in the Videos Box below to see what it feels like to go through the **Bobcaygeon Lock** and the **Kirkfield Lift**.

"What Does It Feel Like Going Through a Lock?"

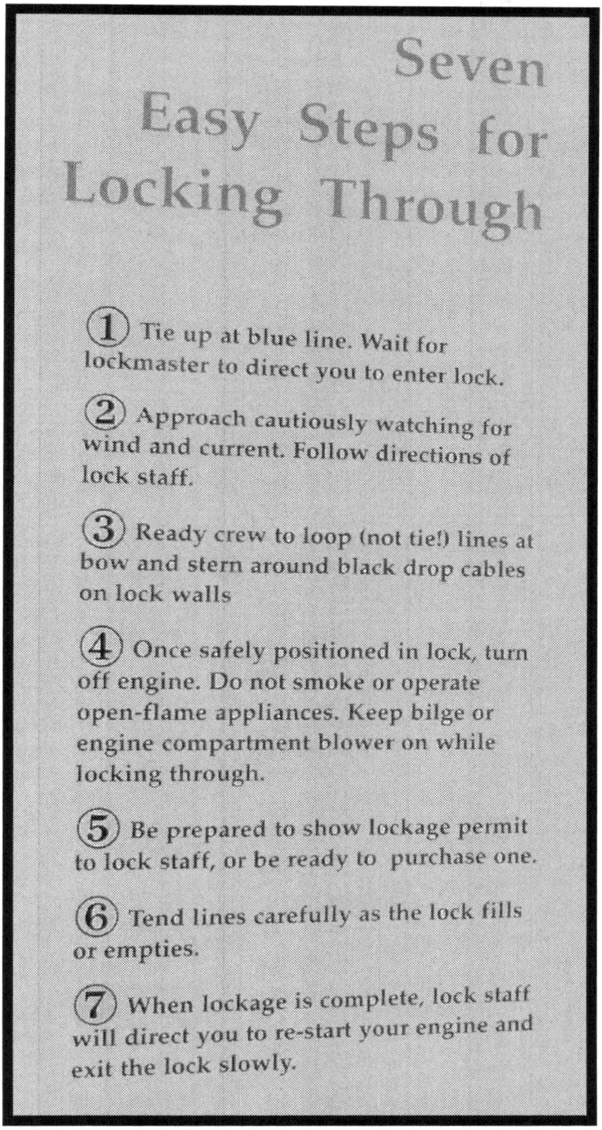

Seven Easy Steps for Locking Through

① Tie up at blue line. Wait for lockmaster to direct you to enter lock.

② Approach cautiously watching for wind and current. Follow directions of lock staff.

③ Ready crew to loop (not tie!) lines at bow and stern around black drop cables on lock walls

④ Once safely positioned in lock, turn off engine. Do not smoke or operate open-flame appliances. Keep bilge or engine compartment blower on while locking through.

⑤ Be prepared to show lockage permit to lock staff, or be ready to purchase one.

⑥ Tend lines carefully as the lock fills or empties.

⑦ When lockage is complete, lock staff will direct you to re-start your engine and exit the lock slowly.

Figure 16 - Seven Easy Steps Sign Posted at All Locks

Navigation Aids and Tour Our Houseboat

We used navigational charts and a GPS to follow the Trent-Severn channel.

Figure 17 - The Pilot and Navigator Work Together

The houseboats are advertised for novice boaters, and the houseboat companies provide you (and require) an orientation course to include:

- Demonstrations on handling the boat (including docking it, starting/stopping) followed by each customer steering the boat thereby validating their hands-on abilities.

- Navigational skills to safely get you from here to there

- Location of all safety gear, onboard fire prevention, man-overboard procedures

- Channel markers, and river etiquette when overtaking and passing others (horn signals, etc.)

- A Final sign-off checklist of all things covered – and items located on the boat.

The entire training course is geared (before you cast off) to make your excursion a safe and rewarding adventure.

I recommend at least one driver feels comfortable in big boats.

I would not recommend this trip for a complete boating novice by her or himself. Going through the locks, docking, and navigating requires boating experience.

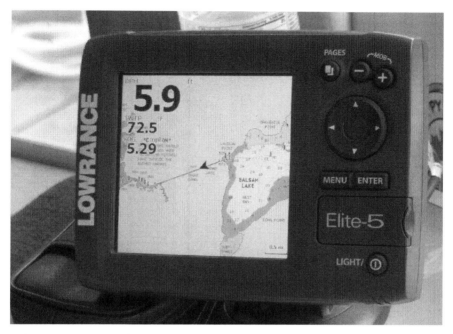

Figure 18 - Our GPS - Where are we and how fast are we going?

My friend Dundee is a qualified boater on a variety of large boats. He is very comfortable with steering and navigating our 40-foot houseboat. Myself, I have a 19-foot deck boat, but admittedly it took me a while to calm my nerves on this "slow-moving barge."

This houseboat was a large, slow to turn boat. Initially, I was a bit nervous driving and navigating our 40 foot long and 14-foot wide houseboat into and out of the lock areas. Dundee's guidance and calming instructions was a major plus for me when I was "Captain" of the boat.

History and Specs of The Trent-Severn Waterway
Construction began in the Kawartha Lakes region in 1833 with the lock at Bobcaygeon marking its beginning. It took over 87 years to finish the entire Waterway and only until after 1920 could a boat

travel the whole route between Lake Ontario and Lake Huron.

The navigation channel runs an average depth of six feet from start to finish. The conventional locks water levels vary by 20 feet or less in raising and lowering boats, whereas the Kirkfield Lift is 49 feet and the Peterborough Lift is 65 feet.

Peaking at Balsam Lake, the system takes the traveler 600 feet above Lake Ontario and 250 feet above Lake Huron's, Georgian Bay.

Standard lock dimensions are 120 feet long by 32 feet wide. The two exceptions are the Big Chute Marine Railway at 100 feet long by 24 feet wide and Port Severn at 84 feet long and 23 feet wide setting the limits if you wish to traverse The Trent-Severn Waterway from one end to the other.

"Did you spend all your time on the houseboat?"

There are many places to enjoy on the Trent-Severn, and I cannot possibly discuss them all here. I will, however, refer to three that are special to me.

The first is the *Buckhorn Canoe Company*. Dundee and I discovered this unique canoe building company owned and operated by Dick Persson.

Dick's company builds, restores and outfits traditional all-wood, wood-canvas canoes, and small boats. We were immediately impressed with Dick's extensive historical knowledge of restoration of old watercraft, old canoe companies, and their boat and canoe models. His shop and showroom were museums unto themselves.

Go to Dick's website (http://www.buckhorncanoes.com/) and read his passion and unique perspective for the history, research, building, repair, restoration, outfitting and use of wooden canoes.

Ottertail Paddle – Pros and Cons and How It Is Made
With Dick's permission, I did an interview and blog video of his comments on the differences between the Otter Tail and Beaver

Tail paddles. My blog post - **The Ottertail Paddle - "Pros and Cons" and "How it's Made,"** (http://tiny.cc/c4c11y) **had over 80,000 views on my blog and Youtube.com**

- My next "must share" is my swimming in Burleigh Falls. I wanted so much to swim at least once on our trip, and this was my opportunity. The below Special Memories of Trent-Severn Waterway video has my brave five-foot ledge jump into Burleigh Falls.

- Last, but not least, I strongly recommend a visit to the magnificent Canadian Canoe Museum (http://www.canoemuseum.ca/ in Peterborough, Ontario. This huge museum has exhibits and hands-on demonstrations of canoe and kayak building. Found throughout the museum is the history of the native peoples of Canada and the historical importance that canoes and kayaks have played in the development of Canada's more remote wilderness areas.

    See a below brief video of special moments at the Buckhorn Canoe Company, swimming Burleigh Falls, and the Canadian Canoe Museum at the blog post.

Never Say, "I wish I had locked the Trent-Severn Waterway"

The Tent-Severn Waterway was a wonderful and memorable experience, and now Cathy, Linda, Dundee and I will never have to say, "We wish we had house-boated the Trent-Severn Waterway in Ontario Canada.

References to the Trent-Severn Waterway

- Trent-Severn Tool Kit
  http://www.trentsevern.com/newsite/

- http://en.wikipedia.org/wiki/Trent%E2%80%93Severn_Wa
  terway

- http://www.thetrentsevernwaterway.com/#top

- http://www.ontariowaterwaycruises.com/kawartha.html

- http://www.thetrentsevernwaterway.com/
- http://www.happydayshouseboats.com

- http://www.buckhorncanoes.com

- The Waterway (Kawartha Region Lock Dimensions)
  http://www.thewaterway.ca/kawartha_locks.html

Blogs and Videos Available for Trent-Severn Waterway

- **Outdoor Adventures Blog: The Trent-Severn Waterway** http://tiny.cc/jwc11y
- **Special Memories of Trent-Severn Waterway** http://tiny.cc/8wc11y
- **Bob Caygeon Lock** http://tiny.cc/9xc11y
- **Kirkfield Lock** http://tiny.cc/czc11y
- **The Ottertail Paddle - "Pros and Cons", "How it's Made", and "Let's Give it a Test"** http://tiny.cc/c4c11y

---

Paddling the Allagash Wilderness Waterway

A Father-Son Paddling Trek

Ten of us just returned from paddling the Allagash Wilderness Waterway (AWW) in northern Maine. The ninety-eight-mile AWW is composed of streams, rivers, and lakes, and shines as the brightest among the jewels of Maine's wilderness state parks and historic sites.

This was a father-son trip with four dads and five sons. Linwood "The Loon" Parsons (http://www.loonsnest.biz/) was our guide. Loon's knowledge of the history and special sites around the Allagash meant many side trips and informative lectures on the unique history and lore of the Allagash Wilderness Waterway.

We entered the AWW at Indian Pond Stream on Saturday, July 11th and exited Saturday, July 18th at Allagash Village where the Allagash River and the St John River meet.

Wildlife

A special treat for me was hearing the "snort" sounds of a moose. One evening a cow moose and her calf spent nearly an hour across the river from our camp, and we heard her many snort calls to her calf.
Each day we saw moose, and we stopped counting moose at twenty-five.

We saw many Bald Eagles, the national emblem of the United States and a spiritual symbol for native people. At one campsite a pair of eagles perched in trees across the river from our camp and made frequent screams as if warning us to stay away. We stopped counting at ten pair.

Figure 19 - Shush…a Moose

Figure 20 - Look…There's an Eagle!

A loon Landing

A very unusual sight was seeing a loon land within a foot of our moving canoe. We spotted the loon coming toward us from afar, and we expected it to land. I have seen loons land hundreds of times, but what was unique this time was the loon did not land but kept approaching us head-on. It kept coming and coming as if it was going to collide with us.

The loon reminded me of seeing a seaplane coming in low and long with its proud chest up and no legs showing.

Finally, after much anxiety on our part thinking the loon did not see us, the loon smoothly settled within a foot

Figure 21 - Experiencing a loon landing

of our canoe and became one with the water – all this without making a ripple. Wow! What a sight to see.

Chase Rapids
This was my son Tim's and my third trip into the AWW in six years, and the water level was the highest and fastest we had seen. My earlier trips required us to frequently exit our canoe due to the low water conditions. This time we fought headwinds on Eagle and Long Lakes. Chase Rapids is five miles of Class 1 and Class 2 rapids with many thrills. We did short stretches of class 2 rapids over Long Lake Dam and below Allagash Falls.

My biggest thrill was paddling with my son, Tim. We did the first three days with me in the stern, including Chase Rapids. On day four, we switched ends of the canoe for the remainder of the trek. Tim's ability to read fast moving water, along with his paddling strength, resulted in an adventurous, fun, and safe trip through the rapids. Our last day, the eighth, it poured rain, but since we were on our way out, the rain getting any of our gear wet was of no consequence.

Figure 22 - Eyes Focused Ahead in Chase Rapids

Figure 23 - Notice the Loaded Canoe with Camp Gear

Figure 24 - Time to Camp for the Night

Gourmet Meals

Figure 25 - Steak and Hot Dogs!

Our meals were simply delicious, well planned, and cooked by "The Loon". Rib-eye steaks and potatoes cooked over our open fire pit are just a sample of our eight days of gourmet dining. And since one of the paddlers was a "hotdog eater," our chef accommodated him for his own "special tastes."

Allagash History and Our Itinerary
Without a doubt, the Allagash Wilderness Waterway rates as one of the grandest wilderness areas east of the Mississippi. Its mystique draws canoeists from all over America and the world. First roamed by native Abenaki Indians in search of food and furs, then in the 1800s by lumbermen in search of virgin timber for logs and pulpwood, it is today visited by the adventurist paddler seeking a deep wilderness experience.

The Allagash Wilderness Waterway is rich in historical points of interest from those by-gone eras. It abounds in wildlife of every description, from the majestic Moose to the ubiquitous White-throated Sparrow. Extending some 98 miles (normally) end-to-end, but can be extended to a trip 125 miles by starting at Johnson Pond and thereby including a run down Allagash Stream. The Waterway offers the canoer both lake and river paddling environments.

Our trip began at Indian Pond Stream, which flowed into Eagle Lake, and then proceeded northward for eight days ending at Allagash Village on the Canadian border. "Pongokwahemook", an Indian name meaning "woodpecker place" and today called Eagle Lake, is a most interesting spot on the Allagash. We pitched our tents at Thoreau campsite on Pillsbury Island, the northernmost point reached by Henry David Thoreau in his expedition of 1853. It is from this base encampment that we launched our exploration of the "Tramway" that connects Eagle Lake with Chamberlain Lake and of the old locomotives that ran between Eagle and Umbazooksus lakes in the early 1900's lumbering era. A strange sight indeed to see these 90 and 100-ton locomotives sitting alone in this vast wilderness.

By now, everyone's paddling skills have become finely tuned and in two days or so, we will be running the canoes down famous Chase Rapids, a beautiful and exciting run of nearly 5 miles ending at Umsaskis Lake. As the river enters Umsaskis Lake it meanders through an attractive marsh where we see moose feeding on the plant life. Canada geese often stop over here on their great migrations up and down the Atlantic flyway.

We next cross Round Pond, the last pond on the Waterway and spend the next few days being carried along by the current through easy rapids as the Allagash River descends to join the Saint John River.

Trout fishing at the mouths of the many brooks and streams offered Eric and Garrett the opportunity to wet a fly. That evening Garrett shared his 14" brook trout cooked over our campfire.

We portage the most awesome spectacle on the river; 40-foot high Allagash Falls, a thundering, boiling cauldron of power and beauty.

Figure 26 - Overlooking Allagash Falls

Fourteen river miles below Allagash Falls through class 1 rapids, the Allagash River delivers us back into civilization, and our wilderness river adventure becomes a treasured memory.

A special notation on this trip. We had planned this trek two years ago, but one of the Dads was diagnosed with throat cancer. We had made all the arrangements, and two weeks before the trek, we had to cancel the trip as he began aggressive treatment. Two years later, cancer-free, he and his two sons, made his Allagash Wilderness Waterway dream come true.

Never say, "I wish I had ..."

We now never have to say, "I wish I had paddled the Allagash Wilderness Waterway."

Figure 27 - A Father-Son Trip to the Allagash

For more information go to Allagash Wilderness Waterway **http://www.maine.gov/cgi-bin/online/doc/parksearch/index.pl**) and Maine Bureau of Parks **http://tiny.cc/58l6sw**

Video References for Allagash Wilderness Waterway

- Blog: Paddling the Allagash Wilderness
  http://tiny.cc/48ze5x
- Video of Pictures from Allagash Wilderness Waterway
  http://tiny.cc/vxze5x
- Videos of Paddling over Long Lake Dam, Allagash Falls, and Canoe Poling the Allagash
  http://youtu.be/7OANcEldsUA
- The Loons Nest
  http://www.loonsnest.biz

Ballad of the Allagash Wilderness Waterway

(To the tune of "Oh Lord, won't you buy me a Mercedes-Benz" by Janis Joplin)

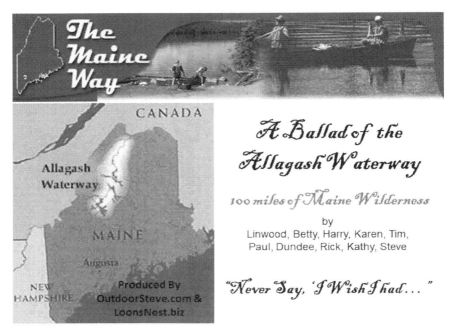

Figure 28 - Ballard of the Allagash by its Paddlers

Introduction

This Allagash Wilderness Waterway Ballad video was prepared from participants' memorable moments of expeditions guided by Registered Master Maine Guide Linwood Parsons and his wife Betty.

Without a doubt, the Allagash Wilderness Waterway rates as the gem of Maine's wilderness areas.

The Ballad of the Allagash Wilderness Waterway

(Kathy)
Oh Lord, won't you buy me a big can of Ben's.

I'm out in the woods now,
The flies never end.
Got bitten all over,
No help from my friends.
Oh Lord, won't you buy me a big can of Ben's.

Oh Lord, won't you buy me a bed of my own.
A mattress and box spring
That's not on the ground.
Last night I got bruises,
I slept on a stone.
Oh Lord, won't you buy me a bed of my own.

Oh Lord, won't you buy me a roll of TP.
Those baked beans of Betty's
Are getting to me.
Been wiping with leaves
Til I got poison ivy.
Oh Lord, won't you buy me a roll of TP.

(Linwood)
Oh Lord, won't you buy me a deputy's badge.
We helped save two druggies
At Little Allagash.
Ole Andy was naked,
And Tara was scared.
Oh Lord, won't you buy me a deputy's badge.

Oh Lord, won't you buy me new waterproof gear.
"Dry bags" became "wet bags"
When we sank to our ear.
We swam down the rapids
A chasin' the beer.
Oh Lord, won't you buy me new waterproof gear.

(Betty)

Oh Lord, won't you buy me a few more good years.
To paddle with Linwood
And Harry mit beers.
Chase Rapids with Karen
Without many fears.
Oh Lord, won't you buy me a few more good years.

(Karen)
Oh Lord, won't you buy me an instant campfire.
No sawing of firewood,
No stripping of bark.
No pleading with Linwood
Or Harry to lite it.
Oh Lord, won't you buy me an instant campfire.

(Harry)
Oh Lord, won't you buy me a brand new spruce paddle.
Chase Rapids are coming,
Excitement is high.
Cross draw, sweep, and a pry,
Til we all finished dry.
Oh Lord, won't you buy me a brand new spruce paddle.

(Steve)
Oh Lord, won't you buy me a Maine Master Guide.
To show us the Allagash,
In swagger and stride.
And teach us canoe rescue,
And a loon landing and more wildlife bona fide.
Oh Lord, won't you buy me a Maine Master Guide.

Oh Lord, won't you buy me a Chickadee and a Loon.
The bread in the Dead,
Cornish hens in the coffee can.
Folger's Black Silk,
and a pudding lid spoon.

Oh Lord, won't you buy me a Chickadee and a Loon

Oh Lord, won't you buy me a campsite to rest.
Spruce gum for the rookie,
Counting moose at its best.
A swim though the rapids,
Flint and steel for our test.
Oh Lord, won't you buy me a campsite to rest.

Oh Lord, won't you buy me a Long Lake Dam
A dam to portage if you can,
Or paddle at risk and I'll be dam.
A spike waiting to rip the canoe,
Tim and Steve paddled be dammed.
Oh Lord, won't you buy me a Long Lake Dam.

(Tim)
Oh lord take me down to the Allagash now.
Take me to the north woods,
Where the moose runs wild and proud.
To see the eagles soar,
As I relax on the shore.
Oh lord take me down to the Allagash now.

Oh Lord, won't you buy me some rapids right now.
The "V" through the rocks
will guide us somehow.
The draw stroke shall save us
with a quick turn of the bow.
Oh Lord, won't you buy me some rapids right now.

(Dundee)
Oh Lord, won't you buy me more beer.
To help me create more cairns made of stone,
And the whistles of willow,
And the white birch bark stars.
So much more to create, so

Oh Lord, won't you buy me more beer!

Oh Lord, won't you buy me a big ole white sail.
I'm on Eagle Lake and,
The wind never fails.
My arms ache from paddlin',
Oh, S#%t is that hail?
Oh Lord, won't you buy me a big ole white sail.

Oh Lord, won't you buy me a big ole fat fish.
I'll gut him and skin him,
Then he'll land in my dish.
An eighteen inch Brookie,
Now that'd be my wish.
Oh Lord, won't you buy me a big ole fat fish.

Oh Lord, won't you buy me a bigger Canoe.
'Cause the one I have now,
Just simply won't do.
Need more room for the beer,
for the hard strokin' Crew.
Oh Lord, won't you buy me a bigger Canoe.

Oh Lord, won't you buy me some stars in the Sky.
They look near at hand,
yet, are so high.
I'm just a lightening bug seeking a mate,
in the heavens above, but I'm feeling spry.
Oh Lord, won't you buy me some stars in the Sky.

Oh Lord, won't you buy me paddlers so grand.
Dundee is prepared,
And navigates first hand.

Timothy skilled in the stern,
When the river gets tough he insures the turn
Oh Lord, won't you buy me paddlers so grand.

Oh Lord, won't you buy me a campfire recipe.
Garret flint and steel,
Tim saws wood fire-to-be.
Linwood's cuisine is five-star,
Lobster and eggs benedict are the par.
Oh Lord, won't you buy me a campfire recipe.

Oh Lord, won't you buy me "Never say I wish I had ..."
For eight days we were in awe of the Allagash and the Loon,
Our skills grew as we paddled in tune.
Coolers with names of rivers,
All are lifetime of memories delivered.
Oh Lord, won't you buy me a "Never say I wish I had ..."

References

- **Video Blog**: The Ballard of the Allagash Wilderness Waterway **http://tiny.cc/s7d44x**
- Tim Priest Reflects on Treks Guided by Loon Parsons **http://tiny.cc/y9d44x**
- The Allagash Wilderness Waterway: A Father-Son Paddling Trek http://tiny.cc/wbe44x
- Nine videos of the Allagash **http://tiny.cc/see44x**

Tim Priest Reflects on his Maine Paddling Treks Guided by Linwood "The Loon" Parsons

Figure 29 -Tim Reflecting on Linwood and Betty

Tim Priest Reflects on his Maine Paddling Treks Guided by Loon Parsons (http://tiny.cc/y9d44x) is a recently identified video made by Frank Crosby as he interviewed Tim Priest heading for eight days of paddling and tenting on the 92-mile North Maine Woods Allagash Wilderness Waterway in July 2009. We call this particular trek a *Father-Son trip* as the expedition of ten was made-up of four Dads and their sons and one friend.

Tim has been on many wilderness paddling trips guided by Master Maine Guide Linwood "The Loon" Parsons and his wife Betty "The Chickadee". Tim shares his reflections on Linwood and Betty and his Maine North Woods trips.

The video (http://tiny.cc/y9d44x) includes pictures from the Father-Son Allagash Wilderness Waterway trek.

Figure 30 - Chickadee and Loon Parsons

Thank you to Frank Crosby for sharing this interview.

References

- Video and Blog: Tim Priest Reflects on his Maine Paddling Treks Guided by Loon Parsons http://tiny.cc/y9d44x
- Paddling on the Allagashh Wilderness Waterway http://tiny.cc/wbe44x
- http://www.outdoorsteve.com
- The Loons Nest http://www.loonsnest.biz
- The Ballad of the Allagash Wilderness Waterway http://tiny.cc/s7d44x

Hike Grand Canyon Bright Angel Trail Down to Indian Garden and Back to the South Rim

Figure 31 - Bright Angel Trail

Last summer I had the privilege of being in Grand Canyon National Park in northern Arizona. Certainly, as an outdoor enthusiast, I had to walk more than the Canyon's Rim Trail. My friend JK recommended a hike into the Canyon to Indian Garden via the Bright Angel Trail. The estimated hiking time was 6 to 9 hours for this 9.2-mile hike down and back to the south rim.

My enthusiasm for hiking into the Canyon was cautioned by my fears of:

1. My fear of height. The south rim of the Grand Canyon is nearly 7,000 feet above sea level. The thought of looking over a drop-off of thousands of feet was admittedly something I was not sure I could face.

2. Meeting Mules on the Bright Angel Trail. There are frequent mule trips passing hikers on Bright Angel Trail. Could I squeeze close enough to the mountain side to let mule riders pass me on the Trail?

Figure 32 - "Mules ahead" is Common on Bright Angel Trail

3. The width of the Bright Angel Trail. Would the Trail down into the Canyon be so narrow as to force me to hug the mountain?

4. On Thursday morning at 6:40 am I began my hike on the south rim at the Bright Angel Trailhead. Two and a half hours and 4.6 miles later I reached the Indian Garden. The hike down was fabulous, and I frequently stopped in awe of this incredible landscape and to take pictures and "smell the roses" of my America's beautiful country.

The four ½ hour return trip from Indian Garden to the rim was quite the challenge. The only thing that kept me going was I knew I had a six-pack sitting on ice in my cooler!

Figure 33 - Looking Up from Indian Garden

I believe the main reason for my exhaustion on the return trip from Indian Garden to the south rim was because I had not trained at 7,000 feet above sea level. My daily Bedford, New Hampshire training runs were at an elevation of 275 feet.

Lessons learned from my six plus hour hike from the south rim on Bright Angel trail to Indian Garden were:

• Height. My fears were for naught. The width of the trail was four to six feet, and most often the cliff side of the trail had trees and rocks that eliminated any fear of falling hundreds or thousands of feet

• The width of the trail was more than enough to accommodate mules passing. I had three groups of mule riders pass me on the way up. As they passed I simply sat on the mountain side with plenty of room to relax, drink water, and take pictures, as you will see in the video.

• The three rest areas (Mile-and-a-Half Resthouse, Three-Mile Resthouse, and Indian Garden) all had water sources for refills of my water bottles.

• The dust from the limestone was choking and blinding. Following another hiker up the trail put me in a dust cloud, and I had to wait until the hiker was way ahead before I continued my trek. The mules passing generated even more dust. Certainly, a person with breathing issues needs to be very aware of this situation.

• Shade was plentiful in my morning trek down. However, my journey back to the rim started around 10 am and shade was less prominent, and the bright sun was hot, resulting in sweat mixed with suntan lotion (a mandatory item) burning in my eyes.

• There were four-foot timbers every three to four feet on the trail to prevent trail wash away. This meant on the return to the rim I had to constantly lift my feet six to twelve inches with every step. My thighs began aching before I reached the Three-Mile Resthouse.

• My approach to the hike back was to divide my trek into three phases: (1) Hike from Indian Garden to the Three-Mile Resthouse, (2) Hike from the Three-Mile Resthouse to the One-and-a-Half-Mile Resthouse, and (3) Hike from the One-and-a-Half-Mile Resthouse to the Canyon's rim.

There are over 200 heat-related rescues in Grand Canyon National Park each year and most of them on the Bright Angel Trail. So, a word to the wise.

Down is Optional – Up is Mandatory

Hmm, I trust the below picture of **Down is Optional, Up is Mandatory**, will cause you to ask yourself, "What does **Down is Optional – Up is Mandatory** mean?" Well, as noted, hiking down the Canyon can be essentially an easy stroll. Your main concern is to lift your feet so as not to trip over the log sections and rocks. Thus "Down is Optional" means go down the canyon knowing you must be able to climb back up – thus "Up is Mandatory" means you are responsible for getting yourself back up to the canyon rim.

Figure 34 - Sign at Three-Mile Resthouse

"**Up is Mandatory**" means **BEFORE** you go further down into the Canyon you must understand and accept all the barriers that can prevent you from later returning to the rim.

Here is an incomplete list of barriers to making a safe return to the rim (which is 7,000 feet above sea level):
- Your body must be at a good level of cardio fitness.
- You will be returning up the same 4.6-mile trail – and that distance in itself can be difficult.
- The climb back to the upper rim means the constant lifting of your legs and the hurt of your thighs.
- Minimal shade.
- Constant clouds of dust from the path and certainly when mule trains pass – you will be breathing dust into your lungs – even if wearing filtering scarfs.
- You must stay hydrated – means constantly drinking water.

Thus, the choice to go DOWN is a life-threatening decision made BEFORE you leave the top.

The steep plunge is made somewhat easier through switchbacks curling down the mountain. The need to replenish water is a lifesaving concern in a desert environment. Water replacement in May is no issue as my 4.6-mile descent of the Bright Angel Fault to Indian Garden had three springs. Only Indian Garden has water year-round. You still need to carry your water – and constantly replenish at each water stop.

Memorable Moments

• As I hiked, I began thinking this trail would be runnable, similar to my winter wild experience described here in an earlier blog post. Then, just before the One-and-a-Half-Mile Resthouse, I was passed by a person running. A few minutes later I met him at the Resthouse. We introduced ourselves, and he said he was 63 years old and "out for an early morning run." He turned around at this point and ran upward toward the rim.

• As I neared Indian Garden, the trail leveled off, and I would run a bit – both to reduce the time to Indian Garden as well as to change my gait and vary the use of different leg muscles.

• On my return to the rim, I could see a woman walking very slowly in front of me. She was stumbling and frequently stopped to grasp the wall. She appeared to me to be in trouble. I caught up with her, and we spoke as we rested against the wall. I asked her if she needed any assistance, and she replied "No." We both were near finishing, and I waited for her near the Bright Angel Trailhead. We did a high-five. Certainly, she was close to not understanding, "**Down is Optional – Up is Mandatory.**"

• Because of my early morning start, almost my entire down hike was in the shade. However, my return hike was mostly in the sun - and it was very hot.

• Going down I did not touch the wall. On my trek back, I frequently would use the wall to help support my upward progress - and the wall was cool. I kept thinking a hiking stick would be nice about now.

Enjoy my video and hike into the Grand Canyon to Indian Garden and my return to the south rim.

I never have to say, "I wish I had hiked Bright Angel Trail into the Grand Canyon"

References for the Bright Angel Trail
- **Blog and video: Hike from South Rim of Grand Canyon's Bright Angel Trail Down to Indian Garden and Back to the Rim** http://tiny.cc/qphx1y
- **Wikipedia Bright_Angel_Trail** http://tiny.cc/o2kx1y
- **Canyon Explorer – Bright Angel Trail** http://tiny.cc/lalx1y
- **7 of most dangerous hikes in America – Bright Angel Trail** http://tiny.cc/76kx1y

Sea Kayaking and Camping on the Maine Island Trail

My cousin Linwood suggested I join the Maine Island Trail Association (MITA). (http://www.mita.org/) The Maine Island Trail (MIT) is a 375-mile chain of over 180 wild islands along the coast of Maine. The MIT is a must do for any outdoor enthusiast.

The Planning Phase

Figure 35 - Maine Island Trail Map of Our Trip

Kayaking and camping on islands in the Atlantic Ocean is not something one does on a whim. Who would like to go with me? When do we go? Where do we put-in? Where do we park the car for three days? Which islands do we camp on? Do we need fire permits? Do we need camp site reservations?

I invited my regular camping and paddling buddies, and Dundee was the sole positive responder. Dundee and I selected Stonington on Deer Isle as our put-in because it offered a plethora of islands close to shore for our maiden trip.

I emailed the office of the Maine Island Trail Association with questions:
- **Island fire permits** - There is a telephone number in the MITA app (http://www.mita.org/app/) and hard copy guidebook (http://www.mita.org)
- **Camp site reservations** -There is no need for camp reservations on any of the islands - a MITA member has access to all sites on the trail, at any time, unless the guide descriptions indicate otherwise)
- **Put-ins available** - The Deer Isle overview page of the guide has a list (we selected Old Quarry Ocean Adventures http://www.oldquarry.com)

Linwood sent emails on maps (http://www.charts.noaa.gov/OnLineViewer/13313.shtml) for nautical navigation charts. He cautioned us to plan transits from the islands and mainland using a favorable following tide flow. Tides can be 2 to 4 knots in some of those channel passages, and if we end up bucking the tidal flow, we won't make much headway toward our destination and may run out of energy and daylight.

He sent us tide charts (e.g., http://www.maineboats.com/tide-charts/tides?t=augstn10) as tide knowledge is critical for camp site and campfires since the fires must be below the high tide line. The velocity of flow is maximum at mid-tide and slackens toward either end, reaching null at the direction of change. In the

Stonington areas, the tide will run about 12 feet (give or take the phase of the moon effects). We needed to remember to drag our kayaks a boat length or two above the high tide mark. When the tide rises 12 plus feet, we do not want to find our transportation has gone out to sea.

Figure 36 - A Good Navigator with a Map and Compass

Our gear included compasses, relevant guides and charts, the MITA guidebook, and a plastic water resistant nautical chart.

Packing our kayaks for our three day paddle meant tough decisions on what to bring and what to leave. My wife Cathy thought we would never pack the gear we had readied, but indeed we managed without sinking our kayaks.

Our Itinerary

Hells Half Acre Island on Wed Night and Steves Island on Thurs Night with a 4 pm Fri Return to Old Quarry.

Figure 37 - Our Put-In at Stonington, Maine, Located on the Southern Portion of the Island of Deer Isle.

I sent emails to friends to follow our progress on their email with Google Maps (the app is called **Where's My Droid** (http://www.wheresmydroid.com/). I also downloaded an app called **My Tracks** (http://www.mapmytracks.com/) to follow our island trail paddle.

Day 1 – Wednesday

We registered our itinerary with Old Quarry. The Old Quarry staff were extremely accommodating with information on selecting alternative islands to camp on (e.g. "too buggy", "be careful of lobster boats when crossing channels and between islands", etc.)

Figure 38 - Old Quarry Ocean Adventures

We had a smooth put-in at Old Quarry, and with a smooth paddle, we were at Hells Half Acre island in just over thirty minutes. We were in awe of the island and the view of the bay. We took a walk about this two-acre island, and located a nice spot on the east end of the island and pitched our tents on two wood platforms.

Our initial plan was to save a camping spot by pitching our tent and then doing some paddling to other islands. However, we were in awe of this paradise, and after some adult beverages, we decided to cool it for the night right where we were. This proved to be the right decision as shortly after we landed a three-masted schooner, the "Victory Chimes," with five sails full, tacked into our harbor. It was a magnificent sight.

Figure 39 - "Victory Chimes" from Hell's Half Acre Island

Dundee was the chief chef for this evening's dinner. We made a campfire below the high water line, and he proceeded to prepare beans and franks — fabulous meal.

The sunset was dreamlike on this beautiful summer evening with a gentle breeze.

On Wednesday night we went to sleep surrounded by beautiful islands with clear skies and overhead stars.

Day 2 – Thursday

We awoke Thursday morning on an island in the middle of the ocean! We were completely engulfed in pea soup fog!

We had a lazy breakfast hoping the fog would clear. It did not.

At 10 am we decided to use our map and compass skills and find our way to Steves Island. Dundee's experience at reading a nautical chart and steering by compass was impressive.

Figure 40 - The Fog

I felt comfortable with Dundee leading the way, but I must admit it was a weird feeling paddling into pea soup fog and hoping to find our next marker to know we were on course to Steves Island.

It took us about an hour to paddle to Steves from Hells Half Acre, as we meandered between a few islands enjoying this surreal experience of fog paddling. We could see about thirty feet ahead, so when we located an island, we paddled around it so as to take in the scenic pleasures of the spruce and granite topography along its shoreline, and if truth were to be told, to be sure we could recognize the island on our navigational map so we knew where we were.

Figure 41 - Paddling Away from Hell's Half Acre Island

When we found Steves Island, we were met by a couple, Taylor and Catherine, who had spent the prior night there, and because of being fog bound today, they intended to spend another day on Steves trusting that Friday's sun would burn away the fog.

We found a delightful campsite to pitch our tents. We toured this rock-bound island, with balsam trees in the middle. Of course with the fog, our views off the island were essentially nil. We could hear lobster boats but did not see them.

During the day, four kayakers in beautiful hand-made sea kayaks found the island for lunch. Interestingly, I knew one of the kayakers, so it was fun talking old times. They had all the appropriate navigation equipment for foggy weather, and after lunch left to make their way back to their campsite at another MITA Island.

A Fresh Mussels Feast

Given we were now friends with Taylor and Catherine, we invited them to join us for Steves Island fresh mussels and pre-dinner Hors D'Oeuvres. The **Video References** box below offers a link to our ocean mussels feast.

Figure 42 - Mussels Bed at Low Tide at Steves Island

Figure 43 - Steves Island and Steamed Mussels

Day 3 Friday

We awoke at 5:30 am Friday hearing the working lobster boats getting an early morning start. The fog was lifting, and we knew the day would be clear. Around 9 am we began to be surrounded by views of the islands, as indeed they had been depicted on our map.

Figure 44 - An Early Morning Working Lobster Boat

At 10 am we started a gentle paddle back to our Old Quarry take-out via Crotch Island and Stonington. We left Steves Island with wonderful memories of ocean mussels and new and old friends. Crotch Island used to be a stone quarry and is loaded with monstrous granite cut stones. A lot of the granite blocks used in the construction of many government buildings and monuments in our nation's capital were mined off this island.

We paddled along the shorefront of Stonington harbor, and around 1 pm we pulled into our take-out.

We reported our return at the **Old Quarry Ocean Adventures** office, and after buying three freshly caught Maine lobsters, we headed home to New Hampshire.

Shared Learning

• My Droid Incredible ran out of power in less than 7 hours after its full charge, so my expectations for **Where is my DROID**, and

> ### Video References Paddling the Maine Island Trail
>
> - Blog: Sea Kayaking on the MIT
>   http://outdooradventurers.blogspot.com/2010/08/sea-kayaking-and-camping-on-maine.html
> - Hells Half Acre's Island Pea Soup Fog
>   http://www.youtube.com/watch?v=k4G4KmqLlp8&feature=player_embedded
> - Eating Ocean Mussels on Steves Island
>   http://www.youtube.com/watch?v=NhfMKal5DWo&feature=player_embedded
> - Old Quarry Ocean Adventures
>   http://www.oldquarry.com/
> - Maine Island Trail Association
>   http://www.mita.org

My Tracks was a big negative (although some friends used GPS My DROID on day one and it worked great.

• Always bring a water-resistant nautical map and compass – and certainly know how to use it BEFORE you go

• Join the Maine Island Trail Association (MITA)

• Most assuredly I will return many times to enjoy and explore the 200 plus islands cared for by the Maine Island Trail Association (MITA) membership.

• Enjoy the below **Video References** taken on MIT

• Never say, "I wish I had paddled the Maine Island Trail."

Ocean Kayaking in the Deer Isle Region of the Maine Coast – Stonington to Isle au Haut

The Deer Island Region of the Maine Island Trail

The Maine Island Trail (MIT) is a 375-mile chain of over 180 wild islands along the coast of Maine. In mid-July friends Dundee, Cully, David and I did a three day paddle on the MIT in the Deer Island Region. The Deer Isle Region extends from Stonington south to Isle au Haut and east into Blue Hill Bay. We tented two days on the two acres Steves Island (the name by coincidence.)

We put-in at Stonington, Maine at the Old Quarry Ocean Adventure campground. See the video below for exciting footage of our trip, including a Google Earth map of our MIT route.

Photo by Randy Hess
Steves Island, Maine
July 22, 2014

Figure 45 - Steves Island Campsite

Special notes on our trip

- **Over the years, the pronunciation** of "Isle au Haut" has drifted considerably. Nowadays, people who have spent time on the island pronounce it "i-la-HO."

- **Dundee was both our Chef and Navigator**. He is top-notch in both areas.

- **Where are we in the Atlantic?** A map and compass are mandatory in this Deer Island area consisting of a 40 offshore island archipelago.

Figure 46 - Packing Kayaks from Quarry Ocean Adventures

Admittedly we had moments where we were questioning the name of the islands we could see in the distance. Certainly, when fog is present (frequently), you either stay on a known island, use your map and compass to get to your next island destination, or back to the mainland.

- **Disposal of human waste**
  - The Maine Island Trail Association (MITA) requests all island visitors carry off solid human waste and dispose of it safely on the mainland. The Maine Island trail Guide lists several good carry off methods to help you deal with human waste on the Trail. We chose the Crap Wrap method.

Figure 47 - All Trash is Carried Out

- **Water**
  - We brought our potable water. The islands we visited had no drinking water - and remember, we were in the ocean.
- **Day 1 Old Quarry Campground to Steves Island**
  - A 4.6-mile paddle from Old Quarry Ocean Adventures campground to the 2 acres Steves Island where we camped for two nights
  - Met Randy and son Steve from Lancaster, PA
  - First come – gets the first camp. Steves Island is 2 acres and has three sites – ten max occupancy
  - Put-in and parking at Old Quarry Adventure Campground
  - 90 plus minute paddle from Old Quarry to Steve's Island.
  - Dave caught mackerel (cooked over a campfire.

Figure 48 - Map Quarry Ocean Adventures to Steves Island

- **Day 2 Steves Island to Isle au Haut and return**
  - The day starts with Chef Dundee cooking McNestlers for breakfast.
  - 11 mile round trip paddle from Steves Island to Isle au Haut. The paddle trip was close to 5 hours with gusts of wind and choppy seas.
    - Went ashore at Harbor Island.
    - Paddled by Merchant Island, Pell Island, Nathan Island to the Isle au Haut Thoroughfare.
    - Had lunch outside Island Store.
    - The reversed route back to Steves Island.

- Mussels from Steves Island for a seafood feast. (A warning here about Red Tide). Invited Randy and Steve to dinner.

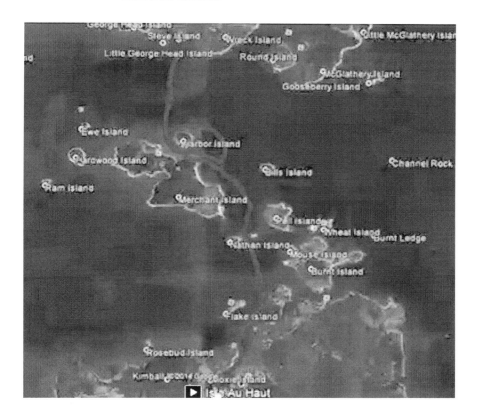

Figure 49 - Map Steves Island to Isle Au Haut

- **Day 3 Steves Island to Crotch Island quarry and Stonington with takeout at Old Quarry Adventures**

- Our 6 mile paddle passed by the George Head island sandbar in a whoop-de-doo surfing wave. We visited Crotch Island, once a world renowned granite quarry. We went up the "crotch" past hills of waste chunks of granite. We saw osprey and eagles. We continued along the shoreline of the town of Stonington with its many wharfs of commercial lobster and fishing operations. Lobster boats have the right of way and we learned this quickly as our final hour coincided with lobster boats returning en masse to sell their day's work.
- With expectations of rain and windstorm on Wednesday night, we decided to curtail our trip. After coffee and orange juice, we had a burrito breakfast of pita bread, eggs, cheese, and salsa.
- Crotch Island and stone quarry. At the turn of the century, Crotch was one of 33 major island quarries along the Maine coast. They provided work for an estimated 10,000 to 15,000 people, creating a boom-town atmosphere in nearby coastal towns. Crotch Island is an active remnant of what once was a dominant industry and colorful part of Maine's past.

- Crotch Island's 450 acres are littered with the rusted relics of its past, and dotted with hills of waste rock,

Figure 50 - Crotch Island Osprey Nest

chunks of granite that didn't break right and couldn't be used. A steam-powered Brown hoist crane with a 40-foot boom stands to rust near the V-shaped inlet that gives Crotch Island its name. We saw an osprey nest on a hoist crane.

For those interested in more detail:
- **Island fire permits** - There is a telephone number in the MITA hard copy guidebook. There is also a mobile phone app http://www.mita.org/app
- **Camp site reservations** -There is no need for camp reservations on any of the islands - a MITA member has access to all sites on the trail, at any time, unless the guide descriptions indicate otherwise)
- **Put-ins available** - The Deer Isle overview page of the guide has a list (we selected Old Quarry Ocean Adventures http://www.oldquarry.com)

The Maine Island Trail Association (MITA)

The Maine Island Trail Association (http://www.mita.org/) MIT is a must membership for any outdoor enthusiast considering an ocean paddle.

As a member of the Maine Island Trail Association (MITA), I enjoy the benefits of a MITA e-newsletter and a MITA Guidebook. Dundee, Cully, Dave and I used this guidebook with its maps and island descriptions to plan our three days 22 mile sea kayak paddle in the Deer Island region of the MIT.

References

- **Ocean Kayaking in the Deer Isle Region of the Maine Coast - Stonington to Isle au Haut**
  http://outdooradventurers.blogspot.com/2014/07/paddling-deer-isle-region-of-maine.html
- **Sea kayaking and Camping on the Maine Island Trail Outdoor Steve's Blog post of August 2010**
  http://tiny.cc/u2j44x
- **Deer Isle Region paddle, Bedford Community TV**
  https://www.youtube.com/watch?v=4FIMlGYn9K0&feature=youtu.be
- **Maine Island Trail Association**
  http://www.mita.org/
- **Maine Island Trail App**
  http://www.mita.org/app
- **Senior Hiker Magazine**
  https://www.seniorhikermagazine.com/

Rowing through the eyes of a Beginner

Figure 51 - Lake Sunapee Rowing Club Lessons

"Never say I wish I had …" is an expression that has always motivated me. All summer I passed a road sign announcing, ***"Rowing Lessons Lake Sunapee Rowing Club. Next class starts on August 3."*** I had watched snippets of racing shells on the Merrimack River, TV, and in summer Olympics. I decided this was my time to say, "Never say I wish I had rowed a shell".

Figure 52 - www.LakeSunapeeRowing.com

I spoke to a friend who I knew was taking rowing lessons with the LSRC – and she sent me the website with a note of encouragement to join.

I registered for the Novice classes – three weeks of classes – three times a week – two hours each class. The LSRC provides the boats (also known as shells). Rowing is often referred to as **crew**.

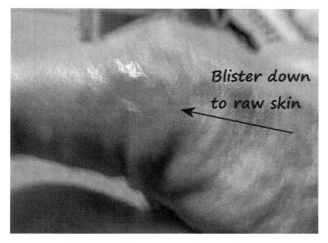

Figure 53 - A Rowing Blister

Figure 54 - An 8+ Sweep with Mount Sunapee in Background

Our coach, Brenda, is just an amazing instructor with knowledge, skills, and a lot of patience. Brenda makes each class fun with personal instruction for each student, and a wealth of education on learning the language and techniques of rowing.

Enjoy the video of this novice student and my classmates as we team and row together never to have to say, "I wish I had learned to row."

Figure 55 - Shoe Stretchers and Sliding Seat

Bedford Community Television (BCTV) is playing a 30 minute video (see below) detailing Steve's novice rowing experience. The dates and times of playing are published on BCTV. All community TV stations are welcome to use this video by contacting BCTV or by communicating directly with Steve.

The below references are shared for each reader's more intense research into the fascinating sport of rowing.

Distinction from other watercraft
"The distinction between rowing and other forms of water transport, such as canoeing and kayaking, is that in rowing the oars are held in place at a pivot point that is in a fixed position relative

to the boat, this point is the load point for the oar to act like a second class lever (the blade fixed in the water is the fulcrum). In flatwater rowing, the boat (also called a shell) is narrow to avoid drag, and the oars are attached to oarlocks at the end of outriggers extending from the sides of the boat. Racing boats also have sliding seats to allow the use of the legs in addition to the body to apply power to the oar. Racing shells are inherently unstable, much like racing kayaks or canoes."

Two types of rowing

- In *sweep* or *sweep-oar* rowing, each rower has one oar, held with both hands. This is generally done in pairs, fours, and eights. In some regions of the world, each rower in a sweep boat is referred to either as *port* or *starboard*, depending on which side of the boat the rower's oar extends to. In other regions, the port side is referred to as stroke side, and the starboard side as bow side; this applies even if the stroke oarsman is rowing on bow side and/or the bow oarsman on stroke side.
- In *sculling* each rower has two oars (or *sculls*), one in each hand. Sculling is usually done without a coxswain in quads, doubles or singles. The oar in the sculler's right hand extends to the port side, and the oar in the left hand extends to the starboard side.

Figure 56 - LSRC Lessons include the Eight+, Quad Scull, Doubles, and Single

My first boat was a quad scull. A **quad scull** is a rowing boat designed for four persons who propel the boat by sculling with two oars, one in each hand. This four seater quad was 45 feet with a weight of 200 lbs. Its cockpit width is 20 inches. Our two oars were 9' each.

My second boat was a single scull one seater 24 feet in length, 75 lbs., and a 20 inch wide cockpit designed for a single person who propels the boat with two 9' oars, one in each hand.

My third boat was a double scull two seater, somewhat similar to a single scull but has two rowers.

My fourth boat was an Eight (8+) 65 foot shell with 8 rowers and a coxswain. We did what is called a sweep or sweep-oar rowing where each rower has one 12 foot oar held with both hands. As each rower has only one oar, the rowers have to be paired so that there is an oar on each side of the boat. Sweeping is in contrast to sculling with my quad and single boats where a rower has two oars, one in each hand.

Some special attire is needed for rowing. Snug-fitting shorts and shirts are best as loose fitting clothing could get caught in the oars and seat tracks. Compression type shorts are ideal. Dry socks are also a must. Socks should be synthetic or wool to help ensure that feet stay warm while wet and will help prevent blistering from the hull's shoes.

Personal Insights of a Novice Still Learning to Scull and Sweep

- As I was canoeing, this week it hit me why canoe instructors always say, "Keep your paddle in the water during rough conditions." As sculling and sweeping oar blades in the water stabilized the boat, so does the canoe paddle blade!

- In canoeing and kayaking, the paddlers face the bow. In sculling and sweeping rowers face the stern. Thus, the rower in the bow in the quad, double, and single need to frequently turn around to see where they are going. The bow person not only has to row BUT has to make sure we are heading in the right direction and away from obstacles.

- In learning to row the instructor does not usually have everyone row at the same time. Initially, I thought this was to give me a rest. Later I realized while not rowing I still had a critical task keeping my blades on the water to stabilize the boat for the other rowers.

- In the eight, quad and double if I made a mistake, the rowers stabilized the boat for me. In the single this was my responsibility - otherwise, I would capsize.

Bedford Community Television (BCTV) has accepted the below 30 minute video detailing Steve's novice rowing experience. The dates and times of playing will be published shortly. All community TV stations are welcome to use this video by contacting BCTV or by communicating directly with Steve.

References
Blog and Video: ROWING through the eyes of a novice
http://tiny.cc/exd31y

Lake Sunapee Rowing Club
http://www.lakesunapeerowing.com

Glossary of Rowing Terms
https://en.wikipedia.org/wiki/Glossary_of_rowing_terms

Single scull
https://en.wikipedia.org/wiki/Single_scull

How to position hands on oars
https://www.youtube.com/watch?v=o3MdSkh2s2o

Rowing technique with diagrams on the rower
https://www.youtube.com/watch?v=W8a9nKkp1OM

Natural Rowing Technique
https://www.youtube.com/watch?v=9BAXGFwcVaY

Getting into a capsized single and double
https://www.youtube.com/watch?v=VYfvuXcSuqs

Recovery to Catch: How to Position Your Hands and Hold Your Oars
https://www.youtube.com/watch?v=o3MdSkh2s2o

Sweep Rowing
https://en.wikipedia.org/wiki/Sweep_(rowing)

Coxswain
https://en.wikipedia.org/wiki/Coxswain

Head of Charles Regatta
http://www.hocr.org/the-regatta/competitors/registration/

Paddling the Northern Forest Canoe Trail
Section 6: The Clyde River - Island Pond to
Pensioner Pond

Three friends and I spent four days paddling the Clyde and
Nulhegan Rivers and Spectacle Pond – parts of what the NFCT
calls section 6. Island Pond is the highest point in the NFCT, and it
serves as the headwaters for the Clyde River, which flows 40 miles
northwest to Lake Memphremagog and leads to the Saint
Lawrence River. Island Pond, through Spectacle Pond, is also the
headwaters for the Nulhegan River, which flows east to the
Connecticut River.

The referenced blog and video will focus on the Clyde River.

Figure 57 - Section 6 Clyde River
We tented at Brighton State Park at Spectacle Pond shoreline for
four days.

Figure 58 - Campsite at Brighton State Park, Spectacle Pond

Water Conditions

- On Day One the Clyde River water was clear and moving slowly from our Island Pond put-in to Ten Mile Square Road take-out. Paddling from Island Pond to Five Mile Square Road was five miles of zigzagging and took us about four hours. We overcame many obstacles such as downed trees in the river, beaver dams, Class I-II boulder fields from a washed out logging-era dam, and walls of wood debris and blow-downs. The water level exposed many of the felled trees and was a challenge to our kayak and canoeing skills to overcome these barriers without portaging. The width of the river from Island Pond to Ten Mile Square Road was narrow (ten to twenty feet wide).
- Day Two was an all-day drenching, soaking rainstorm, and we only managed a brief evening paddle on beautiful Spectacle Pond passing the NFCT sign to portage to the Nulhegan River.

- On Day Three we continued from our Ten Mile Square Road take-out nine miles to Pensioner Pond. Certainly, the previous day's deluge had an impact on the Clyde River width and speed which overflows with high water levels. We estimated a 3 to 4 mph current that moved us along. This Day Three section had more marsh and fewer trees than Day One from Island Pond to Ten Mile Square.

Places to get answers for questions on conditions on the Clyde:

- We used the highly recommended NFCT online **Trip Planner** (http://www.northernforestcanoetrail.org/tripplanner/) to plan and map our trip. We also purchased the **NFCT Lake Memphremagog to Connecticut River Section 6** water protected map - and referred to it frequently throughout our paddle.

- The **Island Pond to Upper Clyde** reference has a very good **Trip Summary** of paddling miles and times. (**http://www.northernforestcanoetrail.org/media/Island Pond And The Upper Clyde.pdf**). Get answers to such questions as "How long does it take to paddle from Island Pond to Five Mile Square Road, and then to Ten Mile Square Road? How long does it take to paddle from Ten Mile Square Road to Pensioner Pond?"

Want to know what it feels like to paddle the Clyde River? What does the countryside look like? What obstacles may be encountered? Want to see Tim, John and Dundee paddle a short section of Class I – II boulder field rapids?

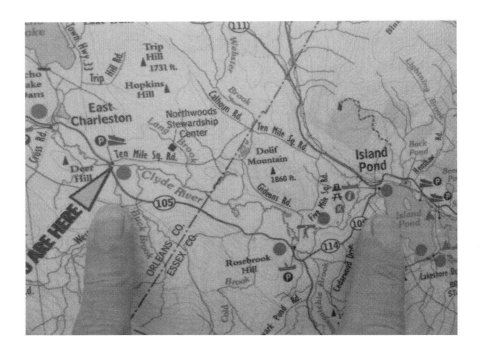

Figure 59 - Map of Island Pond to Ten Mile Square Road

Before you watch the below video let me get you psyched for watching my friends go through the rapids.

Normally, as we approach log dams and other obstacles in the river, we slow and check the area for our approach, and then go through one person at a time, waiting to make sure each person safely gets through before the next person goes. When we know rapids are ahead, we stop before the rapids and scout the best way to go through the rapids.

About four miles from our put-in at Island Pond, I was the first person through one of the many fallen trees blocking the river, and I intended to paddle clear of this obstacle and wait for my fellow paddlers. However the fallen tree was on a bend, and when I made it through the barrier on the bend I immediately found myself upon what looked like Class II white water without a place to pull out and wait for the next paddler.

Mainly I was committed to these rapids with boulders and small drops, not really knowing how rough they were nor how long they would last. I was safely able to make it through this two hundred yard set of rapids – and as you will see next, my friends did likewise. Enjoy the short movie clip made when I ran back on the riverbank, too late to warn my friends of their upcoming surprise.

Clicking the below video reference shares my excitement filming my friends negotiating rapids.

Figure 60 - Our whitewater paddlers

So what is the Northern Forest Canoe Trail (NFCT)?
The NFCT is a living reminder of when rivers were both highways and routes of communications; the Trail is a celebration of the Northern Forest. The Trail is 740 miles of historic waterway traveled by Native Americans. It begins/ends in Fort Kent Maine, and travels through Maine, New Hampshire, Vermont, Quebec, and ending/beginning in Old Forge, New York.
http://www.northernforestcanoetrail.org.

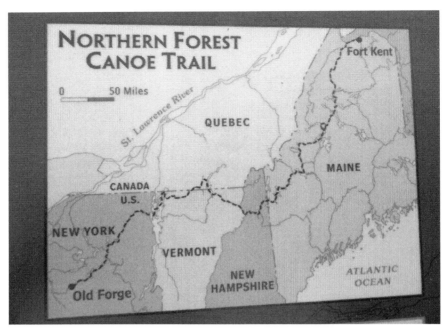

Figure 61 - Map of Northern Forest Canoe Trail

The NFCT is a journey through the landscape of the northeast. The land speaks of its history – of rocks and ruins, people and plants, and natural and economic forces at play. The sections of the NFCT that friends and I have paddled are:

- The Allagash Wilderness Waterway
- Lake Umbagog; Androscoggin River
- Lake Memphremagog
- Connecticut River
- Moose River and Attean Pond on the historic "Moose River Bow Trip"
- Umbazooksus Stream
- Clyde River, Nulhegan River, and Spectacle Pond

- Four Days in Northern New Hampshire with Family and Friends Hiking, Paddling, Tenting, and Moose Sighting.http://outdooradventurers.blogspot.com/2012/07/four-days-in-new-hampshire-of-family.html

- Exploring Lake Umbagog – a Gem in the Great North Woods http://outdooradventurers.blogspot.com/2010/09/exploring-lake-umbagog-gem-in-great.html
- Paddling the Allagash Wilderness Waterway http://outdooradventurers.blogspot.com/2009/07/paddling-allagash-wilderness-waterway.html
- **Paddling the Northern Forest Canoe Trail Section 2: Long Lake to Village of Saranac Lake** http://tiny.cc/ma9o1y
- **Three Generation Paddling in Saranac Lake** http://tiny.cc/pke01y

Special 24 Minute Clyde River Video: Clicking http://tiny.cc/ze954x presents the Northern Forest Canoe Trail ordeal of a writer/cameraman who is occupied as a kayaker on the Clyde River in the Northeast Kingdom of Vermont.

References
Video and Blog: **Paddling the Northern Forest Canoe Trail Section 6: The Clyde River - Island Pond to Pensioner Pond** http://outdooradventurers.blogspot.com/2013/06/paddling-northern-forest-canoe-trail.html

- Northern Forest Canoe Trail http://www.northernforestcanoetrail.org
- Island Pond and the Upper Clyde http://www.northernforestcanoetrail.org/media/Island_Pond_And_The_Upper_Clyde.pdf
- NFCT online Trip Planner http://www.northernforestcanoetrail.org/tripplanner/
- OutdoorSteve.com http://www.outdoorsteve.com
- Blog: Outdoor Enthusiast http://outdooradventurers.blogspot.com/
- Paddling the Northern Forest Canoe Trail: The Clyde River from Island Pond to Ten Mile Square http://youtu.be/ZF6KswIEPHM
- Brighton State Park, Vermont http://www.vtstateparks.com/htm/brighton.htm

Paddling the Northern Forest Canoe Trail Section 2: Long Lake to Village of Saranac Lake

Welcome to the Northern Forest Canoe Trail. The NFCT is a living reminder of when rivers were both highways and routes of communications. The Trail is 740 miles of historic waterway traveled by Native Americans. Its west to east direction begins in Old Forge, New York, and travels through Vermont, Quebec, New Hampshire and ends in Fort Kent Maine. The non-profit that established the Trail divides the trail into 13 sections and offers detailed maps for each of these sections.

Figure 62 - Take-out at Village of Saranac

Our journey was Section 2 in the Adirondack and Saranac region of northern New York. We began at the Long Lake bridge paddling in a north-east direction and ended 42 miles and 3 ½ days later at the Village of Saranac.We hired Adirondack Lakes & Trails Outfitters to drive us to the put-in so we could leave both our vehicles at the Flower Lake take-out – thus saving ourselves two plus hours when we were homeward bound.

Our trip included transfers through two hand-operated locks to convey paddlers between waterways, and three very demanding portages totaling 11.5 plus miles.

Our 3 ½ day itinerary:

- Day 1: A 15 plus mile paddle on Long Lake, then a 1.6-mile portage around Raquette falls – which took three trips totaling 4.8 miles - with our day ending at the Palmer Brook lean-to on the Raquette River.
- Day 2: Raquette River to Stony Creek Ponds, a 1.1 mile Indian Carry portage - which took five trips totaling 5.5 miles – followed by the .4 mile Bartlett Carry into Middle Saranac Lake to our campsite on Norway Island. This was a twelve miles paddling day.
- Day 3: We paddled through the Upper Locks into Lower Saranac Lake to our campsite on Partridge Island. About an 8 mile paddling day.
- Day 4: Lower Saranac Lake to First Pond into Second Pond and through the Lower Locks of the Saranac River into Oseetah Lake, and then into Lake Flower for our final take-out at the Village of Saranac Lake. An 8 mile paddling day

This Section 2 water highway has no fresh drinking water sources. Dehydration can be a major issue. We restocked our drinking water at night boiling lake water with our Jet Boil. Also, it rained our second night, and we directed rainwater from our camp tarp to our cooking pans hence to our water bottles – thus saving Jet Boil fuel.

Figure 63 - Passing through the Locks of NFCT Section 2
More specifics of our Section 2 paddle, portages, and locks can be found in a day-by-day 50-minute web link video at Bedford Community TV **http://tiny.cc/ydb64x**.

Day 2 – Palmer Brook Lean-to to Norway Island, Middle Saranac Lake

We arose in our Palmer Brook lean-to campsite with the smell of fresh coffee. Dundee was up early. John followed asking "How do you want your eggs and bacon?"

Gary, a Park Ranger, visited our camp and emphasized issues of dehydration, particularly on the two upcoming portages at Indian Carry (1.1 miles) and Bartlett carry (.4 miles). He advised us on maps of Section 2 and reminded us to be sure our campfire was completely out before we left camp.

Given our first day had a very demanding 1.6 mile portage that we had to do three times for 4.8 miles (carry the canoe, return to take-out, carry backpacks), we decided at Indian Carry the four of us would carry one canoe. This proved to be really exhausting, as we did five trips over the 1.1 Indian Carry trail (carry the 65 lb old town, walk back, carry the 72 lb Grumman canoe, walk back, and carry the backpacks). These five trips totaled 5.5 miles.

Throughout our portages, we continually drank water every ten minutes or so to prevent dehydration. Even so, we were exhausted by the time all our canoes and gear were at the Upper Saranac Lake put-in.

Indian Carry revealed a very moving token of New York hospitality. As we were lugging the 65 lb Old Town, and we were really exhausted with at least another half mile to reach the Upper Saranac put-in, a fellow waved as he went by us in his truck. Lo and behold he backed up, rolled down his window, and asked, "Do you want to put those canoes in my truck?"

Brian, you are an angel!! He saved us at least an hour of portaging – and certainly provided the physical relief we needed. I gave Brian my OutdoorSteve business card and told him to send me an email so I could mail him a signed copy of **Outdoor Play: Fun 4 4 Seasons**.

We paddled on the Upper Saranac for an hour and came to Bartlett's Carry. We were now sharing our two bottles of remaining fresh water – like in rationing. And we had the Bartlett .4 mile carry left for at least 1.2 miles, AND if we had four people for each canoe, we had nearly two miles left! After our grueling human transport of 5.5 miles at Indian Carry (due to four of us per canoe), our exhaustion told us to return to two people per canoe to eliminate an extra one-mile portage.

We finished Bartlett Carry still alive and entered Middle Saranac Lake. It was about an hour's paddle to Norway Island, our campsite for the night. Amen!!

Our Norway Island campsite (#74) was perfect. It was the only campsite on the island and had pine trees growing amongst the rocks.

The ranger at Palmer Brook told us about a coming storm that evening, so we immediately put up our tents, and then a tarp over the campsite table. Indeed that evening we had a terrible rain storm with lightning and wind. Once the camp was set up, Dundee took a Middle Saranac Lake cool, clear water swim. The rest of us were too exhausted.

I dreamed about our canoes being washed away, paddles gone, and tarp down. I was too exhausted to get out of my tent. My fears were for naught as in the morning the site was calm and everything was in its rightful place.

Day 3 We paddle today from our Norway Island campsite on Middle Saranac Lake to a Partridge Island campsite in Lower Saranac Lake
We started our day with another great breakfast by Chef John. We appreciated John's menu planning, food acquisition, and certainly, his meals were fit for royalty.

Similar to our prior two days, we have been abused by mosquitos, black flies and whatever flying bugs we met on our trip. I am not a DEET person and had been wearing a long sleeve jersey as well as a full body netting. One section we paddled before the locks, turned into a serious humming sound – and by that I mean bug sounds at a high and steady pitch. It was like we were immersed in a swarm of vibrating insects. What a surreal experience.

Today would be the self-operated Uppers Lock from Middle Sarnanc Lake to Lower Sarnanc. Enjoy our first lock transition as we thoroughly appreciated the experience of going from a higher lake to a lower lake – bypassing a severe set of rapids.

After passing through the Upper Lock, we paddled another hour to our campsite for the night on Partridge Island. It was my turn to go swimming in this beautiful clear Lower Saranac Lake.

As you will see in the 50 minute video link on Bedford Community TV **http://tiny.cc/ydb64x** we were more relaxed on Day 3 as we had our strength back with no portages and plenty of potable water. Our relaxation time included:

- Starting our campfire with sparks
- Sharing how we eat our pudding without a spoon when on our camping trips.
- Learning to tie quick release knots for putting up and taking down our tarp
- Walked to ledges on the island to view the beautiful sunset.

Day 4 – Our last day on Section 2 of the NFCT in the Adirondacks and Saranac. We paddled from our Partridge Island campsite through a second hand-operated lock to Oseetah Lake and then to our take-out at the Village of Saranac on the north end of Flower Lake.

We estimated Partridge Island to be about 8 miles or 3 hours of paddling to our take-out at the north end of Flower Lake.

Yesterday, when we passed through the Upper locks, I was in the canoe being lowered. Today was Tim's turn to experience this unique procedure transiting the Lower Lock, that feeling of our canoes and gear being transported via water from Lower Saranac Lake to Oseetah Lake.

No lock operator was present at the lock and Dundee operated the manual controls while John and Tim paddled into the locks – and I documented their transition with videos. The whole descent would take about 30 minutes – mostly waiting for the lock to fill – and then empty and gently hand our canoes and gear, and us, into lower Oseetah lake.

The paddling was easy and we soaked in the wilderness and beauty of the Adirondacks. We saw deer, huge rock formations, and shared highlights of our Saranac paddle. We all agreed, the portaging of our 65 lb and 72 lb canoes was the toughest part of the trip. On our next trip requiring extensive portages, we definitely would rent 40 lb canoes.

After we finished at the Village take-out, we went to the NFCT Kiosk and signed the NFCT log book.

Never say, "I wish I had paddled the **Northern Forest Canoe Trail Section 2** in the Adirondack and Saranac wilderness."

References

Video and Blog: Paddling the Northern Forest Canoe Trail Section 2: Long Lake to Village of Saranac Lake http://outdooradventurers.blogspot.com/2014/06/paddling-northern-forest-canoe-trail.html

Adirondack Lakes & Trails Outfitters

http://www.adirondackoutfitters.com/

Adirondack State Park

https://en.wikipedia.org/wiki/Adirondack_Park

How long does it take to boil drinking water?

http://modernsurvivalblog.com/health/how-long-to-boil-drinking-water/

Northern Forest Canoe Trail

http://www.northernforestcanoetrail.org/

OutdoorSteve.com

http://www.outdoorsteve.com

Figure 64 - Overview of NFCT Section 2 Trip

Goffstown Giant Pumpkin Weigh-off & Regatta

Figure 65 - Giant Pumpkin Weigh-Off & Regatta

"Pull over, there's a giant pumpkin in the river with a person sitting in it!" my wife said as we were passing over the Piscataquog River in Goffstown, New Hampshire. She had spotted a weird scene. Lo and behold there were several giant pumpkins on the river - and they appeared to be racing each other! We were in the midst of the Goffstown Giant Pumpkin Weigh-off and Regatta.

Jim Beauchemin is a volunteer organizer of the Goffstown Giant Pumpkin Weigh-off and Regatta. I saw Jim's license plate, and I asked him, "What do **1,314 LBS** mean?" He enthusiastically told me his giant pumpkin had won first prize at the 2005 Topsfield Fair and his plate number was the weight of his winning giant pumpkin.

Figure 66 - Winner of the Largest Giant Pumpkin - 1,465 lbs

Because of my prior year glimpse of this unique parade of giant pumpkins on the Piscataquog, and Jim's enthusiasm for this hobby/sport, I made it my quest to see this year's Goffstown Giant Pumpkin Weigh-off and Regatta "upfront and personal."

Here is the whirlwind tour of my two days at the Giant Pumpkin Weigh-off and Regatta:

The New Hampshire Giant Pumpkin Growers Association (NHGPGA) Hosts the Weigh-off

o Front-end loaders carry the giant pumpkins for the weigh-off from their pallets to the scale.

o Jim Beauchemin was the narrator and skillfully kept the crowd's enthusiasm throughout the weigh-off and educated them to giant pumpkin growing.

o Bruce Hooker of Belmont, NH was the winning grower. His

pumpkin weighed 1,465 lbs

The Goffstown Giant Pumpkin Regatta is a Boat Race on the Piscataquog River

o Because an excessive amount of rainfall in a short period this summer caused many giant pumpkins to grow too fast and split, there was a fear among the Regatta organizers that there would not be enough pumpkins to use as boats this year. Thankfully, several of the growers donated giant pumpkins for use in the Pumpkin Regatta.

At 2 pm the giant pumpkin boat building started

Figure 67 - Giant Pumpkins Carved for Electric Motor

o Bruce Normand expertly guided and supervised the process for "Giant Pumpkin" boat carving and river testing.

o The first boat building task is to use a plywood template and a power saw to cut a two foot or so diameter hole in the top of the pumpkin.

o Only the grower is allowed to remove the seeds from the giant pumpkins, as the seeds can be very valuable. I heard anywhere from $800 to $1,600 per seed from winning giants.

o Bolts attach the plywood around the carved opening, and the wood serves as a platform to connect an electric motor.

o Each team has a boat theme. You will see their designs in my video.

Sunday morning each team is assigned a time to test their boats on the Piscataquog River

Figure 68 - Goffstown Fire and Rescue Readies Safety Boats

o The boats are ballasted with sand. Insufficiently ballasted boats tend to tip, or heel, and can result in capsizing.

o The electric motors and batteries were placed on/in the boat.

o The captains take the boats for a maiden voyage.

o This maiden voyage is as much fun to watch as the actual race itself. Some of the captains had never been in a giant pumpkin before, and you could feel the nervousness in the air.
o The support crews were tremendous with their encouragement and support for all contestants.

Figure 69 - A Captain Takes Her Boat for a Trial Run

o Goffstown Fire and Rescue handled water safety. The Goffstown hydro dam is very near to the start of the race. In case of capsizing, to catch the "captains" of each pumpkin from going over the dam, two safety catch lines were strung across the river just upstream from the dam.

o The Goffstown Chief of Fire and Rescue reviewed the safety issues with all captains.

At 3 pm the Cannon Roared and Nine Giant Pumpkins headed toward the Goffstown Main Street Bridge

o Upon the roar of the starting cannon, and with the dam at their backs, the captains aimed their giant pumpkin boats upstream into the strong current. Their target was the Main Street Bridge finish line.

Some of the boats swirled in circles, others seemed to be pushed downstream with the current, and one, specifically the Goffstown News Harry Potter themed boat, kept river left aiming straight at the bridge.

Figure 70 - A Boat Captain Fires T-Shirts to the Crowd

o The Giant Pumpkin Eater suddenly appeared upstream honking its horn with water hoses spraying the boats. Indeed some of the boats reciprocated with their hoses. We had a Regatta "Battle on the Piscataquog" – all in fun.

o To fire up the river-bank spectators, some of the boats used air-cannons to shoot Goffstown Regatta monogrammed t-shirts into the crowd.

Figure 71 - Giant Pumpkin Eater Puts the Fleet Under Attack

o The winner of the 2011 Giant Pumpkin Regatta was the Harry Potter themed boat of the Goffstown News. Actually, all the boat captains are winners. Meeting the challenge of steering a near-thousand pound pumpkin, seated on their battery with knees up, and reaching back in an awkward position to steer and throttle – showed me that there should be nine trophies awaiting all finishers of the Giant Pumpkin Regatta.

An international flair was present throughout the two days as a TV crew from Germany did interviews and videos.

Figure 72 - And the Winner is Harry Potter!!

- Thanks to the support of the New Hampshire Giant Pumpkin Growers Association and countless sponsors and volunteers throughout Goffstown, the Giant Pumpkin Weigh-off and Regatta has become the signature event for Goffstown Main Street. I can't wait to attend next year.

I now will never have to say, "I wish I had watched the Goffstown Giant Pumpkin Weigh-off and Regatta".

References

o Jim Beauchemin's Discovery Channel DVD, "**The Secrets of Growing Champion Giant Pumpkins**", is available at https://www.createspace.com/209048. It is an entertaining presentation with a wealth of information on growing giant pumpkins.

o **Excess Rain, Lack of Growers** http://tiny.cc/djq74x
o **Goffstown Reviews the Seedy Fleet** http://tiny.cc/oev74x

o New Hampshire Giant Pumpkin Growers Association http://www.nhgpga.org/

o Goffstown Main Street http://www.goffstownmainstreet.org/

o World Record Giant Pumpkin is 2,009 lbs as of October 1, 2012, held by Ron Wallace of Greene, RI.

Video Reference Goffstown Giant Pumpkin Regatta

- **Blog: Giant Pumpkin Regatta** http://outdooradventurers.blogspot.com/2011/10/goffstown-nh-giant-pumpkin-weigh-off.html
- **Video Giant Pumpkin Weigh-off and Regatta** http://www.youtube.com/watch?feature=player_embedded&v=upwOo6B9JBo

---

Paddling the Waters of Quetico Provincial Park

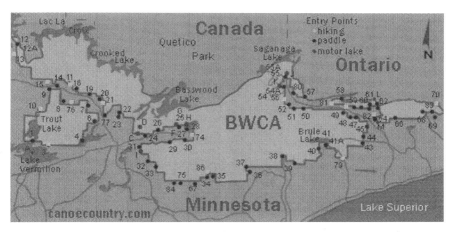

Figure 73 - Map: BWCA – Minnesota and Ontario

Quetico Provincial Park is a region of isolated Canadian wilderness straddling the Canada - United States border between southwestern Ontario and northern Minnesota. Quetico is composed of over 1 million acres of forests and thousands of miles of water routes. A permits is required for each visitor.

In mid-September, three outdoor enthusiast friends and I paddled a six-day 35-mile loop in the Quetico Provincial Park region of Ontario.

We all agreed we had the most physically and technically demanding portages we have ever attempted. We balanced these challenges against seeing some of the most beautiful wilderness, pristine water, and wildlife in the country. Indeed, the boundary waters provided us with a very memorable and impressive paddling experience.

The Portages

Figure 74 - Canoe Shoulder Yoke for One Person Carry

We had seventeen portages for eight-plus portage miles. (See the **Video References** below to see my spreadsheet for the lake sequences, their portages, and the portage distances).

My son Tim and I were in an 18' 6" 43 lbs kevlar ultra-light Wenona canoe and Dundee and his son Paul in a similar model canoe. The portages were through dense woods with extremely narrow and rough granite rocks of all sizes and shapes, up and down hills, over fallen trees, mud, and water.

At each portage, one person from each canoe carried the canoe on their shoulders using a leather padded neck yoke. I portaged the canoe five times, whereas Tim did the other 12 portages. Dundee and Paul likewise worked a similar type of division of labor to carry the canoe at each portage. Our backpacks (in each canoe - a food pack and two packs for each of our personal gear) averaged 50 plus lbs for the first few days until the food weight eased.

Figure 75 - Beginning a Gear Portage

To get the full feel of our physical effort of the seventeen portages, you must realize the four of us had to make three trips each across the portage. Because of the narrow and rough terrain and its length, each canoe was carried by one person, while their canoe partner carried the food pack. We then returned over the portage for the remaining gear to carry our packs, and other hand carried gear such as paddles, fishing poles, tent, dry bag, and maps.

We had no injuries of a hernia, sprained ankles or whatever. Amen!

As you see from the portage spreadsheet, our first day of paddling had the three longest portages, and since it was our first day, we had the heftiest weight of our entire trip. I must confess - after we selected a campsite on the Meadows Lake island, set up our tents, and went for a much needed refreshing swim - we all took a one hour nap. Exhaustion was upon us. After that we began preparations for dinner.

Our Team

Figure 76 - Dundee and Paul Paddling Lake Agnes

Paul, our Meal Planner and Chief Cook did a fabulous job in providing wonderful meals. My son Tim shared with Paul the meal preparation, camp setups, cleanup, etc.

Dundee was the navigator with excellent map reading skills and keeping us on our water trail as we paddled through fifteen or so lakes. There were no trail signs or lake signs – our only guidance was the detail map and our compass showing the portages– and Dundee's innate sense of direction and recognition of where we were located on the map.

As the days passed, we realized we were following a waterway highway as we portaged from lake to lake in a very logical manner.

Figure 77 - Just in Time to Get Out of the Rain and Snow

On all five of our evenings, we slept on islands - as we felt this would provide more security from bear and wolves.

Wildlife and Indian Pictographs
We saw a variety of wildlife, including eagles, loons, mink, beaver, otter, grouse, signs of moose, heard wolf calls, and had warnings of black bear from Quetico rangers, but no sightings.

We saw ancient Ojibwe Indian pictographs (paintings on the lakeside granite) and petroglyphs (images etched into the granite) along the lakeside cliffs. We had bought a book, **Magic on the Rocks** by Michael Furtman on the Pictographs of Quetico, and we read the book in camp to educate ourselves on these little understood Ojibwe artifacts (http://tiny.cc/3ww74x).

Figure 78 - Paul Points to Ojibwe Pictographs

Figure 79 - Can You See the Four Pictographs Paul Sees?

Louisa Falls

We swam the first two days – day one off our island campsite in Meadows Lake and the second day in the middle of Louisa Falls - a one-hundred-foot waterfall flowing from Louisa Lake into Agnes Lake. Halfway down the falls is a neat natural bathtub including a stream of water for a great back massage from the rushing water into the tub.

The following day we had a brief flurry of snow and cold rain, and of course, swimming was over. We fished as we paddled, but caught nothing of a size we could eat.

Forest Fire

There was a massive forest fire in the area - we could see and smell distant smoke from our island campsite on Summer Lake, but we were not in any danger. The Quetico ranger at Prairie Portage told us they generally leave these lightening started fires to burn out by themselves, as they are a natural process of the wilderness ecosystem.

Rough Water and Cold Weather

Figure 80 - From swimming to freezing within 24 hours

From Swimming Weather to Freezing Weather – Be Prepared!
We had three days of on and off heavy rain showers (including one shower of hailstones and snow) and 30 mph wind gusts and high waves as we crossed a few of the lakes. You ask, "Why did you cross in such rough conditions?" Well, we needed to seek a campsite for the night. These paddles required seasoned and strong paddlers, and thankfully we were all up to the task. There were no flips. Amen.

The Water
The Boundary Waters and Quetico lakes are pure, clear and pristine waters. Given the fact that the lakes were gouged out by the movement of mile-thick glaciers thousands of years ago, the water depth frequently dropped off close to shore as the lakes are carved within granite mountains.

A question we frequently asked before the trip was "where do we get our drinking water while in the Quetico waters? Certainly boiling or purification tablets are the wisest recommendation for drinking any lake water. However, as we spoke to those who regularly paddle these waters, the feedback was "as you paddle in deep water, push your empty water containers as far down into the water as you can reach and then open the cap. Replace the cap before you bring the filled bottle back up. This water was of course boiled during cooking and using for hot beverages, but we drank directly from the bottles in which we stored the water.

Start a Campfire with Flint, Steel, Tinder – and Practice
One evening we played "survivor man" and started our campfire solely by use of flint and steel. A shower of sparks is needed to start a fire along with proper tinder (http://survivalcache.com/fire-tinder/) and - practice, practice, and practice. I had brought a **FireSteel Scout** tool (www.lightmyfire.com) composed simply of flint and steel.

It's about as basic a process as you can ask for... people have been lighting fires with flint and steel for many, many years. But, again, it does require practice and the use of both hands.

I did start the fire with this tool, but I won't be throwing away my lighter and hand washing alcohol until I practice some more. The **FireSteel** makes a handy item in my pack for emergencies. It does work in wet weather, but, it does take a knack.

Paul was the matchless fire starting expert in the group. Below, Paul demonstrates to how to start a fire with flint and steel. As Paul pointed out to us, the key is proper tinder i.e. (dried leaves, wood shaving chips, or, preferred if available, birds nests, birch bark, and dry mosses) – and practice, practice, and more practice.

Figure 81 - Flint, Steel and Tinder – and Practice

Trip Preparation
We entered the Canadian waters at the Prairie Portage location into Quetico Provincial Park via a water taxi tow on Moose Lake from Ely, MN. To assure the entry date we wanted, we needed to apply for an entry permit five months before our preferred date. There is a limited number of entry permits for each day. Piragis Northwoods Company in Ely coordinated our permit application,

outfitted us with two We-no-nah canoes, maps, food backpacks, and a large Duluth type backpack that could handle what I had originally packed into three dry bags. No motorized vehicles or power boats are allowed within the Quetico wilderness area.

Our Paddling Route

Figure 82 - Piragis Outfitters Shuttle us to Prairie Portage

Our six day water route was a loop of fifteen lakes within Quetico. From the Prairie Portage Ranger Station entry, we paddled north to Sunday Lake, then east to Meadows Lake, and then north on Agnes Lake until we reached the portage to Silence Lake. We looped back to Prairie Portage via the lake route known as the "S" chain of lakes: Silence, Sultry, Summer, Noon, Shade, West, South, and then to Basswood, Burke and Bayley Bay.

Although we passed through the northern Minnesota Boundary Waters Canoe Area Wilderness (BWCAW) as our canoes were towed with the motorboat, technically we did a Quetico paddling trip.

A Trip for the Physically Fit with a Planned Route

Our experience in the waters of Quetico taught us:

(1) You need to plan your portage route in agreement with the physical condition and paddling experience of your group. Develop your route considering portage length and portage frequency;

(2) This trip is for the physically fit outdoor enthusiast;

(3) You need strength and endurance paddling skills to handle long mileages and paddling amongst heavy wind and rough waves;

(4) A strong back for heavy, lengthy, and rough portages;

(5) Have at least one member of your group with map and compass reading skills. Remember Quetico has no trail signs or markers;

(6) Outdoor menu planning and cooking skills (at least one person);

Figure 83 - Our Take-out at Prairie Portage

(7) An ability to set up a campsite, start a campfire in different weather conditions (at least one person);

(8) A team mentality to work together in grinding and varying terrain and weather conditions and with camp setups;

(9) In our late September trip, we went swimming one day – and the next day had to take shelter because of a snow and rain storm. Bring clothing appropriate for the time of year and any unpredictable changes in weather extremes;

(10) A sense of humor and enjoyment of the wonderful outdoors.

Figure 84 - A Big "Thank You" to Drew, Piragis Northwoods Outfitting Manager, for his outstanding advice and gear.

We all gained an appreciation for the beauty, tranquility, and isolation of the Quetico area. Will we return? Yes - absolutely!

Now, I never have to say, "I wish I had paddled the boundary waters of Minnesota and Canada."

References

- Piragis Northwoods Outfitters http://www.piragis.com/
- Canoe On Inn http://www.canoeoninn.com/
- Bearwise http://www.mnr.gov.on.ca/en/Business/Bearwise/
- Boundary Water Canoe Access http://www.bwca.com/
- Boundary Waters Canoe Area & Quetico Provincial Park Canoe Trip Routes http://www.canadianwaters.com/boundary-waters-canoe-area-quetico-provincial-park-canoe-trip-routes/
- Mckenzie Maps http://www.bwcamaps.com/
- Quetico Provisional Park http://en.wikipedia.org/wiki/Quetico_Provincial_Park.
- **Senior Hiker Magazine** https://www.seniorhikermagazine.com/

Video References Paddling Boundary Waters of Minnesota and Ontario

- **Blog:** Paddling the Waters of Quetico Provincial Park in Ontario http://tiny.cc/4px74x
- Video of Boundary Waters Portages http://tiny.cc/jtx74x
- Spreadsheet of lake sequences, portages and portage distances http://tiny.cc/e0x74x

---

Campfire: How to Cook an Egg in an Onion

Why is campfire cooking a **Bucket List** story? Because my blog video has "gone viral" with **over 50,000 YouTube views (http://tiny.cc/9tb94x)**.

A Great North Woods paddling and tenting trip to northern New Hampshire's Lake Francis allowed me to take my campsite breakfast cooking experience a bit further. Paul Tawrell's book, **Wilderness Camping and Hiking,** described a method of cooking an egg over an open campfire in an onion. Being one never to say, "I wish I had cooked an egg in an onion over an open campfire," I decided to try Paul's recommendation.

Figure 85 - Egg in an Onion Cooked in Campfire Ashes

Figure 86 - The First Taste of Egg Cooked in an Onion

Figure 87 - The Egg AND Onion are Both Eaten!

Two more campfire tips: 1) an Egg in an Orange; 2) a Banana Split

Want more campfire cooking treats? These two are from my
fellow outdoor enthusiast, John. John usually assumes

responsibility to plan and cook our meals for our outdoor treks. This trip he wanted to do "something different."

Through a browser search, he found a site for cooking an egg inside an orange over an open campfire. The result was delicious.

Figure 88 - Cook an Egg in an Orange

John further impressed us by serving a campfire breakfast banana dessert. Slice the banana and skin lengthwise, and then put bits of chocolate in the slit. Place this combination inside aluminum foil and heat in the campfire ashes for a few minutes. Indeed, it is a banana sundae!

Go to the **References** below to see videos of these unique campfire breakfast treats: egg in an onion; egg in an orange; and chocolate banana split.

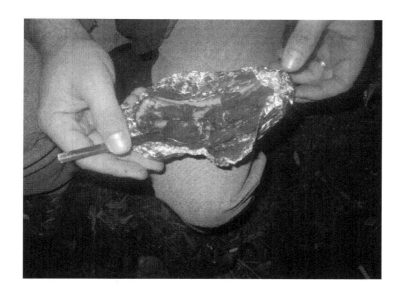

Figure 89 - Banana Sundae Prepared on Open Flame

References: Campsite Chats
- **Blog and video: How to Cook an Egg in an Onion http://tiny.cc/jiap2y**
- **Video: Cook an Egg in an Onion Over an Open Campfire http://tiny.cc/9tb94x.**
- **Blog and Video: Orange and Banana - Never say, "I wish I had Paddled the Swanee River" http://tiny.cc/odyq2y**
- **Video: Using an Orange to Cook an Egg http://tiny.cc/qmap2y**
- **Starting Your Campfire with Rotten Birch Bark http://tiny.cc/5pap2y**
- **Wilderness Camping & Hiking, Paul Tawrell, 2008 http://tiny.cc/opxq2y**

How to Become an Outdoor Enthusiast

"Everyone must believe in something. I believe I'll go outdoors." – S. Priest

Outdoor Play "Fun 4 4 Seasons" Volume II enthusiastically portrays a daily commitment to the outdoors for health and fitness. This book is full of personal "how does it feel" insights and references for the reader to learn more.

The message is to get outdoors and do something. Often your quest starts in your neighborhood and community. Do not worry about reaching the top of the mountain - concern yourself with staying on the path. The only competition you have is the task at hand.

Exercise has proven to make you healthier both physically and mentally. Committing daily outdoor activities, such as walking and running, add to your endurance for all outdoor activities. Best yet, your body will be stronger with exercise, thus avoiding many injuries. So how do you get started being an outdoor enthusiast?

Some people can be discouraged from exercising by not knowing what to do or how to do it. Those who were athletic in childhood may be frustrated by how their abilities have deteriorated over time. Certain individuals need to try new activities so they won't be comparing themselves to others or earlier performances.

This first section is an introduction to the primary intent of this book - to promote the outdoors as a component of one's daily life. I will suggest a process to become an outdoor enthusiast for those who hesitate because of age, limited time, family commitments, or knowledge of an activity. I have used this process to get where I am today.

The middle sections are divided into the seasons of the year: **Spring**, **Summer**, **Fall** and **Winter** with glimpses into my outdoor feelings and shared learning with supporting web references and videos. These sections are taken from my blog – **https://outdooradventurers.blogspot.com**. These posts provide a peek into outdoor places and Internet sites for research and preparation.

The **Places to Play in Northern New England** section provides web references to local activities and clubs to join as incentives to learn and participate.

The last section, **The Beginning**, is my personal story of how I went from a couch potato with a limp from a torn Achilles tendon injury to a daily outdoor enthusiast.

You are only limited to an outdoor activity by boundaries set by yourself. Just by following simple steps, you will be well on your way to expanding your horizons and removing barriers and boundaries to enjoying the outdoors and a healthier you.

In my case, I will start the "beginner" reader with walking outdoors or on a treadmill. Progression to outside exercise is presented as distances between telephone poles. I will explain "telephone poles" later.

First, like all advice on exercise, it is strongly recommended you get your physician's approval.

Second, it is OK for a family member or friend to join you in this endeavor, BUT DO NOT WAIT because of their schedule. Rely on no one but yourself. No excuses.

No matter which outdoor exercises you choose, you need to get your cardio system in shape. Your heart is the engine that requires preparation and tuning. You can do this with both exercise and proper eating habits.

Frankly, in my case, the key is exercise and the eating habits will follow naturally. The more exercise I did, the better my eating awareness and habits became. This chapter does not focus on food. It addresses exercise, and in particular talks about gradually working up from simple and short walks, and the intensity and duration of the exercises will be determined over time.

Start Right Outside Your Home

What is great is you can start right outside your home! For safety's sake, remember to ALWAYS walk and run on the sidewalk, or on the side of the road facing oncoming traffic.

Keeping a diary of each day's progression, including how far you went, the method of exercise (walk, run/walk, run) will help motivate you when you see the progress you are making.

Next, RESIST TEMPTATION TO GO FASTER AND FURTHER. If you do, you will most assuredly be injured.

Okay, let's get started.

> **Day 1**: Go outside and walk the distance between two telephone poles, then walk back home.
> **Day 2**: Go outside and walk the distance between three telephone poles, then walk back home.
> **Day 3**: Go outside and walk the distance between four telephone poles, then walk back home.
>
> Continue this progressive program for days 4 and 5. If you have breathing problems, or get exhausted, do not add the extra distance.
>
> **Day 6 and 7**: Rest. Skip only two days a week. Light rain is no excuse for not accomplishing your day's goal.
> **Day 8**: Go outside and run the distance between two telephone poles, then walk back home.
> **Day 9**: Go outside and run the distance between four

telephone poles, then walk back home.

Day 10, 11, 12: Run six, eight and ten telephone poles respectively (yes, you have increased the number of poles).

If you have followed this fixed schedule, you will feel the urge to get into your car and measure your distance. Do it!

Now develop your own plan to reach one mile in six weeks.

Some frequently asked questions on getting started:

- How far is the distance between two telephone poles? ANSWER: Well, I have 60 paces (about 60 yards) between the poles on my street. No telephone poles? ANSWER: I just gave you a distance.

- What if I feel good and want to go further and faster? ANSWER: DO NOT, I repeat, DO NOT try walking or running beyond the specified distances. People, feeling good, try to go further and faster. THEY GET INJURED, and then they are set back for months. DO NOT, I repeat, DO NOT try to get ahead of this schedule.

- What if I am injured, such as with shin splints or a sore knee? ANSWER: Then back off a bit from your running distance and do more walking. As your injury pain subsides, return to an increased schedule. Try not to skip a day of running or walking, unless you feel the pain is causing the injury to worsen.

- Do I need a particular shoe or sneaker to start? ANSWER: Nope - no excuses. Get outside. When you reach day twelve, you are now ready to buy sneakers or running shoes.

- Do I need sweat pants, shorts, or polypropylene clothing? ANSWER: Nope, again no excuses. Get outside. When you reach day twelve, you are now ready to look like a runner – buy yourself some running shorts, a light jacket, and long lightweight pants.

- Do I need a hat? ANSWER: Yes. Old, new, torn or whatever. You need a hat to protect you from the sun and rain. Get outside.

Four reminders to becoming an outdoor enthusiast:

1. Be sure to follow the schedule of this program.

2. RESIST TEMPTATIONS TO GO FASTER AND FURTHER, or else, guaranteed, YOU WILL GET INJURED.

3. Be consistent in doing your walking and running - No excuse for missing a day.

4. Do not let weather, lack of an outdoor companion, or fancy clothing deter you.

To get a sense of how another person did with this program, it took Outdoor Steve six weeks before he ran one mile without stopping to walk. After that, he never exceeded one mile for the next year. After a year, he began to increase his distance. As he gained confidence in his physical conditioning, he complemented his running with other outdoor challenges. His accomplishments have included cycling, hiking, swimming, canoeing, kayaking, triathlons, biathlons, cross-country skiing, and marathons.

When presented with an outdoor opportunity, such as a one-week paddle on the one-hundred and seven-mile Allagash Wilderness Waterway, do I say, "I have too many things to do?" Or do I say, "Yes!" because this is an excellent opportunity to enjoy my sons and friends? The work and home chores will be there when I get back.

Most of these short scenarios are from my **Outdoor Enthusiast** blog (http://outdooradventurers.blogspot.com/). Each post has Internet references "what, where, why and how" so the reader can do much more than read about one person's outdoor quests.

As you read the short stories and click on the self-taken videos in this book, let your body and mind experience the wonderment of personal enlightenment and outdoor play.

My accompanying blog videos give you the feeling of "being there." For example, I describe with text what it is like to cross the fabled and dangerous Knife Edge Trail on Mt Katahdin. Through the accompanying video from my Go Pro chest camera, you "feel" what it is like to hike this one mile 18-inch wide trail 5,000 feet above sea level.

My mission is to motivate and encourage families and individuals to make the outdoors a key component of their daily life.

Get on your bike. Go hiking with your family. Run with a neighbor. Take telemark ski lessons. Try an Ottertail paddle. Take swimming lessons. Go spinning on your bike. Visit a museum. Go to an Audubon seminar.

Never say, "I wish I had gone outdoors with family and friends."

Warning Signs, Survival, Safety and First Aid

Survival, safety, and first aid can never be assumed. I felt a need to emphasize **Survival**, **Safety** and **First Aid** in this section with my upfront and personal experiences.

This section is not a medical primer. I am not a physician. Other than Wilderness First Aid courses, I have minimal medical training. Given all this, I have faced situations in the wilderness where I do not want to put my friends and myself into critical positions. At times I had to make health and medical decisions to prevent, treat, and care for injuries when trained medical personnel were not immediately present. I want to share these avoidance and treatment situations with you.

To further emphasize this topic, I begin with trailside warning signs I have seen. To me, large warning signs are worth "a thousand words." My companions and I pause and read, and discuss them. The selected signs below have many meanings and interpreted *in a critical, significant, consequential, momentous, weighty, far-reaching, major, grave and severe ways*.

Read the signs – get their message. Then read the sign a second time. Later you will learn about my injuries and experience, and why these signs are critical to every outdoor enthusiast.

Figure 90 -This sign is at the beginning of the Bright Angel Trail on the Rim of the Grand Canyon

After hiking **DOWN** the Bright Angel Trail from the rim of the Grand Canyon[2] to Indian Garden in 2 ½ hours, and then **UP** the same 4 ½ mile trail back to the rim in 4 1/2 hours, I truly experienced this warning. I have promoted and edited this sign in my lectures to **CAUTION – IN IS OPTIONAL – OUT IS MANDATORY** when I talk about hiking into the woods. And when I talk about climbing in the White Mountains of New Hampshire, I edited the sign to warn, **CAUTION – UP IS OPTIONAL – DOWN IS MANDATORY**.

---

[2] **Blog and video: Hike from South Rim of Grand Canyon's Bright Angel Trail Down to Indian Garden and Back to the Rim** http://tiny.cc/k5an1y

Figure 91 - Sign on 18 Mile Moose Alley - Great North Woods of New Hampshire

This **Brake for Moose sign**[3] is no joke. The same for **Moose Crossing** and **Bear Crossing**. I have had too many friends who have hit or been hit by a moose – and were seriously injured. You see this sign, you slow down, and you become alert. Moose and bear do have a habit of following the same paths, so when you look at the sign, you know moose and bear have been reported in this area – keep alert!

---

[3] **Blog and video: Four Days in Northern New Hampshire with Family and Friends Hiking, Paddling, Tenting and Moose Sighting**
http://tiny.cc/n6an1y

Figure 92 - White Mountain trail sign as you go above tree line

This sign says it all, "THE AREA AHEAD HAS THE WORST
WEATHER IN AMERICA. MANY HAVE DIED THERE FROM
EXPOSURE EVEN IN THE SUMMER. TURN BACK <u>NOW</u> IF
THE WEATHER IS BAD".

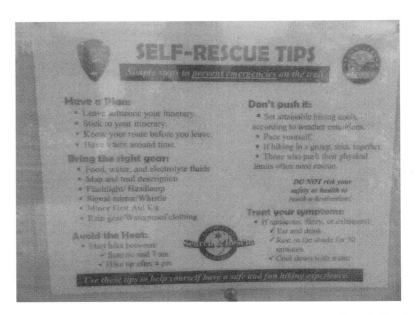

Figure 93 - Grand Canyon sign for 1) Have a Plan, 2) Don't Push it, 3) Bring the right gear, 4) Avoid the Heat, and 5) Treat your symptoms

Below the Self-Rescue Tips sign was an article of the death of a 24-year marathoner who died in the Grand Canyon of dehydration.[4] The message was 1) unprepared for extreme heat, 2) excessive distance and 3) lack of water. She may have lived if she had followed the Self-Rescue Tips. The story she leaves should save the life of others who practice the Self-Rescue Tips.

---

[4] **A Story is Worth a Thousand Words: Death at the Grand Canyon: How a Story Can Save Lives**
https://robbiesenbach.com/how-a-story-can-save-lives/

Preventive success! Grand Canyon's response to search-and-rescue overload http://tiny.cc/5qbn1y

Figure 94 - Tuckerman Ravine Ski Area - a high avalanche area

Tuckerman Ravine[5] [6] is isolated on the east side of Mt. Washington in the White Mountain National Forest, is famous for its daredevil spring skiing, snowboarding, mountaineering, ice climbing, and hiking. Moreover, Tuckerman's isolation and its treacherous conditions and terrain can be risky – and even fatal. Read the sign before skiing and hiking Tuckerman's Ravine.

---

[5] **Blog and Video: Fantastic Mid-week Trek to Tuckerman Ravine** http://tiny.cc/ccbn1y

[6] **Tuckerman Ravine** (http://www.tuckerman.org/tuckerman/tuckerman.htm)

Figure 95 Winter and Spring Warning for Mt Washington

The White Mountains is notorious for hikers, ice climbers, and skiers – Be aware – read the signs

Figure 96 - Bicyclist - Please Pass Carefully. It's The Law

Bicyclists and vehicle drivers must be aware of State laws for a minimum distance when passing a cyclist. It's the law!

For example, in New Hampshire[7]:

265:143-a Drivers to Exercise Due Care When Approaching Bicycle. – Every driver of a vehicle, when approaching a bicyclist, shall insure the safety and protection of the bicyclist and shall exercise due care by leaving a reasonable and prudent distance between the vehicle and the bicycle. The distance shall be presumed to be reasonable and prudent if it is at least 3 feet when the vehicle is traveling at 30 miles per hour or less, with one additional foot of clearance required for every 10 miles per hour above 30 miles per hour.

Figure 97 - Paddlers, boaters and swimmers need to read signs - they can save your life[8]

---

[7]**2017 New Hampshire Revised Statutes**
Title XXI - MOTOR VEHICLES
Chapter 265 - RULES OF THE ROAD
Section 265:143-a - Drivers to Exercise Due Care When Approaching Bicycle. http://tiny.cc/utbn1y

[8]Kennebec Turbine Tests **http://tiny.cc/gubn1y**

Figure 98 - Are you ready for Katahdin? What if I'm not ready?

Figure 99 - Knife Edge Trail - DO NOT HIKE THIS TRAIL IN BAD WEATHER[9]

The Knife Edge Trail can be the hiker's choice on Mt Katahdin's last section to get to Baxter Peak and the northern terminus of the

[9] **Blog and Video Knife Edge Trail to Baxter Peak at Northern Terminus of Appalachian Trail** http://tiny.cc/iwbn1y

2,200 mile Appalachian Trail. Many hikers, after hiking six hours from their Roaring Brook campsite, get to Pamola peak and gasp at the Knife Edge's dramatic, treeless narrow spine made up of jagged rocks and sheer drops for 1.1 miles, and decide to turn around. Other hikers reach the trail, and the weather forces them to turn back. The Knife Edge is considered the most dangerous trail in the northeast.

Be prepared by reading the "Are you ready for Katahdin" sign, and you will have a most rewarding and bucket list accomplishment hike that you will brag about for years.

Have I had injuries?

Yes, many. Injuries go with being an outdoor enthusiast for over 50 years. Here are some:

- Torn Achilles Tendon playing pick-up basketball with co-workers. Took me over one year to overcome a serious limp and to begin to trust my limited Achilles tendon in active exercise.
- Many sprained ankles
- Many knee pain injuries
- Torn shoulder ACL from learning to telemark ski
- Hip pain from worn shoes
- Torn shoulder rotator cuff from demonstrating to my sons I could still throw a baseball.
- Hamstring pulls can be caused by extending myself trying to run faster, not stretching before vigorous exercise, and from not enough cross-training between injuries.

Have I had situations where I put myself in conditions where wrong decisions or tough circumstances could be a threat for getting lost, injured or worse? Yes. Read as I share some these.

Here are my stories in detail – no examples here – only my real-life experiences.

Lessons learned in the White Mountains of New Hampshire

Figure 100 - Sign at the start of a trail in White Mountain National Forest is not to be taken casually

My son Tim and I were taking friends on a hike up Tuckerman Ravine Trail with our destination the summit of Mt Washington. Too many inexperienced hikers are lost in this area of the White Mountains of New Hampshire. We emphasized to our group the importance of suitable clothing and staying together.

It is important to bring proper gear as weather conditions can quickly turn dangerous in the form of severe wind, rain, cold, snow, thunder and lightning, etc. And, the temperature difference between a starting point at Pinkham Notch hut and the top of Mt Washington can vary significantly ... no matter what season of the year.

It was July and we started at the Route 16 Pinkham Notch AMC hut with temperatures in the high 80 degrees, but on top of Mt

Washington temperatures can be significantly lower and high winds are no unusual.

Too many hikers get lost in the White Mountains. The warning signs at the start of trails in the White Mountain National Forest is not to be taken casually.

I told my group of the temperature changes to make sure they all carry a set of warm clothes. And DO NOT wear cotton as it does not dry out quickly if wet. I warned them of directional trail signs – and to stay together in at least groups of two or more – and when reaching a trail junction, to wait for the rest of the group. I wanted no one to get lost from the group.

I repeated the above warning the morning of our hike. What happened was nearly catastrophic for me. We reached the top of Mt Washington, and two of our group were missing. What do I do? Do I report them missing? I decided to wait for 15 minutes. After this period and they did not show, I deemed them to be lost and it was time to report them to the rangers to initiate a rescue search.

As I approached the office of the ranger, who comes around the corner but the two missing people from my group… as if they had successfully reached the summit of Mt Washington. They both said they were freezing… and asked if we have extra clothing. They also "assumed" they knew the trail we were taking to the summit … when they took a more roundabout route … thus appearing to us to be lost because they did not wait when they came to a fork in the trail. Was I upset!

LESSONS LEARNED: 1) When you instruct your group to have warm clothing with them … BE SURE TO visually see the clothing! 2) REPEAT, by a verbal response, when coming to at a trail junction … "WAIT for the rest of the group".3) You cannot depend on cell phones as they run out of batteries or there is usually no cell service where you are going.

Mt Garfield, a broken arm, headache, and nauseous, and no basic first aid knowledge

This hike was supposed to be a pleasant two-night stay in the White Mountains. The plan was to hike on Friday up Mt. Garfield, a 4,000-footer on the Appalachian Trail; stay in our tent, and hike on Saturday to the Zealand Falls AMC hut for an overnight stay by beautiful Zealand Falls. We never made it to the Zealand hut as we had two incidents for which we did not plan.

Our first incident involved two young men in our group who were eager trailblazers, and quickly left our group behind as they hiked uphill with minimal breaks … and, which we learned later, drinking no water. When the rest of us reached the campsite, five and a half hours had passed since we started the hike.

We found the boys at the campsite with headaches and nauseous.

They both were shivering more than was normal, and I began to get a bit nervous, as their condition appeared to be getting worse. We made hot soup and hot chocolate for them. We quickly put our tents in the site's lean-to shelter and encouraged them to get in their sleeping bags, stay warm, and sleep. Thankfully, after an hour, the boys were feeling better.

As I would later learn, their headache and nauseous conditions probably were caused by dehydration and altitude change, which can occur because they climbed too quickly to this 4,000-foot campsite without stopping to drink water. Their youthful aggressiveness to "get there first" caused classic symptoms of high- altitude dehydration which most likely could have be avoided had they been drinking water every ten to fifteen minutes.

Our second Mt Garfield hike incident occurred the next day as we cautiously made our way down the snow and ice-covered Garfield Trail. Suddenly Joe yelled. I turned just in time to see him fall, savagely smashing his right forearm on top of a football-shaped rock. Joe laid there in obvious pain. He was very pale, and his eyes expressed immense pain. The only treatment we offered Joe was to rest 5 minutes before we continued our 5-hour hike to the trailhead.

It is suggested Joe's arm needed medical attention, but having little first aid knowledge in our group, we did not know enough to put a precautionary splint on his hurting arm.

When we reached the trailhead, we immediately brought Joe to a hospital, and X-ray films of Joe's arm revealed he had a broken his arm.

The boys' illness and Joe's accident made me realize someone in our group should have first aid training. The next Spring, I took a three-day Wilderness First Aid course sponsored by the Dartmouth College Outing Club at Moosilauke Ravine.

With some knowledge of wilderness first aid, we may have prevented the boys' headaches and nausea by warning them to drink water, as we practiced, every 10 to fifteen minutes of the hike. We also might have better protected Joe's arm with a splint and then putting a bandage around his shoulder to hold the arm in a stable position.

LESSONS LEARNED: 1) Since we make many wilderness trips, at least one our group needs to take a Wilderness First Aid course[10] 2) Learn how to make an emergency splint 3) Always bring water on a hike, AND, make sure each person in the group drinks at least every 10 to 15 minutes. 4) Learn signs of dehydration – and be aware altitude sickness can come from dehydration caused by lack of frequent drinking of water. 5) So important to stay hydrated when hiking and with altitude. You can gauge your level of hydration by looking at your urine color. Dark yellow urine is a sign you are dehydrated. 6) Some people use a camelback reservoir. Very helpful to stay hydrated without having

---

[10] Dartmouth Outing Club https://outdoors.dartmouth.edu/doc/

to stop every 10 minutes or so to get the water bottle out of your pack.

RICE[11] = Rest + Ice + Compress + Elevate

The knowledge learned at my Dartmouth Outing Club sponsored wilderness first aid course is applied many times. Here are two of those times I used RICE.

- o Saranac Lakes – we spent three days camping on islands, paddling through locks, swimming, and cliff jumping. On our last evening in the Saranac area, one of our group sprained his ankle, and his ankle was quite swollen. Fortunately, we still had ice left in our coolers, and I used an ace bandage and wrapped a package of ice around the ankle – loosening the bandage every 20 minutes. Since we were leaving for our canoe take-out the continuing of the compression bandage, elevation and rest were not as often as I preferred. However, once back home the ankle was checked by a clinician, and our RICE did help.
- o Automobile racing – Tim and I were invited as guests of John, a high-performance driving instructor, to watch cars run at the New Hampshire Speedway. As John began to remove the cracked brake rotor of his racing Corvette, the wrench slipped on the nut and John's forearm smashed against the frame – "Ouch!" Immediately we did RICE and John was able to continue with his instructor responsibilities with his arm wrapped.

Dehydration

---

[11] What Is the RICE Method for Injuries?
https://www.webmd.com/first-aid/rice-method-injuries#1

When on a training hike on Mt Monadnock, six of us started the Pumpelly Trail in Dublin, NH[12]. One of our group was a seasoned hiker who had climbed all the 48 New Hampshire four-hundred thousand footers. However, we did not know he was not in shape for this hike, and as we progressed on the hike, I noticed he never drank water when the group stopped and drank water … usually ever ten minutes. About an hour or so into the hike we began climbing up and over large boulders and cliffs. I noticed my friend appeared to be stumbling, and once he stumbled back dangerously close to the edge of a cliff. He was advised to drink water, and he said he did not need it. After a second near drastic slip, we realized he needed to return to the trailhead.

He at first resisted returning to the trailhead, he but finally consented, and another friend would accompany him back to the trailhead. The rest of us continued to the top of Monadnock. An hour or so later returning on the trail, we caught up to the two hikers … they were still at least an hour from the trailhead and car. We were told our friend had fallen a few times on the trail, and still would not drink water. He also had not urinated. I knew he had dehydration. We begged, cursed, and yelled at him to drink water. He adamantly refused all water. Finally, when within a mile of the trailhead he finally sipped some water.

His friend took him to the Emergency Department where they diagnosed dehydration as the cause of his hallucinations and personality change. Later that evening I received a call from my friend apologizing for his actions on the hike

LESSON LEARNED: Even though I recognized he probably was dehydrated I could not get him to drink water. Waiting until you are thirsty is too long a wait for water on a hike or other long-distance exercise.

---

[12] Pumpelly Trail http://tiny.cc/eebq1y

Making an Overnight Snow Mound Shelter at Gulf of the Slides

A friend and I took a weekend snow-shelter building course from the Appalachian Mountain Club at Pinkham Notch, NH. I had two learning experiences.

- o **Do not pack your snow shelter** – We received instruction to build a mound snow shelter. Our instructor on Friday evening taught us in Step 1 to NOT PACK the snow as we pile the six-foot mound of snow. Simply shovel the snow into a pile. Once the pile is built, then we gently tap and shape the snow into a mound.

  However, the next day when it came time to build the mound shelter, we were not going to have a "weak" snow shelter that would fall in on us ... so with each scoop of snow, we taped it down. The results ... when we finally were ready to remove the snow from inside the pile – we had a six-foot pile of ice! Took us forever to shape the inside of the mound as we had to remove most of the snow/ice from inside the pile by digging a tunnel under the pile and removing ice/snow from the inside.

- o **Pee Jar** – When sleeping comfortably in our mound shelter, and it came time to relieve ourselves (urinate), we had to crawl outside the hut in ten degrees Fahrenheit and cold boots and deep snow. Next time we do this, I will remember to bring a "pee jar."

Figure 101 - Gulf of the Slides Mound Snow Hut

LESSONS LEARNED: Listen to your instructors – they are sharing their experience for a reason.
Ibuprofen Warning

In drafting my first outdoor book,[13] I described my frequent use of Ibuprofen. I take ibuprofen medication both to prevent and treat the injury. I innocently was taking too much and too frequently. My primary care physician explained to me the possible issues with too frequent and too much Ibuprofen. Some athletes recommend specific brand names, but I have tried various brands of ibuprofen, and each seems to work equally well for my body. I am cautious and aware that too much ibuprofen can be harmful. Taking ibuprofen, in my opinion, means striking a balance between how much you are hurting, the number of tablets to take, and frequency of application.

I must offer a warning with non-steroidal anti-inflammatory drugs (NSAID). Every year in the United States, over 20,000 people die

[13] **Outdoor Enthusiast: Never say, "I wish I had ... "© 2009 by Stephen L. Priest** www.outdoorsteve.com
ISBN - 144043840

from complications from NSAIDs. The widespread use of NSAIDs has meant that the adverse effects of these relatively safe drugs have become increasingly prevalent. Most of these effects are dose-dependent. The two main adverse drug reactions (ADRs) associated with NSAIDs relate to gastrointestinal (GI bleeding) and renal (renal failure) effects. Bottom line here is to consult with your physician and read up on NSAIDs before taking them. Pay attention to dose and length of use.

Short courses of ibuprofen are fine for acute injuries. But long term and excessive use of more than three times a day are not recommended. Also taking it with a meal or food helps to alleviate some of the GI side effects. Also (especially seniors) should check with their doctors before taking ibuprofen as it is not allowed with certain medications like blood thinners.

LESSON LEARNED Be careful to not take excessive medications

Change in equipment, training, and technique.

I believe many body injuries occur because of outside influences such as "changes" in your habits, shoes, type of exercises, and length of exertion. Here are my personal experiences:

- While running (I run three to four days a week) I felt a pain in my knee. What change may have caused this? Given this has happened to me in the past, I suspected it was time to change my running shoes. I inspected the shoes and saw one heel significantly worn on the side. I changed to a new pair of shoes – and within one day no pain in my knee.
- I was doing long-distance running. I had a chance to buy very quality running Brand X shoes. A few days after wearing them I began to develop shin splints. Very painful. I went back to my previous running shoes (nothing wrong with them – only I thought more expensive shoes could make me run faster … they do not.) and the shin splints went away. A week later I

went back to my "faster" Brand X shoes – and lo and behold shin splints again.

- I was running one day with a friend, and he told me he had shin splints. I asked him what shoes he was wearing – and guess what … he was wearing Brand X!

LESSON LEARNED – with a new injury look for a "change" – this may have caused the injury because your body was not used to a drastic change. The lesson is two-fold, besides looking for a change, ask a friend who also partakes in the same outdoor activity.

Worn-out Shoes

I try to squeeze as many miles out of my running and hiking shoes as I can. One indicator I use to determine when to change shoes is when my hip begins to hurt. The next day I change to a new pair of shoes and lo and behold I am good for another four to six months before my body tells me "time for a new pair of shoes."

Some experts recommend changing shoes every 300-400 miles. I rarely keep track of miles run and change shoes by listening to my body (or looking worn heels). Certainly, I change shoes if I start developing pains, etc. with the shoes

LESSON LEARNED: Listen to your body

Duct Tape

My eyeglass frame broke on the first day of a 5-day paddle. What do I do because I need to read and look for signs? I used duct tape to hold the frame – and it lasted the whole trip.

On another trip, we had a small hole in the bottom of our canoe after hitting a sharp rock. We used duct tape and lasted for our remaining two days.

Figure 102 - Two canoe paddles duct taped
Another trip we broke a kayak paddle. We took two spare canoe paddles, and duct taped them together for a very efficient kayak paddle.

LESSON LEARNED: Always have duct tape available.

Knee Pain

My primary care physician (PCP), also an outdoor enthusiast who runs and hikes among other things, asked me "Do you ever get knee injuries?" Yes. One injury took over two years before I felt the knee was OK.

Here is my knee story. The knee hurt when running too far, so I would alternate biking one day and running the next day. I do not believe in "no pain, no gain." Not wanting invasive treatment for my knee, here is the clinical saga of my attempt to return to running without pain:

- Cortisone is a powerful anti-inflammatory drug used in the treatment of many orthopedic conditions. When delivered by injection to the site of an injury, it can provide reduced inflammation and pain in joints of the ankle, elbow, hip, knee, shoulder, spine, or wrist. I received cortisone in the

midst of a year-long attempt to overcome pain in my knee. For me, it did not appear to work.
- o I received Physical Therapy (PT) for six weeks. It did not appear to work.
- o I twice had, one year apart, three injections of fluid over two weeks. Each time after the 3rd injection, my knee appeared to be fine. However, after a month or so, the knee pain reoccurred.
- o My triathlon club had a speaker from a local Pilate Center. My Pilates trainer, after examining me and having me do a variety of form rolling and exercises, thought my IT band might need strengthening. Below are the two exercise I continue today and believe they were significant in returning to distance running.

Iliotibial (IT) Band Syndrome (ITBS)[14]. Unlike "runner's knee," where the pain is commonly felt around or below the kneecap, ITBS usually presents itself as pain on the outside of your knee. I belonged to a Triathlon Club. At our monthly meeting, we had a Pilates instructor speak to the members on injuries. She had us all stand and squat down to test our knees. I, of course, had a knee issue. I called her the next day and set up an appointment. I explained my knee issue and past treatment, and she put me through a few tests of balance and strength. She then recommended we start with IT band exercises. The two most memorable to me, and of which I have continued for the last four years, refer to the IT Band. This reference explains the side leg raise and clamshell exercises I continue to do at least twice weekly – and believe they help me significantly.

1. SIDE LEG RAISE
Lie on your right side with both legs straight. Slowly raise

---

[14] EXERCISES TO TREAT AND PREVENT IT BAND SYNDROME http://tiny.cc/fwhm1y

your left leg about 45 degrees, then lower. Repeat on both sides. To make this move more challenging, use an exercise band around your ankles to increase resistance. Reps: 20–30 on each side

2. CLAMSHELL

Lie on your right side with your knees bent at a 90-degree angle to your torso. Keeping your feet together, use your glutes to slowly open and close your legs like a clamshell. Keep the motion controlled, and don't allow your pelvis to rock throughout the movement. Use an exercise band just above your knees to increase resistance. Reps: 20–30 on each side

LESSON LEARNED: Regular preventive maintenance training, such as my side leg raise and clamshell, and cross training, can be effective.

Cross-training with Rowing to treat knee issues

As noted, I had a heck of a time with my knee pain. I cut back to every other day running, and I lowered my time running. I am a big believer that all exercise should be 20 minutes minimum to get the heart at a steady pace. I also believe in cross-training such as mixing my hiking, running, paddling, and swimming. I also try to practice my "Never say, I wish I had …." Thus, I took six weeks of sculling/rowing lessons, within the time frame of knee pain.

Lo and behold, after three or so weeks of rowing lessons three evenings a week, I began to realize my knee pain had gone away. Could it be because rowing keeps your knees in basically the same horizontal and vertical motion …push down on the foot pad, straighten knees, and draw knees back to their beginning position? There is no side-to-side motion … as with running or walking.

Essentially you are using and strengthening the knee muscles in a very controlled environment … not like hiking, running, bicycling and swimming. Hmm, I do believe my sculling/rowing has helped strengthen appropriate muscles in my knee area.

Figure 103 - Rowing assists with knee alignment strengthening

LESSON LEARNED: – Sometimes knee pain is from leg muscle weakness and doing other exercises and strength training can help. I believe ITBS **exercises,** rowing, and other cross-training all helped my injured knee to heal.

Canoe Rescue – Practice makes perfect

Briefly, on a canoe trip to the 34-mile Moose River Bow Trip, two of our group flipped their canoe in the middle of Holeb Pond. My friend John and I were nearby, and we quickly paddled over, tied a rope to the overturned canoe, and towed them to shore – an exhausting paddle that took nearly a half hour. My cousin Linwood, a Master Maine Guide, asked, "Why did you not rescue them?" My response was, "We did!"

Linwood then proceeded to tell us we should have righted the swamped canoe in the middle of the lake draining it of water, then getting the two paddlers back in the boat, and letting them paddle themselves back to shore. No need for an exhausting paddle towing an overturned canoe with two bodies hanging on.

At our next campsite, Linwood would teach us how to do this. The next day for *nearly four hours*, myself and six companions, under the tutelage of Linwood, learned and practiced two types of canoe rescue scenarios:

1) **Two or more canoes are paddling together, and one flips over**. The upright canoe assists the capsized canoers by righting their boat, emptying it of water, retrieving their gear, and standing by while they re-enter their boat (even in deep water)
2) **Two paddlers, alone, flip their canoe and need to upright it without outside help**.

The next year the same group of friends and I were paddling across Eagle Lake on the Allagash Wilderness Waterway. Suddenly, one of our canoes capsized in the middle of the one-mile wide lake.

By the time we reached them, the two occupants were swimming holding onto the canoe. Their tents, food, and other camping gear drifting nearby (all protected by dry bags). With hardly a word said, this group, who had practiced the canoe rescue four hours the prior year, immediately began their learned "two or more canoers paddling together" rescue technique. Within minutes, both paddlers were back in their righted and dry canoe with their gear intact, and we continued to our next campsite.

Figure 104 - Practicing Two-Person Canoe Rescue

LESSON LEARNED: The message here is "practice makes perfect." Practice can save your life as you react to your prior training. Practice meant our trip was still fun. Practice meant we had no injuries.

Cairns Prevent Getting Lost on Foggy Mt Washington

John and I had just reached the headwall of Tuckerman's Ravine on Mt Washington. Our next milestone would be'to go to the AMC Lakes of the Clouds Hut, but we could only see dense fog in front of us! If you have ever been in a deep fog, you know that you lose all sense of direction. And our path to the Lakes of the Clouds Huts was to be on a windy rock-step path. We did not want to get lost in the White Mountains. What do we do? The answer is to follow the path marked by rock cairns.

Rock cairns in the White Mountains are for marking trails with minimal disruption to the natural environment. Generally, rock cairns along trails and in the backcountry should only be made by park rangers, trail maintenance volunteers, or trail creators. Unless you are one of these people, you should avoid building rock cairns for fun in places where they could be confused as trail markers.

Doing so could send hikers in the wrong direction by misrepresenting the trail.[15]

Thus, we used a compass, map, and cairns to make our way through the dense fog to the AMC hut. The large cairn just over the headway was our starting point. One of us went in the direction of our compass and found the cairns – 20 to 30 feet apart. We cautiously found our way to the AMC hut.

Figure 105 - Cairns and Fog - Mt Madison

LESSON LEARN: Know about cairns for keeping you on the trail – and respect their use.

Lightning Strike on Moose River, Maine

We were on day two of a Moose River canoe trip. It began to rain, and we could hear thunder in the far distance. Loon warned we needed to get off the river when the lightning and thunder are about five seconds apart (by the laws of physics,

---

[15] What are Rocks Cairns and why you should not build them. https://bearfoottheory.com/what-are-rock-cairns

the speed of light travels 186,000 miles per second and the speed of sound about 748 miles per hour, and by interpretation, a time interval of five seconds between viewing a lightning flash and hearing its clap of thunder, means the storm cell is about a mile away). This is a good rule of observation, but certainly not applicable this day – and NEVER to be trusted.

No sooner than Loon got his "words of wisdom" out of his mouth when "Kaboom!!" Instantly lighting struck so close to those in the front canoe that it surely had to electrify all its occupants. Following closely in the second canoe, my whole body instantly jumped from my canoe seat – and I felt a pulsating pressure from its seemingly shattering impact. My ears were ringing with emptiness. An odor of burnt air was everywhere. My heart paused to see if I was still alive. We had just missed being hit by a lightning bolt. The sensation was as if a bomb exploded in the same room. The lightning dazed us all. Immediately we beached our canoes and looked at each other in wonder. We were still alive. Never had any of us felt so close to the end of our lives – and so thankful for still being alive.

LESSON LEARNED: When you hear thunder or see lightning – **TAKE COVER or GET OFF/OUT OF THE WATER**. And get below treeline if hiking on a mountain

Carry Emergency Gear and Clothing

Appalachian Mountain Club's **Ten Essentials for a Safe Hike** are mandatory[16]. I use this list as a checklist for all my outdoor adventures. People sometimes ask me why I have my day backpack with me. My answer is "My backpack contains the 10

---

[16] THE TEN ESSENTIALS http://tiny.cc/j6aq1y

essentials for a safe hike". I even carry duct tape and a contractor trash bag (emergency shelters).

I enforce these ten essentials for a safe hike by checking each person has their own whistle and flashlight with them – and if not, I loan them one! Packing the "Ten Essentials" whenever you step into the backcountry, even on day hikes, is a good habit. True, on a routine trip you may use only a few of them or none.
AMC's Updated Ten Essential Systems [17]

1. Navigation: map, compass, GPS device, whistle - and know how to use them through practice!
2. Headlamp: plus, extra batteries
3. Sun protection: sunglasses, sun-protective clothes and sunscreen
4. First aid: including foot care and insect repellent (as needed)
5. Knife: plus, a gear repair kit
6. Fire: matches, lighter, tinder and flint striker
7. Emergency Shelter:(can be a light emergency bivy) or contractor bag
8. Extra food: Beyond the minimum expectation
9. Extra water: Beyond the minimum expectation
10. Extra clothes: Beyond the minimum expectation

The extra items from each system that you take can be tailored to the trip you're taking. When deciding what to bring, consider factors like weather, difficulty, duration, and distance from help. It's when something goes awry that you'll truly appreciate the value of carrying these items that could be essential to your survival[18].

---

[17] Note: Steve has edited the AMC Ten Essential list with a whistle, contractor bag, and flint striker

[18] Packing the Ten Essentials http://tiny.cc/n9aq1y

Figure 106 - Microspikes - essential for winter travel

Examples of extra items for winter hiking would be traction equipment such as microspikes (for use on ice) and gaiters in our backpack, and snowshoes on the backpack are essential for deep snow conditions. There are highly recommended backcountry gear.

Figure 107 - Outdoor Steve's Day Pack Contents

See if you can locate the ten essentials in the above Figure of

Steve's personal Day Pack. Notice the flint striker (bottom left of picture). We have had more fun on trips with seeing who can start the campfire with the flint striker. This is not only an education exercise – it is a "practice makes perfect" exercise. Do you notice the two waterproof plastic bags in which all gear put into the backpack is first stored?

Figure 108 - Using a Flint Striker to Light Campfire at Green River Reservoir, VT

LESSON LEARNED: Indeed, I have used my backpack for broken items, cuts, splints, sprains, etc. Search for keywords "lost, injured, killed, and rescued hikers" to teach others the "why" of the 10 essentials. Use the "Ten Essentials for a Safe Hike" as your checklist.

There and Back
To have a safe, enjoyable outdoor experience, and help reduce search and rescue efforts, you need to be prepared. The **Hike Safe**

program[19] was created to educate hikers of all ages, from first-timers to experienced trekkers.

Hiker Responsibility Code[20]
You are responsible for yourself, so be prepared:

1. **With knowledge and gear.** Become self-reliant by learning about the terrain, conditions, local weather, and your equipment before you start.

2. **To leave your plans.** Tell someone where you are going, the trails you are hiking, when you will return and your emergency plans.

3. **To stay together.** When you start as a group, hike as a group, end as a group. Pace your hike to the slowest person.

4. **To turn back.** Weather changes quickly in the mountains. Fatigue and unexpected conditions can also affect your hike. Know your limitations and when to postpone your hike. The mountains will be there another day.

5. **For emergencies.** Even if you are headed out for just an hour, an injury, severe weather or a wrong turn could become life-threatening. Do not assume you will be rescued, know how to rescue yourself.

6. To share the hiker code with others.

LESSON LEARNED: To further emphasize the importance of knowing the **Hiker Responsibility Code**, browse the Internet with keywords: "Lost and injured hikers". Read and share the Hiker Responsibility Code

---

[19] http://www.hikesafe.com/

[20] https://www.outdoors.org/conservation/trails/hike-safe

Outdoor Recreation for Seniors (ORFS)

An Introduction to ORFS

I was thrilled to share my latest **New Hampshire outdoor discovery** at an interview with Ela Ramsey aka "The Pearl Monroe" of WTPL 107.7 FM and her listeners. The below pictures and short videos will give you a taste of our Tuesday ORFS encounters. I also responded to Pearl's questions on "How do you spend your outdoor week?", and "What is the difference between a pond and a lake."

Figure 109 - "The Pearl Monroe" Interviewing OutdoorSteve

In July, my wife Catherine and I joined a fascinating group of kayakers, hikers, and bicyclists, in the greater Lake Sunapee area. They call themselves *Outdoor Recreation for Seniors (ORFS)*. ORFS meets year-round, weather permitting, to do an outdoor activity one to two hours. Their mantra is, "**Make weekly outdoor exercise with us your joyful resolution. Join us each Tuesday at 10 am**."

I learned about ORFS from the monthly newsletter of the Kearsarge Council on Aging (COA) with headquarters located in New London, NH at the Chapin Center. The Kearsarge COA includes nine towns in Sullivan and Merrimack counties [Andover, Danbury, Grantham, Newbury, New London, Springfield, Sunapee, Sutton, and Wilmot]. The attendees at the ORFS paddles and hikes are not limited to residency in these two counties.

Attendance at the Tuesday 10 am paddling and hiking welcomes all active paddlers and hikers 50 to 90+ years young. When someone says, "I am too old", then they do not belong with my young friends and me!

The ORFS monthly email and online schedule lists "every Tuesday" paddles and hikes on different lakes and ponds including lake descriptions and directions for our put-ins and hike starts. While there is no cost to join ORFS, you do need your own kayak or canoe (and paddles and life preservers). Bring water for thirst when paddling, a small lunch for post paddling or hiking, and a small chair for waterside relaxing.

I do get asked if kayaking and canoeing novices can come. My quick response is, "No, but I would suggest if an interested person with no paddling experience wants to learn kayaking or canoeing, they call the COA (**603-526-6368**) and ask if an ORFS member might give individual instruction to them."[21]

Where do I learn about ORFS places to meet?
Contacts, schedules, and directions to ORFS events are on the **Chapin Center COA** website under **Programs**
http://www.coachapincenter.org/programs/outdoor-programs/

A Summer of Hiking, Kayaking, and Canoeing
Kayaking, canoeing, and hiking occur at the same time with gatherings in the same area. The selected ORFS sections below are

my paddling experiences. Our recent choice of a sport has been kayaking. Once in a while, someone uses a canoe.

In the fall, when the weather makes paddling too cold, we all hike.

This summer ORFS paddled and hiked near nine lakes/rivers:

- Pleasant Lake (New London),
- Little Lake Sunapee (New London),
- Goose Pond (Canaan),
- Highland Lake (East Andover),
- Grafton Pond (Grafton).
- Lake Kolelemook (Springfield),
- Lake Sunapee (Sunapee)
- Otter Pond (Sunapee)
- Ompomysonsoosac River & Connecticut River - Norwich, VT.

Figure 110 - ORFS Little Lake Sunapee

Figure 111 - A Swim Break at Little Lake Sunapee
To expand a bit more on how ORFS enjoy the outdoors, when we paddled Little Lake Sunapee, it was so hot we stopped paddling for a bit and we went for an unplanned swim. We were certainly a motley group as some had "official bathing suits", and others went swimming in their street paddling clothes. No matter, we all had a great time ... got cooled off ... and then continued our paddle.

Attendee Residences
Attendees of these outdoor adventures come from all over the New Hampshire and Vermont. Summer visitors regularly join us. As the seasons change to cold weather, the group hikes in the fall, and later depending on snow and ice conditions, we use microspikes, snowshoe and cross-country skis. Some Tuesdays we bowl, and sometimes we tour areas of historical interest such as the Warner, NH Telephone Museum, and the American Precision Museum and Harpoon Brewery in Windsor, Vt.

Figure 112 - Unloading Kayaks

Biking
AND two biking groups ride every Thursday. One group pedals moderately and the other calls themselves "Slower Spokes for Older Folks". Miles differ depending on the routes but can sometimes exceed 20 miles.

I am also a biker and I pedal with these cyclists mostly in the fall.

Summary Outdoor Recreation for Seniors (ORFS)
The Outdoor Recreation for Seniors (ORFS) group at the COA is made up of numerous high-energy seniors whose hiking, alpine and Nordic skiing, kayaking and snowshoeing activities would put many younger persons to shame. As you will see in forthcoming ORFS stories, the ORFS group is active throughout the year.

So, not only are my wife Cathy and I getting outdoors regularly, we have a plan for every Tuesday throughout the year!! No more excuses, "I wish I had known about ORFS".

"Make weekly outdoor exercise with us your joyful resolution. Join us each Tuesday at 10 am."

Readers interested in more information in ORFS can contact The New London, New Hampshire Chapin Center website or the below telephone number

Coachapincenter.org
37 Pleasant St
New London, NH
603-526-6368

References

- **WTPL 107.7 FM Interview with Outdoor Steve**
  http://tiny.cc/t8yj1y
- **COA Chapin Center** http://www.coachapincenter.org
- **Schedule and directions to ORFS events**
  http://www.coachapincenter.org/programs/outdoor-programs/
- **Kearsarge COA New London, NH**
  https://www.yelp.com/biz/the-kearsarge-area-council-on-aging-new-london
- **OutdoorSteve.com** http://www.outdoorsteve.com
- **Lake or Pond?** http://tiny.cc/6hzj1y
- **Senior Hiker Magazine**
  https://www.seniorhikermagazine.com/

Addendum to "The Pearl" Interview – "What about the rest of your "Senior" week?"

Pearl, asks, "I see your Tuesday's are always committed on your calendar, but as a Senior, can you share other outdoor adventures that encompass your week?

First, I do find it difficult to define and categorize "senior." My mantra, **Never says, "I wish I had ..."** has provided opportunities for discovering the outdoors – and personally, I am only restricted from trying an outdoor trek or sport because of limits I impose on myself, and age has rarely been one of those "limits". You will notice in the **Introduction to Outdoor Recreation for Seniors (ORFS)** above, I mention "50 to 90+ years young."

Let me share my outdoor experiences within the past week. Admittedly, this is not a typical week, but a week I did not shy away because I am a senior.

Rowing
You may ask, "Why have you not been biking?" Well, my summer has been busy with other outdoor commitments. I average running three days a week. I have a 22' single rowing scull, and I row two days a week on Perkins Pond. Plus, I am also an active member of the Lake Sunapee Rowing Club (LSRC), and they have evening lessons for me to learn to progress in my single sculling technique. The LSCR also is an opportunity to improve my rowing skills in the doubles, quad, and eight-person (plus coxswain) boats.

[In rowing, the coxswain sits in either the bow or the stern of the boat (depending on the type of boat) while verbally and physically controlling the boat's steering, speed, timing, and fluidity. The primary duty of a coxswain is to ensure the safety of those in the boat. In a race setting, the coxswain is tasked with motivating the crew as well as steering as straight a course as possible to minimize the distance to the finish line. Coxswains are also responsible for knowing proper rowing technique and running drills to improve technique.

A coxswain is a coach in the boat, in addition to following the orders of the team coach, the coxswain is connected to the way the boat feels, what's working, what needs to be changed, and how. A successful coxswain must keep track of the drill, time, pace, words of the coach, feel of the boat, direction of the boat, and safety. During a race, a coxswain is responsible for steering, calling the moves, and responding to the way the other boats are moving. Success depends on the physical and mental strength of the rowers, ability to respond to the environment, and the way in which the coxswain motivates the rowers, not only as individuals but as members of the crew. https://en.wikipedia.org/wiki/Coxswain]

Golf

I know there are only 7 days a week. However, my wife has become an avid golfer, and we have been playing nine holes of golf about once a week. I do double up activities sometimes, such as yesterday I rowed for an hour at 6 am, and then at 11 am my wife and I played nine holes of golf.

Pickleball

In July, I also learned the game of pickleball on a week's visit to my nephew's wedding in California. Admittedly, it took me two days or so to pick up the game.

[**Pickleball** is a racquet sport that combines elements of badminton, tennis, and table tennis. Two, three, or four players use solid paddles made of wood or composite materials to hit a perforated polymer ball, similar to a wiffle ball, over a net. The sport shares features of other racquet sports, the dimensions and layout of a badminton court, and a net and rules similar to tennis, with a few modifications. Pickleball was invented in the mid 1960s as a children's backyard pastime but has become popular among adults as well.]

Running

I try to do a 3-mile run at least 3 days a week. I firmly believe this is a key to my health and keeps me in aerobic[22] shape for my hiking, paddling, swimming, rowing, and whatever other strenuous exercise I come upon.

What is the difference between a lake and a pond?
Interestingly, I frequently get asked, "What is the difference between a lake and a pond?" As taken from the New Hampshire Environmental Fact Sheet[23]:

The term "lake" or "pond" as part of a waterbody name is arbitrary and not based on any specific naming convention. In general, lakes tend to be larger and/or deeper than ponds, but numerous examples exist of "ponds" that are larger and deeper than "lakes." For example, Echo "Lake" in Conway is 14 acres in surface area with a maximum depth of 11 feet, while Island "Pond" in Derry is nearly 500 acres and 80 feet deep. Names for lakes and ponds generally originated from the early settlers living near them, and the use of the terms "lake" and "pond" was completely arbitrary. Many have changed names through the years, often changing from a pond to a lake with no change in size or depth. Often these changes in the name were to make the area sound more attractive to perspective home buyers. Examples of ponds that are now called lakes include Mud Pond to Mirror Lake in Canaan, Mosquito Pond to Crystal Lake in Manchester and Dishwater Pond to Mirror Lake in Tuftonboro.

References
- **WTPL 107.7 FM Interview with Outdoor Steve**
  http://tiny.cc/t8yj1y

---

[22] Aerobic is relating to or denoting exercise that improves or is intended to improve the efficiency of the body's cardiovascular system in absorbing and transporting oxygen. tiny.cc/t7ti1y

[23] Lake or Pond?
https://www.des.nh.gov/organization/commissioner/pip/factsheets/bb/documents/bb-49.pdf

- **Book Review for "*The Boys in the Boat: Nine Americans and their Epic Quest for Gold at the 1936 Berlin Olympics*"** by Daniel James Brown http://tiny.cc/vo8i1y
- **Blog and Video: Rowing through the eyes of a beginner** http://tiny.cc/w5vi1y
- **Pickleball** https://en.wikipedia.org/wiki/Pickleball
- **OutdoorSteve.com** http://www.outdoorsteve.com
- **Lake or Pond?** http://tiny.cc/4dwi1y

++++++++++++++++++++

Hiking Eagle Pond, NH with Poet Laureate Donald Hall

Figure 113 - Poet Laureate - On Eagle Pond

Hiking around Eagle Pond was very personal to me. When the Outdoor Recreation for Seniors (ORFS) had Eagle Pond on their list of Tuesday hikes, I could not wait to experience the same bucolic scenes that former United States Poet Laureate Donald Hall, a poet of the rural life, had seen, walked, and wrote about. Eagle Pond is across the street from Mr. Hall's home.

I became interested in Mr. Hall's work a few years ago when a good friend read some verses from one of his books. The words were absorbing and graphic as I felt the moment of the poem's content

Mr. Hall wrote many books with "Eagle Pond" in the title. My wife and I have read his 2016 book titled, "On Eagle Pond".

Our hike was 3.5 miles and took just over 1 and a half hours. We went in a clockwise direction. It had been raining prior to starting our hike, but mysteriously the rain stopped until we finished our hike.

1. We began our Eagle Pond hike at Eagle Pond Road where it intersects with Route 4.
2. We hiked approximately 1.5 miles took a right on Jack Wells Road.
3. Jack Wells Road is .7 miles and ends on Route 4, and just before Route 4, we took a right onto the Rail Trail for 1.3 miles.
4. The Rail Trail returned to our Start.

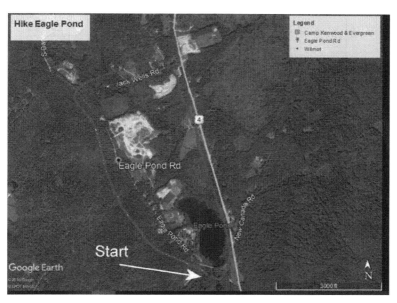

Figure 114 - Eagle Pond, Wilmot, NH Map

Now, I never have to say, "I wish I had hiked around Eagle Pond with Poet Laureate Donald Hall"

References

- **Blog and Video: ORFS Hike Eagle Pond with Poet Donald Hall** http://tiny.cc/5ovi1y

- **Eagle Pond by Donald Hall** http://tiny.cc/vsvily
- **Donald Hall, a Poet Laureate of the Rural Life** http://tiny.cc/dvvily
- **Ox Car Man by Donald Hall** http://tiny.cc/nxvily
- **Sunapee Ragged Kearsarge (SRKG) Trail** http://tiny.cc/nxvily
- **OutdoorSteve.com** https://www.outdoorsteve.com

+++++++++++++++++++

ORFS Hike Northern Rail Trail from Potter Place Depot to Andover's Softball field.

Figure 115 - ORFS Hike Andover Rail Trail

Seven miles past Danbury you pass Andover's Potter Place Railroad Station, restored to look as it did in 1874. The Depot's museum, caboose, and nearby freight house are operated by the Andover Historical Society. In 1 mile, the trail crosses the Blackwater River next to the 1882 Keniston Covered Bridge. Andover stretches along US 4/Main Street roughly between Eagle Pond and Highland Lake.

The Northern Rail Trail includes portions of the Sunapee Kearsarge Ragged Greenway (SKRG)Trail. The SRK Greenway is a 75-mile loop of hiking trails in central New Hampshire. The Greenway Trail System circles the Lake Sunapee area and connects Sunapee, Ragged, and Kearsarge Mountains.

See the video at http://tiny.cc/ljuily

The Outdoor Recreation for Seniors (ORFS) hiked the Andover Rail Trail from Potter Place Depot to Andover's Blackwater Park ballfield. The ballfield has a regulation diamond where some

ORFS played softball while other ORFS cheered them on.

Directions:
Take Route 11 east out of New London towards Andover. After the Route 4 sign, take Route 4 east and turn right down to the Potter Place Park 'n Ride area. Bring ball equipment if you wish and a sense of humor!

References:

- **Blog and Video: ORFS Hike Northern Rail Trail from Potter Place Depot to Andover's Softball field.**
  http://tiny.cc/ljui1y
- **Northern Rail Trail**
  https://www.traillink.com/trail/northern-rail-trail/
- **Sunapee Kearsarge Ragged Greenway**
  http://www.srkg.com/
- **OutdoorSteve.com** http://www.outdoorsteve.com

++++++++++++++++++

ORFS Hike Little Sunapee Associates Trail, New London, NH

Know where you are going

I volunteered to be the leader for the Outdoor Recreation for Seniors (ORFS) hike at the Little Sunapee Associates Trail in New London, NH. Given I had never hiked this area, I had to scout the trails. I went to the New London, NH Conservation Commission website

http://www.nl-nhcc.com/trails/little_sunapee_14.htm for a topographical trail map and trail descriptions.

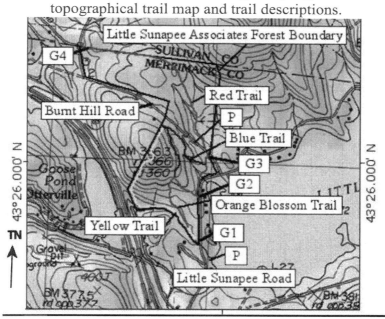

Figure 116 - Little Sunapee Associates Trail Map

Of importance in the topographical map of the **Little Sunapee Associates Forest** would be contour lines, streams, boundary lines such as fences, roads, stone walls, and elevations (hills). And of course, the color-coded marked trails.

The moderately difficult Yellow to Orange Blossom Trail was recommended as a 1½ hour hike for our ORFS group.

I visited the Little Sunapee Associates Forest the week before the ORFS hike to get familiar with the area and locate the recommended Yellow and Orange Blossom trails. This on-site research showed difficulty finding trail signs. The trails also needed maintenance (e.g., hard to see trail signs, down trees across trails and overgrown forest growth). It appeared to me this trail had not been maintained for a few years.

My visit revealed the many pluses of the Little Sunapee Associates Trail outweighed its negatives. The forest has wetlands, a ten-foot rock bed rippling stream from Little Sunapee Lake, unique red cardinal flowers, a moderate hill, different colors of mushrooms, stone walls, and ancient house foundations of farms and land for sheep and crops.

The Yellow Trail is the steepest trail on the property as shown in the trail map profile. The Yellow Trail starts at Gate 1 (G1) on Little Sunapee Road then follows along the brook from Little Sunapee Lake. The trail turns right at the edge of the I 89 rights-of-way where it meets the Red Trail, and both trails proceed together along the wire fence marking the right-of-way with stonewalls and foundations, and ascend nearly 200 feet in a quarter mile, and then plateaus to an intersection with the Blue Trail at Burnt Hill Road. At this point, an option is to exit to Burnt Hill Road. The Blue Trail can be followed right downhill parallel to Burnt Hill Road, and an intersection with the Orange Blossom Trail and proceeds down to an old logging road trail off of G3 on Burnt Hill Road. Right on this logging road ends at an unmarked gate (G2) on Little Sunapee Road.

OK, let's look at the MAP

1. First, we start at G1 on the map (unmarked), which is an opening in the fence, below a posted tree sign, "Yellow Trail."

2. We immediately climb over a large fallen rotten tree, and in 175 paces come to a sign in the folk of the path with a Yellow left arrow and an **Orange** arrow to the right. We continue left on the Yellow Trail.

3. On our left is an outlet stream from Little Sunapee Lake. Think of a poetic bubbling stream flowing over moss covered rocks. We listen to this soothing sound as we silently hike on the path. Red Cardinal flowers in the stream are a hiker's delight - we "stop and smell the flowers".

4. We begin to hear traffic from Route 89.

5. Shortly we come to a wire fence and turn right on the path. We are walking parallel to Route 89N. The steep ascent identified in the Yellow Trail description begins.

6. We are still following the Yellow Trail, but the yellow markers are not plentiful, and we regularly pause searching for a yellow marker ahead.

7. We search for the trail and pause before seeing a triple red paint mark on a tree and then yellow paint on a metal stake. We encounter a farmer's stonewall on the left, and the remnants of what appears to be a foundation. The now Red/Yellow trail gets steeper.

8. After peaking on the hill, we descend and up through a gully and see the road – Burnt Hill Road. Burnt Hill Road could be a bailout road going right to Little Sunapee Road for another right to return to the parking area. We agree to continue with the Orange Trail. Not much chance of getting lost on Orange Blossom Trail because all you need to do is keep Burnt Hill Road in sight on your left.

9. We follow the blue and orange signs, sometimes needing to stop and wander about before locating the next sign. Eventually, we come to an old wood road. Our map shows this old logging road from G3 on Burnt Hill Road. We go right on the old logging road. The road runs parallels to Little Sunapee Road and we hear cars.

We come to Gate 2 (unmarked). We exit at Gate 2 onto Little Sunapee Road, whence we go right and back to our parking area and lunch with our kayaking ORFS friends.

Know Where You Are

Certainly, bring a whistle and a compass. In describing the area of Little Sunapee Associates Forest... it is like a square. If you stay within the square and go in one direction you will come out to an access area. If lost:

- Going East you will come to Burnt Hill Road.
- Go south you come to Little Sunapee Road.
- Go west and you come to the stream, and then go South to Little Sunapee Road.
- Go North you come to Route 89. You then go East to Burnt Hill Road or South to Little Sunapee Road.

Let's Hike the Trail

Figure 117 - ORFS Hike Little Sunapee Associates Trail

Now, I never have to say, "I wish I had hiked the Little Sunapee Associates Forest Trail."

Topographic Map

The distinctive characteristic of a topographic map is the use of contour lines to show the shape of the earth's surface. USGS topographic maps also show many other kinds of geographic features, including roads, railroads, rivers, streams, lakes, buildings, built-up areas, boundaries, place or feature names, mountains, elevations, survey control points, vegetation types, and much more.

A contour line joins points of equal height. Contours make it possible to show the height and shape of mountains, depths of the ocean bottom, and steepness of slopes. Basically, contours are imaginary lines that join points of equal elevation on the surface of the land above or below a reference surface, usually mean sea level. (https://www.usgs.gov/faqs/what-a-topographic-map)

References

- Blog with Videos: ORFS Hike Little Sunapee Associates Trail, New London, NH http://tiny.cc/4yui1y
- http://www.fourseasonssir.com/waterfront/pdfs/little-lake-sunapee.pd
- http://www.nl-nhcc.com/trails/little_sunapee_14.htm
- https://www.usgs.gov/faqs/what-a-topographic-map
- http://www.OutdoorSteve.com

ORFS Winter Hike at Colby-Sawyer College's Kelsey Field Trail

Colby-Sawyer College, New London, NH, provided our weekly Tuesday 10 am winter hike. Hiking the Kelsey Field trail was a first time experience for our **ORFS** hiking group.

Jim was our leader and hike organizer. Leading 20+ ORFS was a responsibility he readily accepted. In fact, he first hiked the trail last October to be sure of its locations and turns, and level of difficulty. The second time he hiked the trail was after a snow and ice storm. He used emails to notify all ORFS to bring their micro spikes or crampons, snowshoes, and trekking poles ... he expected the trail to be mixed ice with snow.

The sky was cloudless with the temperature in the low twenties. A beautiful New Hampshire day for a winter hike.

Figure 118 - Colby-Sawyer College Kelsey Field Trail

The trail was designed and constructed by Professor Leon Malan, Environmental Services, and his students. It was built to be used as an outdoor classroom and a cross country track for the Athletic Department.

The Kelsey Trail had to meet the specifications for a cross-country track. It was opened to the public during Homecoming Weekend, October 2017.

Colby-Sawyer College Event Services office was happy to have ORFS use the trail and also have a delicious lunch in the dining hall. All enjoyed the entire outing.

DIRECTIONS to Kelsey Field Trail: from New London on Main Street, turn onto Seamans Road at 1st Baptist Church. Continue behind CSC and turn right at Mercer Field take the first left and drive to the far parking area. Trailhead is across Seamans Rd.

More Blog Posts on Outdoor Recreation for Seniors (ORFS)

1. Blog and Video: ORFS Winter Hike Put Safety First: Kidder-Cleveland-Clough Trail http://tiny.cc/a10i1y

2. Blog and Video: Christmas Caroling with the ORFS
http://tiny.cc/tz3i1y

3. Blog and Video: Radio Interview with Pearl Monroe -
http://outdooradventurers.blogspot.com/2017/09/

4. **Colby-Sawyer College** http://colby-sawyer.edu/

+++++++++++++++++++++

" Everyone must do something. I believe I will go outdoors with family and friends."

ORFS Winter Hike Put Safety First: Kidder-Cleveland-Clough Trail

Safety First

The **Outdoor Recreation for Seniors** (ORFS) place an emphasis on the closeness of the ORFS group and the importance and caring for each other's physical being. No doubt, they are a family.

- If local schools and the Chapin Center are closed due to weather conditions, then there will be no "Every Tuesday at 10 am" outing.
- Be prepared with proper equipment for the trail and conditions
- Buddy system (For example, do not hike or paddle alone, keep an eye on the first and last person in the group, when coming to a fork in the trail, make sure all in the group know which path to take).
- If you have a cell phone have it fully charged **before** you start – and keep it on.
- If an accident does happen (e.g. sprained ankle), be sure to report it to the COA.

Winter Hike

The below video shares the ORFS 2-mile snowshoe hike in 20 degrees F temperatures in 2 feet of snow. The ORFS were the first on this trail after the storm, making an endurance challenge for all of us. Enjoy the ORFS Kidder-Cleveland-Clough Trail hike.

As I prepared the video of this ORFS winter hike, I wanted this blog to emphasize winter cautions and gear necessary for a safe and fun hike. As the saying goes, "you can never be overdressed or too prepared."

Figure 119 - ORFS Kidder-Cleveland-Clough Trail Winter Hike

A quick primer:

- **Never hike alone.**
- **Always tell someone** where you are going and when you expect to be back.
- **Dress appropriately** – **cotton** is the worst fabric for cold, wet weather. Cotton can kill when wet – meaning it soaks up moisture, and takes a long, bone-chilling time to dry. Dress in layers so you can take off or put on as you need. Wool, silk or polypropylene inner layers hold body heat. Wear a hat (even carry a spare), proper insulated shoes (no sneakers!), and gloves (maybe bring an extra pair).
- **Bring water** and light snacks.
- **A contractor trash bag** (not for trash, but for wearing as emergency shelter or rain gear).
- **Whistle**
- **Map/compass**
- **Flashlight** (extra batteries or 2nd flashlight)

Here are some important winter gear descriptions:

- **Microspikes** (some call them crampons) are best worn on fairly level hiking trails covered with packed snow or ice. They provide that little bit of extra traction that you need when your boot treads stop giving you good grips.
- **Gaiter**: a covering worn over the lower part of the leg to keep the legs and ankles dry when hiking
- **Snowshoes**: usually a lightweight platform for the foot that is designed to enable a person to walk on soft snow without sinking.
- **Trekking Poles**: I'm a big fan of trekking **poles for hiking** because they help reduce the strain on my knees when I walk, they improve my balance when I'm **hiking** over rough ground or crossing streams, and they are useful for establishing a good **walking** rhythm when synchronizing your arms with your feet. Also, they exercise your arms and shoulders.

The above is indeed not all-inclusive. Learn more hiking "musts" from the below references.

References

- **Blog and Videos for ORFS Winter Hike Put Safety First: Kidder-Cleveland-Clough Trail** http://tiny.cc/a10i1y

- **Hiking: Winter Conditions Gear Checklist** http://tiny.cc/g30i1y

- **Recommended Winter Day Hiking Gear List** http://tiny.cc/q40i1y

- **Hike Safe Card** http://www.hikesafe.com/

- **Why Cotton Kills – A technical explanation** http://tiny.cc/up1i1y

- **When do you need snowshoes? Gaiters? Crampons? A winter traction primer** http://tiny.cc/sp2i1y

- **Chapin Center Council on Aging** http://www.coachapincenter.org/index.htm
- **New London, NH Conservation Commission WebSite** http://tiny.cc/ar1i1y
- **The Outing Club** http://www.theoutingclub.net
- **Blog and Video: Christmas Caroling with the ORFS** http://tiny.cc/ar1i1y
- **Blog and Video: Radio Interview with Pearl Monroe - September 6, 2017** http://outdooradventurers.blogspot.com/2017/09/

+++++++++++++++++++++

" Everyone must do something. I believe I will go outdoors with family and friends."

ORFS Hike Dexter Inn and Pine Ridge Road Trails - Sunapee, NH

Members of **Outdoor Recreation for Seniors** (ORFS) had their Tuesday 10 am hike and lunch led by Al and Eileen.

- Al described options for hiking paths: dirt road, paved road, and forest.
- The hike included the trails of Dexter's Inn
- Our trail visited Crowther Chapel
- Eileen shared her bear encounter experience.
- Nancy demonstrated her protection from black flies.
- Al entertained the group with his rendition of rhyme schemes

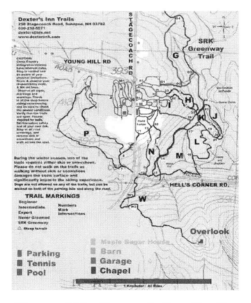

Figure 120 - Dexter's Inn Trails

Directions: from Rte 11 Sunapee, take 103B 1/2 mi, Rt on Stagecoach Rd 1.0 mi, Rt on Young Hill Rd 1/2 mi, L on Pine Ridge Road – go around loop counter clockwise ¼ mi where you see the view.

Figure 121 - Pine Ridge to Dexter Inn - Notice Some ORFS Ready for Black Flies

References

- **Blog and Video: ORFS Hike Dexter Inn and Pine Ridge Road Trails - Sunapee, NH** http://tiny.cc/dmwi1y
- **Dexter's Inn, Sunapee, NH** http://dextersnh.com/
- **Crowther Chapel** http://tiny.cc/k41i1y
- **Sunapee Kearsarge Ragged Greenway** http://www.srkg.com/
- **New London, NH Conservation Commission with 29 Individual Trail Links http://tiny.cc/ar1i1y**
- **2018 New Hampshire Hiking Guide** http://tiny.cc/251i1y
- **Chapin Center COA** http://www.coachapincenter.org/
- **OutdoorSteve.com** https://outdoorsteve.com/

++++++++++++++++++++

Outdoor Recreation for Seniors (ORFS) Hike at Mink Brook Nature Preserve, Hanover, New Hampshire

Let's go hiking with the ORFS! Today's outdoor trek will be in Hanover, NH at the Mink Brook Nature Preserve. Weather is sunny and in the low 70's ...AND the black flies are still sleeping!

The **Mink Brook Nature Preserve** protects habitat for wild brook trout, bears, and many other creatures while offering a natural retreat within walking distance of downtown Hanover. Owned by the Hanover Conservancy, this 112-acre preserve is the result of deep generosity and community spirit. Through the millennia, Mosbasak Sibosis ("Mink Brook" in Abenaki) has been an important center of life for Native Americans and remains so today. (Mink Brook Nature Preserve Map and Guide)

Figure 122 - Mink brook Map and guide

Figure 123 - Entrance Gate - Mink Brook Nature Preserve

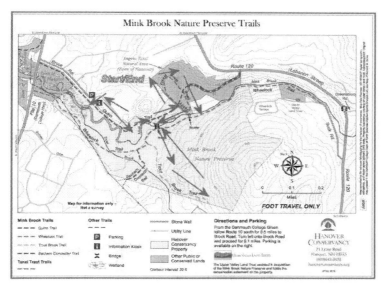

Figure 124 - Mink Brook Nature Preserve Map

The above map's red arrows begin and end at the Parking (P) area and proceed through the wooden gate onto Quinn Trail along Mink Brook; continue on the Forest Loop; cross the Bridge to Trout Brook Trail, and return to the Bridge, and exit at the wood gate on Quinn Trail. Our trek took about 1½ hour.

Who are the ORFS?

The Outdoor Recreation for Seniors (ORFS) group meets every Tuesday year-round at 10 am. In the summer we kayak/canoe, swim and hike. In the fall we hike, and in the winter we snowshoe and cross-country ski. Our trips are from 1-1/2 to 2 hours, followed by lunch.

Directions and location are available for our Tuesday 10 am outings via email and the monthly New London Chapin Senior Center Courier newsletter. To learn more and join, contact the Chapin Senior Center at 357 Pleasant Street, PO Box 1263, New London, New Hampshire 03752 or go to their website at **http://www.coachapincenter.org**

ORFS is a very informal group and participation is for all outdoor enthusiasts wanting guaranteed good exercise with a friendly fun group.

References

- **Blog and Video: Hike at Mink Brook Nature Preserve, Hanover, New Hampshire** http://tiny.cc/yt2i1y
- **Hanover Conservancy** https://www.hanoverconservancy.org/
- **Hanover Conservancy Map and Guide** http://tiny.cc/nx2i1y

More Blog Posts on Outdoor Recreation for Seniors (ORFS)

1. **Blog and Video Posts:** ORFS Winter Hike Puts Safety First: Kidder-Cleveland-Clough Trail
2. Christmas Caroling with the ORFS
3. Radio Interview with Pearl Monroe - WTPL 107.7 Concord
4. Bowling Day for Outdoor Recreation for Seniors (ORFS)
5. An Outdoor Recreation for Seniors(ORFS) Celebration of Spring

+++++++++++++++++++

An Outdoor Recreation for Seniors (ORFS) Celebration of Spring

This Tuesday's 10 am the trek for the Outdoor Recreation for Seniors (ORFS) was a choice of doing a 3-mile hike around Lake Kolelemook in Springfield, NH, or a snowshoe trek on the Protectworth Trail, part of the Sunapee-Ragged-Kearsarge Greenway (SRKG).

My choice was to do the Protectworth Trail, as this would be another opportunity to continue my quest of completing all fourteen sections of the SRKG.

The *Sunapee-Ragged-Kearsarge Greenway (SRKG)* is circle of trail corridors and conserved lands providing hikers with minimally-developed access to the mountains, lakes, vistas and historical sites of the region. The "Necklace Trail" comprises over 75 trail miles, created with the cooperation of landowners and local authorities, through the forests, over mountains and, where appropriate, via old roads, now unsuitable for wheeled traffic but more extensively used as much as two centuries ago.

The Sunapee Ragged Kearsarge Greenway Trail Guide topological Map 4 below shows the Protectworth Trail in Springfield, NH. We trekked on the trail about one and a half hours. This trail is Class VI. In the winter it is groomed for snowmobiles, cross country skiers, and hikers. Besides staying on the main trail, we also added some bushwhacking (making side trails in deep snow).

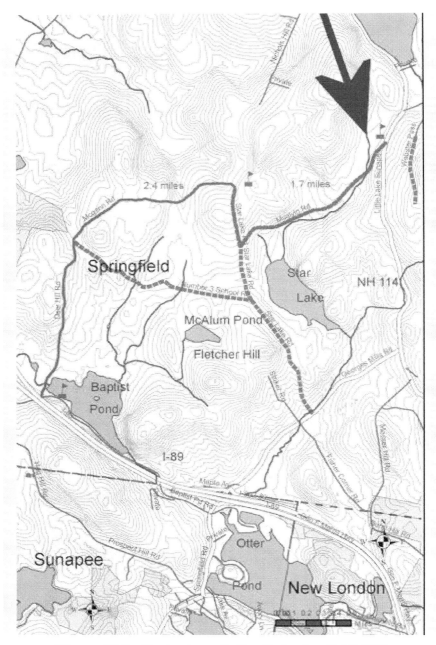

Figure 125 - Protectworth Trail, Springfield, NH

We did not hike the full Protectworth Trail (4.3 miles) today. After 45 minutes on the trail, we turned around and returned to the route 114 trail-head from whence we started. I got enough sense of this beautiful trail, to plan a return to complete the full Protectworth Trail of the SRKG.

Given I chose the Protectworth Trail to snowshoe, the video below gives you a sense of our trek, and then continues to the "party peoples" celebration of spring and new beginnings.

Figure 126 - ORFS Celebration of Spring

References

- **Blog and Video of ORFS Celebration of Spring** http://tiny.cc/xf3i1y
- **Sunapee-Ragged-Kearsarge Greenway Coalition (SRKG and Greenway** http://www.srkg.com/
- **New London, NH Conservation Commission website** http://tiny.cc/ar1i1y
- **Kearsarge Chapin Center Council on Aging** http://www.coachapincenter.org/index.html

+++++++++++++++++++

ORFS Christmas Carol Caravan

Figure 127 - ORFS Celebrate Caroling Senior Residences

ORFS is a very informal group, and participation is for all outdoor enthusiasts wanting guaranteed good exercise with a friendly fun group. The below celebration and sharing shows another side of ORFS.

Today's blog shares our Tuesday 10 am December 19th annual Christmas caroling caravan to two senior residences followed by the ORFS annual Christmas lunch with a Yankee Swap at Flying Goose Brew Pub and Grille, New London. We wear our most lighthearted regalia for this entertaining event! Hats and props provided. No singing ability or books is required, just sing along with the gang!

ORFS Christmas Caroling Itinerary

Meet at Bittersweet Residence on Pleasant Street, New London. Once we organize, we perform skits and singing for a half hour, then socialize with residents over the sweet treats buffet that they provide. Afterward, we head to Lyon Brook condominium community (**http://www.lyonbrook.com/**) and repeat the same show.

After that, we go to Flying Goose Brew Pub and Grille for a meal followed by our traditional Yankee Swap. For those that do not know, in a **Yankee Swap,** each participant brings a wrapped, unmarked gift and places it in a designated area. Participants are given numbers as they arrive, and their names or number is randomly drawn, and they select an unwrapped gift from the pile in that order — with a twist, you can then choose to swap with anyone who drew before you. Watch out for lucky number 1 who gets final pick of everything! In the end, the gift you are holding is the present you take home.

Enjoy the below video of our most rewarding and festive day as ORFS entertain and share their spirit of the season. Merry cheers and a Healthy 2018 to all!

Click **WTPL 107.7 FM** below to see videos and learn more about Outdoor Recreation for Seniors (ORFS) from Outdoor Steve's September 2017 radio interview.

References

- **Blog and Video: 2017 ORFS Christmas Caroling Caravan** http://tiny.cc/tz3i1y

- **Blog and Video: WTPL 107.7 FM Interview with OutdoorSteve** http://tiny.cc/t8yj1y

- **Blog and Video: 2018 ORFS Christmas Caroling** http://tiny.cc/drry1y

++++++++++++++++++

Bowling Day for Outdoor Recreation for Seniors (ORFS)

The winter presents opportunity for ORFS indoor sports, such as bowling. The below blog/video link is a **Bowling Day for ORFS**.

Figure 128 - Meyer Maple Lanes Claremont, NH

- **Blog and Video: Bowling Day for ORFS**
  http://tiny.cc/ao3i1y
- **Chapin Center Council on Aging**
  http://www.coachapincenter.org/
- **OutdoorSteve.com** http://www.outdoorsteve.com

Spring

Two roads diverged in a wood and I – I took the one less traveled by, and that has made all the difference – Robert Frost

Memories of our Mt Washington, Tuckerman's Ravine, and Connecticut Lakes Trip

Figure 129 - Carson - Your Nana Loves You

Figure 130 - United States (New Hampshire) and Canadian Border Crossing

Figure 131 – AMC Pinkham Notch Hut

References

- **Blog and Video of Mt Washington, Connecticut Lakes, and Tuckerman's Ravine** http://tiny.cc/37cj1y

Three Generation Paddling in Saranac Lake

A celebration of high school graduations for Carson and Nicholas on Section 2 of the **Northern Forest Canoe Trail**. We wish them both success in their academic and outdoor endeavors - Carson at the University of Mississippi, and Nicholas in the United States Navy serving our country.

Figure 132 - Carson and Nicholas Saranac Lake

Preparation

- Three canoes and one kayak
- One van carries two of the canoes, one kayak, camping gear, and two people
- One SUV with one canoe, the food, and five people
- Paul and Cheryl did the food for the trip.
- Dundee has the kitchen stuff
- Everyone brings their silverware, drinking cups, flashlights, life jacket, paddle, tent, sleeping bag and other "stuff."
- We will need to buy firewood in New York

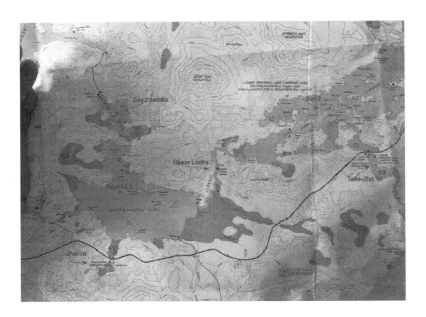

Itinerary
Sunday 6/17 - Leave Sunapee by 9 am.

- Drive to Saranac NY to Saranac Lake Islands State Park Campground on Route 3 for check-in registration (about 1 pm)
- Drive to put in at South Creek Fishing Access site, Route 3, Middle Saranac Lake, unload and drive cars to State Park parking on Lower Saranac Lake and end of trip take out.
- Paddle to Halfway Island on Middle Saranac Lake to set up camp. (at about 4 pm) (Camp site Halfway Island #077)

Sunday 6/17 and **Monday 6/18** - explore Middle Saranac Lake and Weller Pond
Tuesday 6/19 - Pack up and paddle down the Saranac river, passing through Upper Lock onto Lower Saranac Lake and set up camp on Larom Island. (#023)
Wednesday 6/20 – Pack up and paddle to State Park take out on Lower Saranac Lake, load up cars and drive back to Sunapee by around 6 pm.

Trip Highlights

- For the most part, four-day weather was between 60 and 75 degrees - excellent. The exception was Day 1 weather in the evening with heavy rain, but we set up tarps over the camp table, firepit, and tents. Rain no major issue.
- We all went swimming at both islands – water a bit chilly, but once immersed we were fine.
- Day 2 paddling to Weller Pond was very scenic. We explored camp sites, saw pitcher plants, and geese.
- Day 2 return paddle to Halfway Island was a bit of a challenge with heavy swells, white caps, and wind. All accomplished this challenge without incident. Our two recent high school graduates handled the paddling like experienced paddlers with Carson in the stern of our canoe and Steve in the bow and Nicholas in his single kayak.
- Meals all four days were fabulous – thanks to Paul and Cheryl. Paul and Tim were our chefs. Nicholas demonstrated some of his cooking skills. First day afternoon hors d'oeuvres hit the spot after our paddle. Our dinner was steak-tips and Caesar salad. Breakfast each day a choice of eggs with sausage/bacon, bagels, coffee, and tang. Lunches were sandwiches. 2nd night we had pasta and chicken. The third night was sausage and beans.
- We sat on Halfway Island overlooking a ledge for a great sunset.
- Carson and Nicholas went cliff jumping.
- While all three canoes were packed with gear, Paul's blue 18' canoe held the most. Check video pictures of how close the blue canoe's gunnels (the top edge of the side of a boat) were from the waterline.
- Carson and Nicholas rotated between the kayak and canoes to enjoy each boat's uniqueness.
- Used flint and steel to start our camp fire.
- We used the RICE method to treat a sprained ankle
- We experienced another section of the 740 mile Northern Forest Canoe Trail.
- Disclaimer - Due to the importance of this high school graduation celebration, the bog videos are detailed and significantly longer than most of my videos.

Figure 133 - Carson and Nicholas Prep for 40-foot Cliff Jump

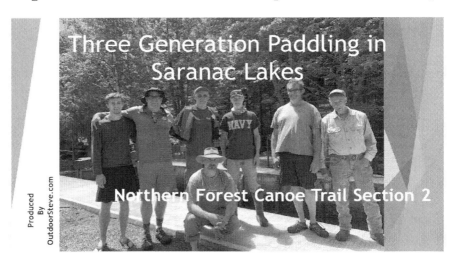

Figure 134 - Three Generations Paddle Saranac Lakes

References

- **Blog and videos of Three Generation Paddle on Saranac Lake** https://outdooradventurers.blogspot.com/2018/06/three-generation-paddling-in-saranac.html
- **Northern Forest Canoe Trail** https://www.northernforestcanoetrail.org/
- **Bedford Community TV - Three Generation Paddling in Saranac Lake** http://tiny.cc/h8wm1y
- Saranac Lake State Park Campgrounds
- **Paddling the Northern Forest Canoe Trail Section 2: Long Lake to Village of Saranac Lake** http://tiny.cc/9axm1y
- **What is the RICE Method for Treatment of Injuries?** http://tiny.cc/mcxm1y
- **OutdoorSteve.com** https://www.outdoorsteve.com

Sky Dive Georgia

My grandson Carson, his father Shaun, and his Uncle Tim celebrated Carson's 2018 graduation from Harrison High School, Kennesaw, Georgia with a tandem sky jump.

They jumped from 14,600 feet. The total jump took approximately 4 1/2 minutes. The free fall was one minute, followed by a three 1/2-minute parachute flight to a safe landing.

Carson will be attending the University of Mississippi this Fall.

Carson's sister, Madison, did the skydive in 2016. She is a senior at Auburn University.

Figure 135 - Carson Skydiving

Figure 136 - Shaun Sky Diving

Figure 137 - Timothy Skydiving

Figure 138 - Madison Sky Diving

Blog and video by a Proud Grandfather and Father - can be seen if References below

Never say, " I wish I had been skydiving"

References

- **Blog and video: Preparation, Pre and Post Interviews** https://outdooradventurers.blogspot.com/2018/05/blog-post.htm

- Sky Dive The Farm https://www.skydivegeorgia.com/

How Close is "Too Close" to a Bear?

I have lived in New Hampshire for many years and have had glimpses of black bears as they crossed my hiking paths or roads. These brief sightings were so quick I was never able to get a picture.

I also heard "Do not get too close to a bear – particularly when cubs are present". With this caution, last Monday I was in my front yard in Bedford, and lo and behold a mother bear with four cubs following, crossed the road ... 100 or so feet in front of me.

With iPhone in hand, I stealthily walked up the road to see if I could spot where the bears entered the leafy green and dark woods. I turned onto my neighbor's lawn outside the forest.

No sooner did I make the turn, when over the knoll ahead was a large growling upright bear facing me with paws up ready to box. The mother was protecting her cubs and warning me to "stay away". With the camera rolling, I was able to get a glimpse of her standing. Then returning to all fours, she lumbered into a dark hole in the forest where she had already cleared her cubs to safety.

This was my first challenge by a bear – and a warning, "do not get too close".

Figure 139 - Warning: Stay Away from a Mother Black Bear

My wife joined me for a view and we watched the bear from the top of the mound ... maybe fifty feet from the dark forest hole where the bear was camouflaged in the woods. We could only see her eyes, nose, and slight body movement. The mother was in front of a tree urging her cubs to climb the tree.

As we silently watched waiting for a better picture, she unexpectedly roared while rushing a few feet out of the woods ... and immediately returned to her black forested cave. She was again challenging us to keep away from her cubs ... and to leave.

This was a more vicious second warning "to leave".

This is when I realized, "too close to a bear", means being within sight of the bear.

We retreated to the road and walked to the other side of the woods. We could see one of the cubs clinging high in a tree. We knew the mother was still below the treed cubs, and we nervously kept an eye on the ground level, anticipating a charging bear from the woods.

It was time to leave before my foolish bravery resulted in personal danger.

My lesson and warning to all my readers are if you want to observe a wilderness bear, stay out of its sight ... as far away as you can. Use your zoom camera lens, and if you do not have a zoom lens, then leave.

Remember, getting close to a bear, means staying out of sight of the bear.

+++++++++++++++++++++

SRK Greenway Trail 7 NH Route 4A to Wilmot Center

The Sunapee, Ragged, and Kearsarge (SRK) Greenway is a 75-mile loop of hiking trails in central New Hampshire. The Greenway Trail System circles the Lake Sunapee area and connects Sunapee, Ragged, and Kearsarge Mountains.

Our pursuit today is shown below: Section 7 topographical map of the SRKG with a descriptive title of **Trail 7 NH Route 4A to Wilmot Center**. This 4.4-mile section involves two trails: the Bog Mountain Trail and Kimpton Brook Trail. This was our first time on section 7, specifically Bog Mountain, for Patty, Jim and myself.

Trail 7 NH Route 4A to Wilmot Center

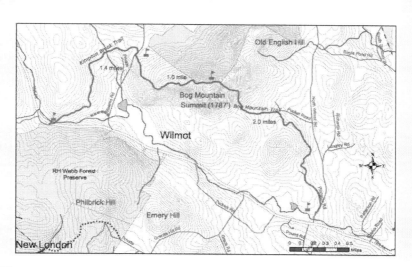

Figure 140 - SRKG Trail 7 Map Route 4A to Wilmot Center

This Greenway map shows our trip marked in green. The Greenway estimated time to hike is 3 hours. On our easterly ascent, we stopped frequently for water breaks, and once for a snack, and took 20 to 30 minutes at the summit. On our hike down to the western trailhead terminus, we stopped a few times for water, and then once for a snack. Our total time for Section 7 was just under four hours.

This section of the SRKG is a mixture of well developed wooded trails and woods-logging roads. Our goal was to summit Bog Mountain, 1,787 feet, starting at the eastern trailhead parking lot at the Wilmot Town Hall. We would be doing all of section 7. For those hikers wanting a shorter hike to the summit, we did cross two major dirt roads, Stearns Road, and Pocket Road cross woods, that could be used to more readily access the summit.

Figure 141 - Bog Mt. Trail Sign, Wilmot, NH

We picked up the bog mountain trail within a minute of walking from the parking lot. This eastern side of the mountain was very rocky, and reminded me of the saying, "Don't take NH for Granite". The trail up to the summit followed a vein of granite exposed centuries ago, reminding me of previous hikes to the White Mountains of NH with plenty of granite outcrops.

For most of the eastern trail up to the summit, the trapezoid signs readily kept us on the trail. The views from the barren summit of Bog Mountain were marvelous. We easily recognized Mt Sunapee and Kearsarge Mountain and their surrounding mountains. Certainly, well worth our trek.

Figure 142 - Sunapee Ragged Kearsarge Greenway Trail Marker
The hike from the summit downward to our western trail terminus was more accessible than the eastern side. However, the trail signs from the summit to the western terminus were not always readily visible. It appears like the signage was made for hikers entering on the western trailhead, as we frequently had to pause to locate the trapezoid signs, and often spotted them only when we looked behind us from whence we came.

We exited the Bog Mountain Trail and crossed Stearns Road onto Kimpton Brook Trail. The Kimpton Brook Trail had large tree blowdowns from winter storms that blocked the trail. Mixed into this, which made the Kimpton Brook Trail hike exciting, was crossing at least four streams by leaping rock to rock, using a blowdown tree, or a hewed log maybe 10 inches in diameter.

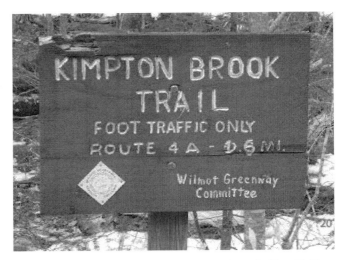

Figure 143 - Bog Mt. Kimpton Brook Trail Sign

We now, never have to say, "I wish I had hiked the SRG greenway section over Bog Mountain."

References
- **Blog and Video: SRK Greenway Trail 7 NH Route 4A to Wilmot Center http:** //tiny.cc/mkqw1y
- **Sunapee Kearsarge Ragged Greenway** http://www.srkg.com/
- New London, NH Conservation Commission with 29 Individual Trail Links http://tiny.cc/8ixm1y
- **2018 New Hampshire Hiking Guide** https://innatpleasantlake.com/2018-new-hampshire-hiking-guide

SRK Greenway Trail 4 Protectworth Trail, Springfield, NH

Figure 144 - Protectworth Trail Springfield, NH

Learning, opportunities, and fun can often come in threes. First was when my wife and I joined the **Outdoor Recreation for Seniors (ORFS)** group with the ORFS emphasis on weekly year-round hiking and paddling in the Lake Sunapee-Dartmouth region.

Through hiking with ORFS, came the second opportunity, discussed in my January 2018 Blog post titled, **New London, NH Conservation Commission WebSite**. The Conservation Commission website listed 29 trail hikes in the New London area.

ORFS introduced me to hikes on the NL Conservation Commission website, leading to my third opportunity to learn about, the **Sunapee-Ragged-Kearsarge Greenway Coalition (SRKG)** and the 14 trails listed in its guide. And yes, there is an overlap of paths between the NL Commission and the SRKG organizations.

Enough said, let me start with my hike and blog post, and that is the 4.3-mile Protectworth Trail in Springfield, NH. Go to the SKRG site and see **Trail Map 4** for a topographical map of the Deer Hill Road to Springfield-New London Road Protectworth Trail.

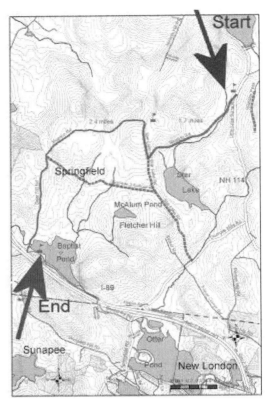

Figure 145 - SKRG Map 4 Protectworth Trail

The ORFS group introduced me to the Protectworth Trail as one of their Tuesday winter hikes. On that day the ORFS hiked one mile of it (actually 2 miles as we snowshoed in one mile, and then backtracked to our starting trailhead). See my **Outdoor Recreation for Seniors (ORFS) Celebration of Spring** reference for more on this ORFS trip.

I was thrilled with this trail because of the snow, blue sky, crisp teen temperatures, no wind, snow-covered tree canopy, and my ORFS friends. So much so that a few days after the hike, I asked my son Tim and friend Mike to join me in hiking the 4.3-mile Protectworth Trail from its start on Route 114 in Springfield, NH, and finishing at its western trailhead on Baptist Pond at the intersection of Stoneybrook Road (also known as Baptist Pond Road) and Deer Road.

The Springfield section of the SKRG is named the Protectworth Trail in honor of the original name given to the land by the Portsmouth proprietors in 1778. This section of the SKRG is a combination of gravel and wood roads. It has a few short steep hills on the class VI roads.

We took two cars – Tim drove to the Deer Road-Stoneybrook Trailhead and parked in an area off Deer Road. Mike and I met Tim there, and we drove in my Jeep to the eastern trailhead on Route 114 to start our trek.

Do we wear snowshoes, microspikes or just our winter hiking boots?

For the ORFS hike, due to deep snow on the trail, we all wore snowshoes and gaiters. They were a necessity because we did some bushwhacking on ungroomed side trails off this class VI trail.

When Tim, Mike and I arrived at the Route 114 trailhead we first checked the trail, and the snow was now packed plus had ice spots. We elected to wear our microspikes.

Scouting the Trail

A few days before the hike, my wife and I scouted the Deer Road/Stoney Road western terminus of the Protectworth Trail by driving to where it ended on Stoney Brook Road, locating the Protectworth trail sign, and driving down the dirt Deer Road.

This would be my first time doing the entire Protectworth Trail, so for safety reasons (do not get lost!) I brought my compass along with the SRKG topo map.

Figure 146 - Map and Compass for Protectworth

SooNipi Magazine Fall 2015 by Ron Garceau

Ron Garceau, a friend and the editor of SooNipi Magazine, had written a nice article in the Fall 2015 issue. The person who had planned the ORFS hike of Protectworth Trail had shared with me the below two pages from the SooNipi article.I do believe if you enlarge the images, you can read these two pages. I share these pages with permission from Ron Garceau. Indeed, Ron's hike was in the fall, whereas our hike was in the winter …covering the same delightful Protectworth Trail.

Protectworth Trail, Springfield, NH

Hiking the Protectworth Trail
Deer Hill Road to Springfield-New London Road (NH Rte 114)
Photos by Ron Garceau

The Protectworth Trail is named after the original name of the land during colonial times. It traverses the hillside on the back side of Star Lake Farm, and is part of the SRKG (Sunapee-Ragged-Kearsarge Greenway).

We hiked this trail a few years ago. Since the length of the trail is 4.1 miles, we opted to leave one vehicle at one end, and start our hike at the other end. So after parking a car at the intersection of Baptist Pond Road and Deer Hill Road, just beyond Baptist Pond, we drove over to Rte 114, where a good parking spot is located, near the beginning of the trail.

A sign greeted us, confirming that we were in the correct place. Along the way, there were signs of life from a hundred years ago. There were old stone walls, a couple of stone foundations, and tree growth that indicated some of the land was once a pasture. The trail was crossed with at least two intersections with other roads. I had brought along a topo map, so we could see where we were in relation to those roads. Our trail continued pretty much west towards Baptist Pond.

Somewhere along the way, we were surprised to come across a man-made field that had Scottish Highland cattle grazing. Our 13-pound terrier-mix decided he should go chase them, but when the first big bull just stood there and looked quizzically at him, the dog smartened up and retreated. (The cattle are being raised by Star Lake Farm.)

Figure 147 - SooNipi Magazine Protectworth

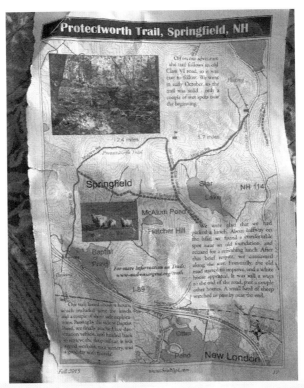

References

- Blog and Video: SRK Greenway Trail 4 Protectworth Trail, Springfield, NH http://tiny.cc/2pqw1y
- Blog and Video: ORFS Winter Hike Put Safety First: Kidder-Cleveland-Clough Trail http://tiny.cc/9tow1y

- .Blog and video: New London, NH Conservation Commission website http://tiny.cc/a1bn1y

- Sunapee-Ragged-Kearsarge Greenway Coalition http://www.srkg.com/alltrailsguide.htm

- Chapin Center Council on Aging http://coachapincenter.org/index.html

- An Outdoor Recreation for Seniors (ORFS) Celebration of Spring http://tiny.cc/p7pw1y

New London, NH Conservation Commission website.

A friend just shared the below **New London, NH Conservation Commission** website. It is a wealth of information for day hikes in the New London, New Hampshire area. What most excited me was the spreadsheet titled, **Individual Trail Links.**Each of the 29 trails listed in the spreadsheet has a link to specific descriptions and directions. Wow!

http://www.nl-nhcc.com/trails/nlcctrails.htm

New London Individual Trail Links

1. Bunker Loop	11. Kidder-Cleveland-Clough	21. Philbrick-Cricenti Bog
2. Clark Lookout	12. Knights Hill Nature Park	22. Phillips Memorial Preserve
3. Clark Pond	13. Langenau Forest Spur	23. Pleasant Lake High
4. Cocoa's Path (SRKG)	14. Little Sunapee Associates	24. Shepard Spring
5. Cook Trails	15. Low Plain	25. Webb Forest
6. Cordingley	16. Lyon Brook	26. Wolf Tree (SRKG)
7. Dura Crockett	17. Messer Pond	27. SRKG Trails 5
8. Great Brook (SRKG)	18. Morgan Hill	28. SRKG Trails 6
9. Kidder	19. Morgan Hill Loop	29. SRKG Trails 7
10. Kidder Brook	20. Morgan Pond	

Visit this most informative and instructive website for trails in the New London area. Many of these New London trails are included in this book such as trails 9, 10, 11, 12, 27, 28 and 29.

++++++++++++++++++

"Everyone must do something. I believe I will go outdoors with family and friends."

Remembering Trips to Maine's Allagash Wilderness Waterway

Figure 148 - Allagash Wilderness Waterway 1998-2001-2009

Maine's Allagash Wilderness Waterway (AWW) is often described as the prime jewel of Maine's wilderness paradises. I have had the privilege of spending three different weeks, paddling and camping in this unique wilderness area. Each of the three trips generally covered the same 100 or so miles of the AWW watershed.

Each trip is planned and guided by Master Maine Guide, Linwood "The Loon." Of significance to me, is that each trip included my son, Timothy. Good friends, John K, Joe R, and Harry, went on two of the trips. Dundee, Paul, Eric, Lennie C, Pat, Rick, Lennie #2, and Jim made one trip.

I composed this montage using pictures from the three trips. My initial goal was to create a 20" x 16" canvas to share AWW highlights in a manner all trip participants could relate on each of their trips.

I wanted each person on a trip pictured on the canvas, and each picture had to generate a unique AWW memory.

The pictures
In the center is a map of the Allagash Wilderness Waterway in northern Maine bordering Canada. One of the exceptional themes about the Allagash is it flows northeast.

1. Linwood and Betty (upper left). Betty did not go on the trips, BUT, without her behind-the scenes work beginning months before the actual trip, and then the after-trip cleaning and repacking of equipment, these trips could not have happened. Think of the time it takes to prepare food for a weeklong trip for six to eight people. Examples of the meals were lobster, steak, breakfast choices, "How do you want your eggs prepared?", and stuffed Cornish hen in a can with peas, potatoes, and onions – one can for each of us cooked amongst our campfire's charcoals!
2. Truly we experienced five-star meals. Packing seven days of three meals a day – in coolers (upper right) named for the rivers Linwood and Betty have paddled. And the coolers contained no ice!)
3. Chase Rapids (below Linwood and Betty) is five miles of class 2 rapids. This picture shows us transferring our gear from our canoes to a ranger van at the head of the rapids. We paddled through the rapids without fear of losing our gear.
4. Tim and Steve paddling over Long Lake Dam. Think of the portage time we saved!
5. Bottom Left – the 2001 crew after a week in the Allagash Wilderness Waterway
6. A selfie as the 2001 crew enjoy morning coffee at Round Pond. We are looking at two moose across the pond.
7. A mother and her calf viewed on our 2009 trip. We stopped counting moose at 25!

8. Bottom center. Our 2001 trip experienced a canoe rescue in the middle of Eagle Lake. Fortunately, "The Loon" on a prior trip had us practice canoe rescues – and within 5 minutes after this trip's spill, we continued, losing only a six-pack of diet soda.
9. "The three cousins" at the top of 40-foot Allagash Falls.
10. Bottom Right. Two rusted locomotives used during the early 1900's for transferring logs from one lake to another on their journey to Millinocket paper mills.
11. Paul and Dundee experience a taste of spruce gum. All first-timers on our trips must experience spruce gum – as chewed by local Abenaki Indians.
12. The crew poses with canoes for the Father-Son 2009 trip (plus driver friends to take us to the put-in and then drive to the town of Allagash to leave trucks for us to return back home at the end of the trip).
13. Middle right. The 1998 crew posing in front of the sign "Leaving the Allagash Wilderness Waterway."
14. The eagles were always plentiful. A joy to experience our national bird.
15. The steak (plus one hotdog for Dundee)
16. Folgers Black Silk coffee. Steve always had one cup of chocolate for breakfast. The rest of the crew would have one or two cups of coffee. The morning routine was to have breakfast with coffee, stow our gear and pack the canoes, and after checking the campsite was without trash (leave it better than we found it), and the fire was out and watered down, we put-in our canoes and away we paddled. Well, on this trip, after the coffee pot was empty, we made the second pot for all. Our put-in for a long-day of paddling was getting delayed because of Folger's Black Silk!

On the third morning, Steve began to wonder why everyone was having a third cup of coffee. So, Steve decided to skip his chocolate and instead have a cup of coffee – and he had one cup – then a 2nd cup, and then a 3rd cup. The Folger's Black Silk was delicious. On all our outdoor trips since, Folger's Black Silk is a MUST.

For more Allagash videos and stories by OutdoorSteve:

- Blog and video: **The Ballad of the Allagash Wilderness Waterway** http://tiny.cc/l3bn1y This Allagash Wilderness Waterway Ballad video is prepared from participants' memorable moments of expeditions guided by Registered Master Maine Guide Linwood Parsons and his wife, Betty.

Reflections on the Allagash http://tiny.cc/c5bn1y
Timothy Priest has been on many wilderness paddling trips guided by Master Maine Guide Linwood "The Loon" Parsons and his wife Betty "The Chickadee". Tim shares his reflections of Linwood and Betty and his seven Maine North Woods trips.

The Allagash Wilderness Waterway: A Father-Son Paddle
http://tiny.cc/u5bn1y
Ten of us just returned from paddling the Allagash Wilderness Waterway (AWW) in northern Maine. The 100 or so miles of the AWW is composed of streams, rivers, and lakes. This was a father-son trip with four dads and five sons. Linwood "Loon" Parsons (http://www.loonsnest.biz/) was our guide. Loon's knowledge of the history and special sites around the Allagash meant many side trips and stories of much historical Allagash lore.

References

- **Blog and videos: Remembering Trips to Maine's Allagash Wilderness Waterway** http://tiny.cc/56ry1y

Bagging Two New Hampshire Four-Thousand Footers in Two Days: Mt Tecumseh and Mt Osceola

My long-term adventurer friend John called and asked if I wanted to hike two days in early November in the White Mountains of New Hampshire He had picked Mt Tecumseh and Mt Osceola, both in the Waterville Valley area, and both described as moderate 4,000-foot mountain hikes.

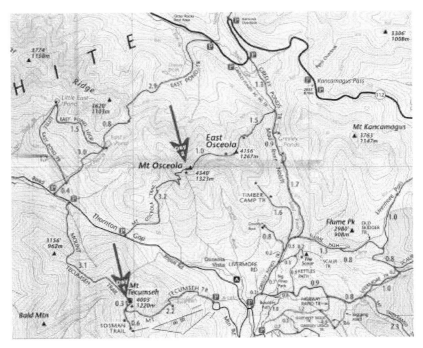

Figure 149 - Two-days and Two Four-Thousand Footers

Timothy, my son and fellow long-term adventurer, and his friend Rob would be joining us for the Tecumseh hike.

Day 1 - Mt Tecumseh

Figure 150 - A Selfie at Mt Tecumseh Trailhead

Mt Tecumseh is 4,003 feet, and the shortest of the 48 New Hampshire 4,000 foot mountains.

The Mount Tecumseh trail ascends Mt Tecumseh, starting at the Waterville Valley Ski area with the trailhead at the top right edge of the parking area. It climbs the east slope of Tecumseh.

Starting at the trailhead sign, we used exposed boulders and rocks to cross a small brook and follow the south side of Tecumseh Brook for 0.3mi., then crossed the brook again to a section along a small ridge. At 1.1 mi., the rock-bound trail drops down and recrosses the brook, then climbs to intersect an old logging road. A view sign points to the edge of the ski slope for excellent views of the North and Middle Tripyramid Mountains.

Continuing upward on the rocky trail, we began to get sights of snow and ice. We carried crampons/microspikes, but we did not put them on. Not wearing our spikes was a bit foolish because it would have made our hike a bit more sure-footed.

Figure 151 - Boulders, snow, and ice beginning at 1 mile

The main trail turns right and follows the rock-strewn road, angling upward along the south side of the Tecumseh Brook valley, then climbs steadily to the main ridge crest south of Tecumseh, where it turns right in a flat area. Here at 2.2 mi. the Sosman Trail enters from the left.

We were not sure whether to follow the Sosman Trail to the summit or the Mount Tecumseh Trail, as both arrive at the summit. We referenced our notes from the AMC White Mountain book and decided on the Mt Tecumseh Trail.

At this fork, we took the Mt Tecumseh Trail as it swings right, descends slightly to circle the base of the steep cone, and finally climbs steeply to reach the summit from the north at 2. 5 miles from the trailhead.

The summit offers a majestic view of 6,288 foot snow-capped Mt Washington, the only mountain covered with snow. We also saw neighboring Mt Osceola, which we will hike the next day,

Figure 152 - Snow-covered Mt Washington from Mt Tecumseh

The White Mountain guide says our trip should average 2 hours and 20 minutes. We took 3 hours with me continually pulling up the rear of our four pack.

Mt. Tecumseh - Sosman Trail
We decided to return to our parking area from the summit by the Sosman Trail, which connects the summit of Tecumseh with the top of the Waterville Valley ski slopes. The Sosman trail sign is clear with an arrow and leaves the summit along the ridge to the south, then turns to the west and switches down the slope with rough snow-ice footing around the rocky nose of the ridge. It merges to the right onto the Mt Tecumseh Trail at .2 mi., then after 120 yds., the Sosman diverges right and follows the ridge south. At .4 mi, it climbs a rocky hump with an interesting view of the Tecumseh summit cone, from which we just came. Just beyond

was another excellent view of snow-covered Mt Washington from a rustic wooden bench. The trail runs south along the ridge, bearing right at .8 mi, and emerging beneath a Waterville Valley ski transmission tower, and the trail comes out at the top of a chairlift. We are about 1.8 mi., from our parking area.

The White Mountain Guide books say the Sosman Trail to the ski slopes to the parking area averages 1hr 45 min. We took 2 hr. Our quads down the ski slopes were unforgiving with cramps and pain. We all agreed, next time no exit via for ski slope hike.

We found the **New England Hiking** site (http://4000footers.com/) site to be an excellent reference in preparing for our hike.

Day 2 Mt Osceola

Mount Osceola is a 4,315-foot mountain located in Lincoln, New Hampshire within a few miles and with a nice view of Mt Tecumseh. Mount Osceola is named after a Native American Tribe leader, Osceola.

The Osceola Trail begins at a parking area on Tripoli Road. Unfortunately, the only two signs we saw were the parking area sign and the trail head sign - both in the same area. After the hike started, including our reaching the summit, we saw no trail signs.

The trail leaves Tripoli Rd. and climbs moderately with rocky footing. At 1.3 mi. It begins to climb by switchbacks toward the ridge top.

At 2.1 mi, a ledge on the left was noted in our notes for a view of Sandwich Mountain.

At 2.3 mi. we crossed a small brook. The trail resumed in switchbacks, gains the summit ridge and turns right, and soon reaches the summit ledge at 3.2 mi, with usually excellent views. Today the summit view was totally fog.

There used to be a fire lookout tower at the summit but was removed in the 1970s. The only remaining signs are three one-foot cement footings. The summit is a large rock slab which is perfect to grab lunch or hang out!

Figure 153 - Summit Mt Osceola

We learned our lesson from the Mt Tecumseh hike, and we wore our spikes going down the same trail we came up.

Figure 154 - A fogged in Osceola Summit

On our trip, we met heavy fog at the summit and missed the views of Osceola, Mount Washington, and other surrounding 4,000 plus footers.

Day 1 Mt Tecumseh

- Elevation: 4,003 feet (1,220 meters)
- Waterville Valley, NH (Grafton County, NH)
- Sandwich Range of White Mountains
- Coordinates: 43°57.99' North   71°33.40' West
- Features: the Cascades, Waterville Valley Ski Area, Limited Summit Views, Loop Hike
- The distance of highlighted hike: 5.2 miles
- The shortest mountain on the AMC's official 4,000 footers list.
- The mountain is named after the Native American Tribe, Shawnee.

Day 2 – Mt Osceola

•Elevation: 4,315 feet (1,315 meters)
•Lincoln, NH (Grafton County, New Hampshire)

•Range: Sandwich Range
•Coordinates: 44°0'5.81" North   71°32'8.21" West
•Easy/Moderate
•Brooks, Cascades, Limited Summit View,
•The mountain is named after a Native American Tribe chief.

References:

1. Osceola https://en.wikipedia.org/wiki/Osceola
2. New England Hiking
   http://4000footers.com/tecumseh.shtml
3. New England
   Hiking http://4000footers.com/osceola.shtml
4. https://en.wikipedia.org/wiki/Tecumseh
5. OutdoorSteve.com http://www.outdoorsteve.com
6. White Mountain Guide 28th Edition Compiled and
   edited by Gene Daniel and Steven D. Smith.
   Appalachian Mountain Club Books, Boston,
   Massachusetts, 2007
   http://outdoors.org/publications/books

+++++++++++++++++++++

"Everyone must do something. I believe I will go
outdoors with family and friends."

Torey Pines

Figure 155 - Playing Torrey Pines in a Torrential Rain

Cathy and I (mostly me) are back-of-the-pack golfers. However, we appreciate this beautiful game. On a recent trip to southern California, we decided to play Torrey Pines Golf Course, the ocean side course for the annual PGA Farmers Insurance Open, and past and future course of the **U.S. Open Championship**.

In summary:

- The temperature was unseasonably cold at 45 degrees and windy.
- Rain is expected.
- Due to the weather, the course is not crowded.
- South Course fee was $110 each plus $25 for a cart.
- Decision time - do we play or not? **Answer - Yes!**
- As we were finishing the second hole of the South Course - life-threatening weather was instantly upon us (check out the video). Horrendous wind, lightning, rain, and hail came down from the sky. **Evacuate the course!**

- We asked for a Raincheck, but the starter said the course had a **No Raincheck Policy.** Decision time: 1) Walk away from our $245 paid fee for two holes, 2) Continue in life-threatening conditions, or 3) Wait in wet clothing in the hope the weather clears. **We chose door number 3 - given this was a lifetime opportunity to play a U.S. Open Course.**
- As we played the tenth hole - the sky again exploded with life-threatening conditions. We both readily agreed we had proved ourselves on this beautiful PGA course - and it was time for a hot shower, warm clothing, and lots of pleasant memories.

Halfway through the 10th Hole - No need to prove ourselves

References

- **Blog and Video: Playing Torey Pines**
  http://tiny.cc/01dj1y

- **About Torrey Pines**
  http://torreypinesgolfcourse.com/about.htm
  Located in La Jolla (pronounced "la hoya"), California, Torrey Pines Golf Course sits on the coastal cliffs overlooking the Pacific Ocean and is recognized as the premier municipal golf course owned and operated by a city. The Torrey Pine is a rare tree that grows in the wild only along this local stretch of the coastline in San Diego County and on Santa Rosa Island.

  It offers two scenic and, due to its yearly hosting of the PGA TOUR's Farmers Insurance Open event, widely recognizable championship 18-hole golf course. It is undoubtedly the most accessible public facility for the die-hard enthusiast wishing to play at a world-renown facility that nearly all golfers know by name.

  Torrey Pines was the site of perhaps the most memorable modern-day U.S. Open Championship, when in 2008, under the typically brutal conditions of this major tournament, injured and hobbling Tiger Woods defeated Rocco Mediate during their sudden death playoff after 90 grueling holes of exciting golf.

Torrey Pines will host the 2020 US Open Championship."

"Everyone must do something. I believe I will go outdoors with family and friends."

Hiking Mt Kearsarge in Central New Hampshire

Mount Kearsarge is a 2,937-foot mountain located in the towns of Wilmot and Warner, New Hampshire. Our ascent to the summit starts at the Winslow State Park parking lot at the northwest slope of Mt. Kearsarge.

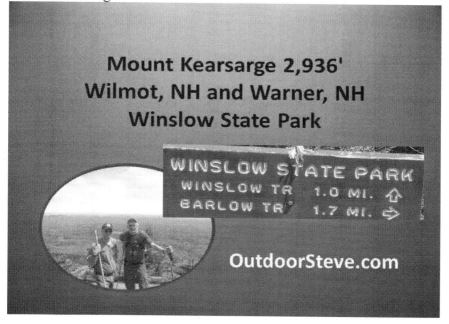

Figure 156 - Mount Kearsarge, New Hampshire

Mount Kearsarge has multiple trails and a bare rockbound summit with an observation fire tower and a cell phone tower.

From the summit on a clear day lies a spectacular view of the White Mountains and Mt Cardigan in the north, the Green Mountains and Mt Sunapee in the west, and the Monadnock Region and the Merrimack Valley in the south. The summit with its towers is a distinctive landmark and is easily seen from its surrounding communities.

Figure 157 - The summit with its distinctive towers landmark

We chose to summit from Winslow State Park with the option of two trails. The Winslow Trail, marked with red blazes, begins at the park's parking area. Winslow Trail climbs for 1.1 miles (1,100 vertical feet) through the forest and over bare granite ledge to the 2,937-foot summit.

The Barlow Trail, marked with yellow blazes, also leaves from the same parking area at Winslow Park and provides a longer, but more gradual ascent to the summit. Several vistas along the 1.7-mile trail afford views of the Andover area, Ragged Mountain, and Mount Cardigan.

Figure 158 - Barlow or Winslow Trail?

We decided to ascend via the longer Barlow Trail and to descend using the much steeper but shorter Winslow Trail. The wet spring run-off and mossy rocks made today's Winslow Trail very slippery.

Early June is the black fly season, and they were plentiful on the day of our trek.

Enjoy this beautiful outdoor recreation of New Hampshire – never say, "I wish I had taken my family to climb Mt Kearsarge."

References

- **Video and Blog Post- Hiking Mt Kearsage in Central New Hampshire** http://tiny.cc/18zo1y
- **Map and more information on Mt Kearsarge** http://tiny.cc/qm0o1y

A Spring Quest to see Tuckerman Ravine

Tuckerman Ravine, is an isolated vast open bowl perched on the southeast slope of Mount Washington, the highest mountain in the Northeast at 6,288 feet. It is one of New Hampshire's unique natural geological formations. In the spring, snow depths in the Ravine can reach 100 feet. Below is a gathering of three of those spring hikes.

Skiing the Ravine is not for the novice or intermediate skier. Tuckerman Ravine can be a hazardous area subject to avalanches and falling massive blocks of ice the size of automobiles.

To see a graphic of Tuckerman Ravine ski routes, go to **Time for Tuckerman** (http://timefortuckerman.com/routes.html). These ski paths from the top of the ravine can reach 40 - 55 degrees in their steeper sections.

Our quest here is to observe downhill skiers ski the Tuckerman Ravine headwall in late winter and spring. It is exhilarating and challenging for skiers, hikers, and those outdoor enthusiast observers, such as myself. The porch deck of Hermit Hut is the place to meet these local "skiing celebrities," and hearing their conquests is worth the 4 to 5-hour round trip hike.

Ski runs in Tuckerman Ravine are steeper than descends at nearby developed ski areas. Adding to the challenge, as noted, Tuckerman Ravine skiers must work for their runs by hiking uphill for 2-1/2 miles or so to reach the ravine. But "Skiing Tuckerman" does boast some of the most challenging terrain in the eastern U.S., making it a magnet for accomplished skiers and snowboarders, and legions of spectators who do the climb to take in the scene.

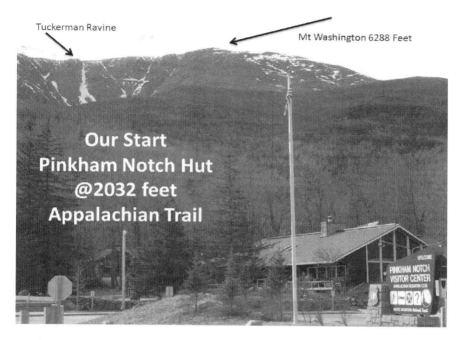

Figure 159 – View of Mt Washington & Tuckerman Ravine from Pinkham Notch AMC Hut

If you are thinking of skiing Tuckerman, you should be an expert skier in good physical condition. The headwall at Tuckerman is between 45-55 degrees and the vertical drop is approximately 1200 ft. The only way to the top is by climbing the headwall. (http://www.out-there.com/tuckerman.htm).

How do I get to Tuckerman Ravine?

The Tuckerman Ravine Trail from Pinkham Notch (el 2,032 ft) on Route 16, leads to to Hermit Lake (el 3,875 ft) at the base of the Ravine. Hiking time to the base depends on the physical condition of the slowest hiker, unpredictable weather, and time of year (snow and ice in winter and flowing streams down the Trail in spring).

Our hikes in the videos are early May with small streams from melting snow frequently crossing the trail for the first half of the trip (1 ½ hour), and then ice and snow for the second half (1 1/4 hour.) Our uphill trips take nearly 3 hours to reach Hermit Hut Shelter from Pinkham Notch Hut. Our downhill hike back to Pinkham Notch via the same trail is about 2 hours.

Skiers carrying their downhill and telemark skis, boots and gear.Hikers, like us, are there for the thrill of the surreal scene of this magnificent, beautiful ravine with a reputation for beauty, avalanche danger, and climbing challenges.

Once reaching the Hermit Hut Shelter, extreme alpine, snowboard, and telemark skiers continue to climb another hour or so up to the headwall of the Ravine's various self-made ski lanes. The **Reference: Blog and videos** show skiers we saw coming down Hillmans Highway, Left Gully, and the Bowl.

Figure 160 - Mike, Steve, and Tim from Hermit Hut

Microspikes or Crampons?

Although the start at Pinkham Notch is on a gravel path, our three visits all met ice at the half-way point, and required microspikes. My videos say we used "crampons" on the trail. We used "microspikes." To learn the difference, go to **Microspikes or**

Crampons? (http://tiny.cc/2bty1y). For most hikers today in the Whites, microspikes have replaced crampons - but some of the older hikers still refer to them as crampons when they indeed are wearing microspikes.

The Tuckerman Ski Patrol runs a reference site for winter and spring travel http://tiny.cc/2z0y1y. The site has daily information from November to Memorial Day on avalanche danger and snow/ski reports for Tuckerman and Huntington Ravines.

Figure 161 - Hillmans Highway and The Bowl

Trek to Tuckerman Ravine. One of Mother Nature's Spring Marvels in New Hampshire

Figure 162 - Warnings and Views of Tuckerman

Figure 163 – Dundee, Steve and Dick Tuckerman Ravine Overlooking Hermit Hut

Tuckerman Ravine

Figure 164 - Skiers on Tuckerman

Shared Thoughts:

A trek to Tuckerman's is a perfect place to bond with your significant other, family, and friends. My wife Cathy and I have made this trek many times, and years ago. Memories of love, emotion, and bonding are part of my Tuckerman experience:

- 10:30 am temperature 82 degrees AMC's Pinkham Hut, 12:30 pm temperature 68 at the base of the ravine.
- We were aware of an air and ground search for a 17-year-old Eagle Scout hiker who had been missing in this area since Saturday. At around noon we heard from a hiker the scout was found safe and in good condition.
- The camaraderie of all skiers was evident throughout the hike as we shared "where are you from", "conditions of your ski", "which side of the ravine did you ski?", and

"Have you heard if they found the scout?"

• We wished a ten-year-old boy "happy birthday" after we learned he and his dad skied Hillman's Highway trail, the longest run in Tuckerman.

• We drank water every ten minutes so as to not get dehydrated. My backpack carries a quart of water, two peanut butter and jelly sandwiches, compass, map, duct tape, ace bandage, contractor trash bags for an emergency overnight, warm clothes, gaiters, winter hat, and gloves. We all wore hiking boots (wearing sneakers on this rocky hike invites a sprained ankle and wet feet).

• After lunch, at the caretaker hut, we started up the right section of the ravine but stopped because of rocks covered with slippery ice and brewing dark storm clouds moving swiftly over the headwall. Since storms come up quickly in this area, we did not hesitate to leave when we saw the threatening conditions.

The New Hampshire Fish and Game Department and the White Mountain National Forest have partnered up to create a mountain safety program called **HikeSafe** http://www.hikesafe.com/.

A large component of the program is the **Hiker Responsibility Code**. The code applies to all hikers, from beginners on a short hike to experienced outdoor enthusiasts on an expedition.

Please practice the elements of the code and help the HikeSafe program spread by sharing the code with fellow trekkers. Creating awareness of HikeSafe will help increase hiker responsibility and decrease the need for Search and Rescue efforts.

Cathy, Tim, Dick, Dundee, Mike, and I, will never have to say, "We wish we had hiked to Tuckerman's Ravine to watch the skiers and enjoy Tuck's majestic wilderness mountain scenery."

Figure 165 - This trail ONLY if you are in top physical condition

References and Videos for "What it feels like hiking to base of Tuckerman Ravine

- **Blog and Video: A quest to see Tuckerman Ravine skiers** http://tiny.cc/6baj1y
- **Blog and Video: Tuckerman Ravine, Southeast Face of Mt. Washington, White Mountains, New Hampshire** http://tiny.cc/ejty1y
- **Blog and Video: Fantastic Mid-week Trek to Tuckerman Ravine** http://tiny.cc/nlty1y
- **Microspikes or Crampons?** (http://tiny.cc/2bty1y)
- **See *Friends of Tuckerman Ravine* for Weather and Trail Conditions** https://www.friendsoftuckermanravine.org/conditions
- **Graphic of Tuckerman Ravine ski routes: Time for Tuckerman** http://tiny.cc/pt0o1y

- **Prepare for Hiking/Skiing Tuckerman with *HikeSafe Card.*** http://www.hikesafe.com/

Kayaking on Lake Coniston, NH

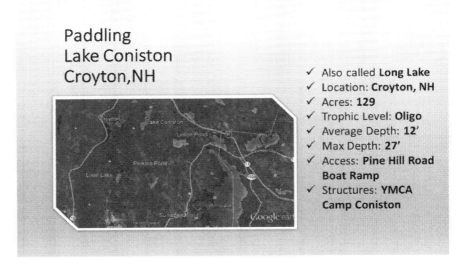

Figure 166 - Statistics on Lake Coniston

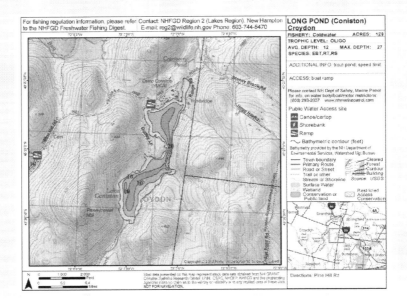

Figure 167 - Map of Lake Coniston Area

Figure 168 - The Dudley Lane Put-in

Figure 169 - Kayaking on Lake Coniston

Figure 170 – Loon Preening

Loons Preening & Bathing

You might think a loon is in distress when you see it preening or bathing, but these are actually important daily maintenance behaviors. I have even believed a loon was maybe dead because it appeared to be floating on its side with no motion minutes at a time – before it finally turned upright again. Here are some key points to help recognize these behaviors:

For loons, daily preening is a necessary maintenance behavior to keep their feathers aligned, waterproofed and in good condition. Individual feathers are like shingles on a roof; their interlocking structure creates a barrier so that water cannot penetrate their skin. Loons and other birds secrete oil from the uropygial gland (also called preen gland) at the base of the tail and work it through all of their feathers. This oil helps keep the feathers in place, like hairspray.

- A loon will often roll onto its side or back and start pulling the breast and belly feathers through its bill. One leg usually comes out of the water and the loon spins in circles while trying to reach these feathers.
- Since loons cannot reach their head and neck with their bills, they rub their head against their back or shoulders after secreting some oil from the preen gland.
- Loons will often flap their wings during and at the end of preening sessions. During a wing flap, a loon rises high up on the surface of the water and with neck outstretched, the bill held high and wings spread, it will flap several times while shaking its head and neck.
- Tail wagging usually follows wing flaps. The loon holds its tail above the water's surface and shakes it from side to side, expelling excess water.
- Preening sessions can sometimes last more than 30 minutes.

Loon Bathing

Bathing is another maintenance behavior that is observed on a regular basis. Loons bathe to help get rid of feather parasites and clean their feathers.

- Bathing involves more vigorous splashing and submerging. A loon may completely roll over while thrashing in the water with partially opened wings.
- One or both wings are often seen flailing in the air and then are slapped back down on the water's surface.
- One or both legs may also be seen flailing in the air.
- A loon may dive backwards, flashing its bright white belly.
- It may intersperse splashing with dipping its bill and sometimes its head into the water to wash its face.

- Loons will often flap their wings during and at the end of a bathing session as well.
- Bathing sessions are often interspersed with periods of preening and may also last more than 30 minutes. A preening or bathing loon is a busy loon. Please make sure that you watch the action with a good pair of binoculars from a safe distance so that your presence does not distract the loon from this essential part of its daily routine.

Loon Calls:

Northern New Hampshire is an area that enjoys the call of the loon – particularly early morning and late evening.

The Wail:

The "Wail" is most frequently given in the evening or at night and can be heard for many miles. This haunting call is not an alarm call but is used to keep in contact with other loons on the same lake and surrounding lakes. The wail is a long, one, two, or three note call in situations where loons want to move closer to one another. Parents will wail to their chicks to encourage the chicks to leave the nest, to approach the parents when they have food, or to emerge from a hiding place. Listen to the "Wail".

The "Tremolo" has been described as "insane laughter"; it is 8 to 10 notes voiced rapidly which vary in frequency and intensity. This alarm call usually indicates agitation or fear, often caused by disturbance from people, a predator or even another loon. Members of a pair will also duet using tremolo calls. This is also the only call that loons make in flight. Listen to the "Tremolo".

The "Yodel" is only made by male loons. It is used to advertise and defend their territory, especially during incubation and chick-rearing. It's also used in territorial situations and aggressive encounters with other birds. Males will also yodel if a predator is seen that may be approaching the chicks, such as when an eagle flies overhead. Yodeling males crouch flat to the water with their head and neck extended and the lower bill just over the water. Listen to the "Yodel".

The "Hoot" call is not as intense or as loud as the other calls. It's a soft, short contact call between birds. Adults will hoot to their mates, and parents will hoot to chicks, enabling them to keep in touch with the whereabouts of the other birds. Adults also hoot to other adults of social groups residing on or visiting the same lake. Listen to the "Hoot".

References

- **Video and Blog:** Kayaking Lake Coniston
  http://outdooradventurers.blogspot.com/2015/07/kayaking-lake-coniston.html
- **Coniston NH Map**
  http://www.wildlife.state.nh.us/maps/bathymetry/coniston_croydon.pdf
- **The Loons Nest**
  http://www.loonsnest.biz
- **Loon Preening and Bathing**
  http://www.loon.org/preening-bathing.php
- **Loon Preservation Committee NH**
  http://www.loon.org/

Summer

I went to the woods because I wished to live deliberately, to front only the essentials of life, and see if I could not learn what it had to teach, and not, when I came to die, discover that I had not lived.
– Henry David Thoreau, Walden

Never say, "I wish I had been in the Lake Sunapee Sailing Day Annual Poker Cruise"

When Bill called asking if Cathy and I wanted to be part of Captain Al's crew in the Annual Lake Sunapee Sailing Day "Poker Run", I could not pass up this unique outdoor challenge. My motivational mantra, **Never say, "I wish I had ..."** had to be answered, "Yes!".

Figure 171 - Lake Sunapee Poker Run Cruise

The ANNUAL "POKER CRUISE" SAILING DAY HOSTED BY THE LAKE SUNAPEE CRUISING FLEET, promotes sailing fun on Lake Sunapee. All sailboats from sunfish to cruisers to racers are welcome to join a "Poker Cruise".

Sailing enthusiasts are invited to rendezvous at the Lake Sunapee Cruising Fleet boat just outside Sunapee Harbor. At the Committee Boat, each sailboat is given instructions, a map of the course and a playing card. Boats will then sail to four marked boats on the upper end of the lake.

At each mark, each sailboat will receive another playing card. Following the "Poker Cruise" each crew is invited to bring their "poker hand" to a reception sponsored by the Lake Sunapee Cruising Fleet at the Knowlton House (LSPA) in Sunapee Harbor. There, prizes will be awarded for the best poker hands and for the best themed crew costumes.

In case you cannot tell, Captain Al's crew costume themes are two-fold, Aliens from Outer space (think "Close encounters of the third kind"), and Spanish neighbors.

References
- **Blog and Video: Never say, "I wish I had been in the Lake Sunapee Sailing Day Annual Poker Cruise"** http://tiny.cc/cmej1y
- 7th Annual "Poker Cruise" Sailing Day http://tiny.cc/goej1y
- Lake Sunapee Cruising Fleet https://lscf.us/
- OutdoorSteve.com https://www.outdoorsteve.com
  +++++++++++++++++++++

Never say, "I wish I had ridden in a race car at New Hampshire Motor Speedway"

Automobile racing is one of the most popular spectator sports in the world. However, until now, my interest was only superficial. Thus, this blog post was difficult for me to write, as high-performance driving was something, I had never paid much attention.

On the flipside, my son Timothy has had a lifelong interest in high speed sports from dirt bike riding, snow mobiles, ATVs, car repairs and automobile shows among his high-speed interests.

Figure 172 - Thank You, John, for a Great Day at SCDA
So why my blog post on high-performance driving? Last winter I met a new friend, John, who shared with me he was a high-performance driving instructor nationally certified who teaches for SCDA, NASA, Porsche, BMWCCA, Audi, JCNA (Jaguar), Ferrari and a host of other clubs/marques across the country. I told John about Timothy's interests in high-performance driving.

Last week John offered to have us join him for demonstration laps and classroom instruction at an event organized and run by the Sports Car Driving Association (SCDA) at which he was instructing. The event would be held at the New Hampshire Motor Speedway, Loudon, NH.

With zero exposure to high performance driving, Never say, "I wish I had …" popped into my mind. My call to Timothy was eagerly accepted, followed by my confirmation email to John.

With this background to the reader, you can expect this post is not a "how to", but an "Hmm … interesting" insights from a neophyte on performance driving.

The SCDA provides the driving enthusiast the opportunity to experience high performance driving in a safe and controlled environment. Events are strictly driver educational events - they are non-competitive and are not timed events. All novice drivers - those who have never been on a track - must ride with a certified instructor in the right seat.

As non-certified drivers, neither Timothy nor I drove on the race course. However, we did get the full passenger effect.

Pit Crew

John had trailered his Corvette, and he had to change a brake rotor on his rear wheel before the day started. This is when John's new Pit crew of one – Timothy - used his car and jump cables to help start John's corvette.

As we watched John began to remove the cracked brake rotor, the wrench slipped on the nut and John's forearm smashed against the frame – "Ouch!" This was not a small hurt, and Timothy, who is a Journeyman Printer at the Boston Globe and responsible for maintaining the presses, and has replaced brakes on his own car, jumped in and worked with John to replace the broken brake rotor. In less than 10 minutes the car was ready for the track.

Novice Classroom Instruction

John suggested we start the day by attending the Novice classroom instruction. The instructor had a screen of the track with a number assigned for identification to each section of the track. The instructor briefly described the awareness of each section pointing out critical areas, and to "keep your eyes off the wall". "Focus only on the apron". [The apron is an area of asphalt or concrete that separates the racing surface from the infield.]

Walking tour of the Pit

While John attended to his instructor responsibilities, Timothy took me on a walking tour of the pit providing me his insights. This stadium can hold nearly 100,000 fans on a race day, the largest sporting event in New England, but was essentially empty today with about 100 or so SCDA students at this event.

The Two Videos

Below is the blog reference containing two videos. The first video is a summary of our day: Timothy pit crews for John; we attend the novice class; a walkabout of the pit; observe the racers from various parts of the course; saw a minor incident and the quick response of the emergency personnel and equipment (which is mandatory at such events) respond; saw both black and yellow flags in response to this incident, where the black flag is waved at all corner worker stations, and means that all cars must come into the pits to await further instructions until the incident is evaluated and the track cleared.

John took Timothy on a six-lap drive, but it was difficult for me to video as the fences protect and prevent visitors from getting close to the race track.

The second video is short snippet videos of my 5-lap ride with John driving his corvette. The video starts with Timothy getting strapped in John's car. For my track ride, I hold my camera on the dash as we zip around the 1.6-mile course five times.

A day at the New Hampshire Motor Speedway

NEW HAMPSHIRE MOTOR SPEEDWAY SCHEDULE

TIME	www.scda1.com	
7:30	Gate Opens (sign waiver at gate, then register w/SCDA in Garage 1)	
7:00 - 8:30	Registration & Tech Inspection (Outside Gate/ Garage 1)	
8:00 – 8:15	Instructor's Meeting (Gas Pumps)	
8:30	Driver's Meeting (By Garage Bay 1)	
*** Please arrive at staging lane at least 10 minutes prior to your run group ***		
	ON TRACK	IN CLASS classroom by garage 1
9:00 - 9:30	Instructors	Intermediate 1
9:30 - 10:00	Intermediate 1	Novice
10:00 - 10:30	Intermediate 2 Advanced	
10:30 - 11:00	Novice	Intermediate 2 Advanced
11:00 - 11:25	Intermediate 1	
11:25 - 11:50	Instructors	Novice
11:50 - 12:15	Intermediate 2 Advanced	Intermediate 1
12:15 - 12:40	Novice	
12:40 - 1:05	Intermediate 1	Intermediate 2 Advanced
1:05 - 1:30	Instructors	
1:30 - 1:55	Intermediate 2 Advanced	
1:55 - 2:20	Novice	
2:20 - 2:40	Intermediate 1	Instructors
2:40 - 3:00	Instructors	Novice
3:00 - 3:20	Intermediate 2 Advanced	Intermediate 1
3:20 - 3:40	Novice	Intermediate 2 Advanced
3:40 - 4:00	Intermediate 1	
4:00 - 4:20	Intermediate 2 Advanced	
4:20 – 4:40	Novice	
4:40 - 5:00	Instructors	
	Thank you for choosing SCDA!	
UPCOMING SCDA EVENTS	August 18th: Palmer Motorsports Park 10% for Miata drivers	
	August 25th: Thompson Speedway Motorsports Park 10% off for Lotus drivers	
	August 27th: Lime Rock Park Full Track and SCDA Car Control Clinic	
	September 10th-11th: New Jersey Motorsports Park Drive BOTH tracks!	

Figure 173 - SCDA NH Motor Speedway Schedule

References

1. **Blog and Video: Never say, "I wish I had ridden in a race car at New Hampshire Motor Speedway"**
   http://tiny.cc/66dj1y
2. **Sports Car Driving Association** http://tiny.cc/a9dj1y

3. The New Hampshire Motor Speedway https://www.nhms.com/
4. Survive the Drive https://survivethedrive.org/
5. Glossary of Motorsport Terms http://tiny.cc/99dj1y
6. OutdoorSteve.com https://outdoorsteve.com/

Rowing Lessons with Lake Sunapee Rowing Club

A proud father and grandfather share videos of his two sons and grandson taking July 2016 and July 2015 rowing lessons from the Lake Sunapee Rowing Club (LSRC) http://www.lakesunapeerowing.com.

The 2016 day's class was for the doubles scull and the singles scull. The LSRC provides the boats (also known as shells).

Figure 174 - Lake Sunapee Eight plus Coxswain on Lake Sunapee with Mt Sunapee in background

Our coach, Brenda, is just an amazing instructor with knowledge, skills, and a lot of patience. Brenda makes the classes fun with personal instruction for each student, and a wealth of education on learning the language and techniques of rowing.

Tim and Carson did the doubles scull, while Shaun did the singles scull. Coach Brenda motored between the two sculls giving each one immediate feedback. In addition, while Brenda counseled Shaun and Tim at the end of the evening, she had Carson get into a single scull, and with a brief tutorial, Carson was sent on his way into Lake Sunapee to adjust to the single scull. After Brenda's session with Shaun and Tim, she rowed in a single scull beside Carson to instruct him in his first single scull lesson.

See a nine-minute video of this 2-hour lesson by Coach Brenda.

In 2015 Tim and Carson, and friend Nicholas took lessons in the Eight plus coxswain boat with LSRC. Below is a 5 minute video of the 2-hour lesson.

Now, Shaun, Tim, Carson, and Nicholas have experienced lessons offered by the Lake Sunapee Rowing Club.

So where is OutdoorSteve in his rowing this year?

- I had the privilege of participating in the 2016 Prouty Rowing doubles rowing event on the Connecticut River starting at the Dartmouth College boat house. As representatives of the Lake Sunapee Rowing Club, my teammate Dave and I, under the excellent tutelage of LSRC coaches, trained for the month of June and early July for two hours every Tuesday, Thursday, and Sunday. **http://outdooradventurers.blogspot.com/201 6/07/the-prouty-lake-sunapee-rowing-club.html**
- Along with the Prouty training, a friend asked if I wanted his unused single scull. His offer was readily accepted, and from June till the middle of September, I managed to do a one-hour every other day row in my single scull. The very positive results of this committed training will be discussed in a future blog.

	Shaun	Tim	Carson	Nicholas	Steve
Single Scull	√		√		√
Doubles		√	√		√
Quad					√
Eight Plus		√	√	√	√

What is Rowing/Crew?

Here is the definition by **River City Crew**: The term "crew" is often used when talking about rowing. This term is commonly misused, so this may clarify the truths of the names of the sport. "Crew", as a noun, can refer to either the people in a specific high school or collegiate rowing boat or the entire sport of rowing in high school or college. The term "crew team" is redundant and is not properly used. After college, the term "crew" is no longer used to describe the sport or people in a boat, and "rowing team" or "rowing club" is proper. In the sport of rowing, "crew" is never, ever properly used as a verb, i.e., one does not "go crewing", rather one would "go rowing". When in doubt, the noun "rowing team" or verb "rowing" will always be correct when describing the sport.

Rowing is truly a sport which can be done throughout one's lifetime.

Other Rowing Blog Posts by OutdoorSteve

- **Book Review for "*The Boys in the Boat: Nine Americans and their Epic Quest for Gold at the 1936 Berlin Olympics*" by** Daniel James Brown http://tiny.cc/hq2o1y
- **Rowing through the eyes of a beginner** http://tiny.cc/rs2o1
- The Prouty - Lake Sunapee Rowing Club Participation - http://tiny.cc/zs2o1y
- What is Rowing/Crew? http://www.rivercitycrew.com/about/3127/
- River City Rowing Crew http://www.rivercitycrew.com/

++++++++++++++++++

"Everyone must do something. I believe I will go outdoors with family and friends."

Hiking at Mount Sunapee

"The summit of Mount Sunapee (elevation - 2,743ft.) is reached via ski trails or the Summit hiking trail (Red Blaze). The start of the Summit Trail can be found on the right of the Lower Ridge ski trail, behind Sunapee Lodge.

A number of hiking trails are accessible year-round at Mount Sunapee. These include the Summit Hiking Trail, the Lake Solitude Hiking Trail, and the Newbury Hiking Trail.

You may also hike on any of the ski trails during the summer months. **Ski trails are off limits for hiking during ski area operation, however, you are allowed to cross ski trails during winter operation to access the state hiking trails.** Please look uphill for downhill skiers and snowboarders before crossing the ski trails. Mt Sunapee snowshoe trails are located across the road from Spruce Lodge if you wish to have a shorter and less demanding hike."

For your safety be sure to be prepared when hiking:

- Allow ample time
- Wear sturdy footwear
- Know and heed weather forecasts
- Bring warm clothing and rain gear
- Bring food and water with you

Mt Sunapee Maps & Info
Mount Sunapee State Park Hiking Trails

- Newbury Trail to Old Province Road, Goshen
- Sunapee-Ragged-Kearsarge Greenway
- Friends of Mt Sunapee http://tiny.cc/yt2o1y

Lake Sunapee

"The lake is approximately 8.1 miles) long (north-south) and from 0.5 to 2.5 miles wide (east-west), covering 6.5 square miles with a maximum depth of 105 feet.

It contains eleven islands (Loon Island, Elizabeth Island, Twin Islands, Great Island, Minute Island, Little Island, Star Island, Emerald Island, Isle of Pines and Penny Island) and is indented by several peninsulas and lake fingers, a combination which yields a total shoreline of some 70 miles. There are seven sandy beach areas including Mount Sunapee State Park beach; some with restricted town access. There are six boat ramps to access the lake at Sunapee Harbor, Georges Mills, Newbury, Mount Sunapee State Park, Burkehaven Marina, and a private marina. The lake contains three lighthouses on the National Register of Historic Places. The driving distance around the lake is 25 miles with many miles of lake water views. The lake is 1,093 feet above sea level.

The lake's outlet is in Sunapee Harbor, the headway for the Sugar River, which flows west through Newport and Claremont to the Connecticut River and then to the Atlantic Ocean. The lake discharges about 250 cubic feet per second (on average), and the Sugar River drops approximately 800 feet on its 27-mile journey to the Connecticut River."

https://en.wikipedia.org/wiki/Lake_Sunapee

References

- **Blog and video: Newbury Trail to Eagles Nest to Lake Sunapee, NH** http://tiny.cc/2v2o1y

The Prouty - Lake Sunapee Rowing Club Participation - July 9, 2016

Steve and Dave participated in the Prouty rowing event as members of the Lake Sunapee Rowing Club (LSRC), sponsored by Casella Recycling. Under the excellent tutelage of LSRC coaches, they trained us for a month every Tuesday and Thursday evening, and 6 AM Sunday mornings.

Figure 175 - Start of Prouty Rowing

The Rowing event is on the Connecticut River starting and ending at the Dartmouth College boathouse. The rowers go upstream (north) on the beautiful Connecticut River in 5, 10, 15 or 20-mile increments (up and back format). Rowers also have the option of turning around at any time. Steve and Dave started their loop back just shy of the 7 mile marker, returning to the Dartmouth boathouse.

Steve and Dave's total time on the river was under four hours. They estimated their total row to be 13+ miles. None of the **Prouty** events are timed or considered races. The winner of the events is the Norris Cotton Cancer Center.

The Connecticut River is the border between New Hampshire and Vermont.

The brief descriptions below from the Prouty website say it best:

"**The Prouty** is an event of The Friends of Norris Cotton Cancer Center, an organization wholly devoted to raising funds to support innovative cancer research and important patient services at Dartmouth-Hitchcock Norris Cotton Cancer Center.

On July 8-9, 2016 in Hanover, New Hampshire, more than 5,000 participants, and some 1,300 volunteers teamed up to raise more than $3.1 million for cancer care and research in the Prouty, Northern New England's largest charity fundraiser. Money raised at The Prouty goes to support cutting edge research and patient services that help ease a patient's cancer journey.

People from all over the country come together every July to raise funds by rowing on the Connecticut River, walking or cycling through neighborhoods and roads in New Hampshire and Vermont, or hitting the links at the Hanover Country Club.

References:

- **Lake Sunapee Rowing Club** http://www.lakesunapeerowing.com
- **Row the Prouty** http://tiny.cc/002o1y
- **The Prouty** http://theprouty.org/
- **OutdoorSteve.com** http://www.OutdoorSteve.com
- **Casella Recycling** http://www.casella.com/

Other Rowing Blog Posts by OutdoorSteve

- **Book Review for "*The Boys in the Boat: Nine Americans and their Epic Quest for Gold at the 1936 Berlin Olympics*"** by Daniel James Brown http://tiny.cc/hq2o1y
- **Rowing through the eyes of a beginner** http://tiny.cc/rs2o1

+++++++++++++++++++

"Everyone must do something. I believe I will go outdoors with family and friends"

Paddling, Hiking & Camping at Connecticut Lakes & Lake Francis

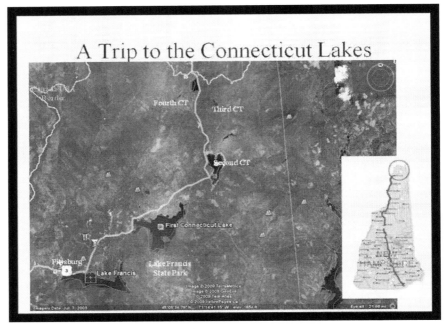

Figure 176 - Route 3 with the Great North Woods circled

Pittsburg, New Hampshire – The Great North Woods

When you say or hear, "Connecticut Lakes and Lake Francis", or "Pittsburg", you are talking about the most northern area of New Hampshire near the Canadian border.

On a Monday in mid-June, John, Dundee, Dick and I drove to the Lake Francis State Park in Pittsburg, NH. Pittsburg has an estimated population of 900 and is the northernmost town in NH and the largest town by area in the state. U.S. Route 3 is the only major highway in the town ending at the Canadian border. Contained within the boundaries of Pittsburg are the Connecticut (CT) Lakes and Lake Francis. These lakes are the headwaters of the 410 mile Connecticut River.

Pittsburg is known for snowmobiling and ATV trails, fishing and hunting, canoeing and kayaking, and its moose. Some of the folks jest, "There are more moose than people."

Pittsburg is an outdoor enthusiast's paradise.

Why are we doing this?

1. To visit Moose Alley and almost assure ourselves of seeing moose.
2. We want to straddle the Connecticut River at its 4th Connecticut Lake headwaters outlet.
3. To enjoy my fellow trekkers and The Great North Woods.
4. Because we never want to say, "We wish we had paddled the Connecticut Lakes and Lake Francis."

Great North Woods Itinerary

Here is our schedule for this four-day paddling, hiking and camping trip:

- Monday: Drive to Lake Francis State Park, set up camp, and paddle the lake as daylight permits. The Park will be our camp site for three nights
- Tuesday: Hike to the 4th Connecticut Lake, paddle the 3rd Connecticut Lake, and continue our Lake Francis paddle.
- Wednesday: Paddle 2nd Connecticut Lake, East Inlet, and Scott's Bog.
- Thursday: Take down our campsite, paddle 1st Connecticut Lake in the morning, and return home in the afternoon.

The Fourth, Third, Second, First Connecticut Lakes, and Lake Francis flow into each other starting with the tiny Fourth CT Lake on the Canadian border. The water connections are small streams with intermittent sections of white water. Paddling these connections is not really feasible due to the narrowness of the stream, its shallow depth, and obstructing rock formations. For each lake, we portage our canoes/kayaks on our car carrier racks.

I used **Google Earth** for maps to orient ourselves and determine distances. **Google** search found the website **Paddling.Net** which had a wonderful article titled, **Connecticut Lakes - Kayak Trip / Canoe Trip.** This article contained a detailed narrative of an earlier trip.

Young's Store was our primary hub for information, food, and adult beverages. "If they do not have it, you do not need it." Next to Young's Store was a wonderful breakfast and lunch café.

The **Buck Rub Pub** is a great place to quench your thirst and have dinner.

They even have their own specially ale - **Buck Rub Brown Ale**!

Figure 177 Buck Rub Pub

Statistics of Connecticut (CT) Lakes

- 4th CT 78 acres (on the Canadian Border)
- 3rd CT 231 acres (fed by the 4th CT)
- 2nd CT 1,102-acres (fed by the 3rd CT)
- 1st CT 3,071 acres (fed by the 2nd CT)
- Lake Francis 1,933 acres (fed by 1st CT)

For detail statistics on the Connecticut Lakes go to http://en.wikipedia.org/wiki/Connecticut_Lakes
Pictures are Worth a Thousand Words

Rather than give a narrative of this beautiful area, I will simply show pictures of the areas we visited. At the end of this section, I have listed references for more detailed information on The Great North Woods for those outdoor enthusiasts that may want to visit this most beautiful area.

Lake Francis

Figure 178 - Put-in at Lake Francis State Park

Figure 179 - Relaxing at the Campsite

Republic of Indian Stream

Did you know that there once was a country between New Hampshire and Canada? Read on.

- For a few years in the 1830s, an area of today's Pittsburg, NH was an independent republic, not part of New Hampshire and not part of the United States.
- The US attempted to tax the 360 inhabitants, and Canada tried to make them serve in its military, so the people decided to establish their own sovereign nation – **The Republic of Indian Stream.**
- The existence of the republic was ended by New Hampshire in 1835.
- The Webster -Ashburton Treaty of 1842 established the border between Canada and the United States.
- Pittsburg is the largest township in the United States, covering over 300,000 acres.

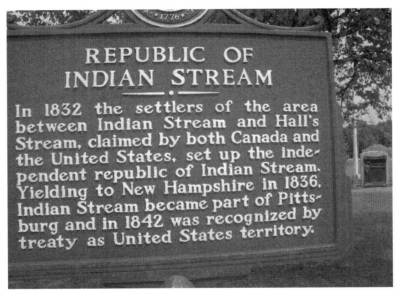

Figure 180 - A Country between the United States and Canada

Fourth Connecticut Lake – Headwaters of the CT River

Figure 181 - A View of the 4th CT Lake

Figure 182 - Steve with one foot on each side of the CT River

Figure 183 - At 4th Connecticut Lake Using the Bug Baffler!

Figure 184 - Straddling the USA and Canada Boundary

Third Connecticut Lake

Figure 185 - Is this 3rd CT Inlet of Water from the 4th CT?

Figure 186 - We Spot a Moose Skeleton on the 3rd CT

First Connecticut Lake

Figure 187 - A Mating Pair of Loons

Figure 188 - Loon Egg on the Man-made Loon Nesting Platform

East Inlet

Figure 189 - Put-in and Take-Out at East Inlet

Figure 190 - Beaver Lodge in East Inlet

18 Mile Moose Alley

I get asked, "What is the best way to see moose in the Great North Woods?" My response is to drive Route 3 (the last 18 miles in NH is nick-named "Moose Alley") and when you spot a stopped car, pull up behind it, as they most likely have spotted moose.

It is safe to say, you will see moose everywhere – including in the middle of the highway – so be careful when driving anywhere in Pittsburg.

"Once you see one, you see them all" is not a valid expression with moose. Each time I see a moose it is a thrill – however, do not get close as these are huge animals. An adult moose can stand close to seven feet high at the shoulder, and males (or "bulls") can weigh as much as 1,500 lbs. Females with a calf are especially dangerous, and during rutting season, a male moose may charge anything. A word to the wise.

Figure 191 - Moose - Scotts Bog from My Canoe

Never say, "I wish I had been to the Great North Woods of New Hampshire"

Video Reference Planning a Paddle to Connecticut Lakes and Lake Francis

- **Blog and videos: Paddling the Great North Woods of New Hampshire** http://tiny.cc/d22o1y
- **Lake Francis State Park** http://tiny.cc/152o1y
- **Buck Rub Pub**
  http://www.buckrubpub.com/
- **Youngs Store**
  http://www.yelp.com/biz/youngs-store-pittsburg
- **Connecticut Lakes – Canoe and Kayaks**
  http://tiny.cc/i72o1y
- **Moose**
  http://en.wikipedia.org/wiki/Moose#Size_and_weight
- **Connecticut Lakes**
  http://en.wikipedia.org/wiki/Connecticut_Lakes

Camp OutdoorSteve Training Youth in Canoe Rescue

An afternoon learning canoe rescue and self-confidence.

My teenage grandson was visiting our camp in Sunapee, NH. We were sitting around a campfire with his Sunapee friends. In the course of our campsite storytelling, I shared with them my experience participating in a canoe rescue on one of my paddling trips to the Allagash Wilderness Waterway in Maine.

The message I wanted to convey to these youths was, "practice makes perfect."

Briefly, on a canoe trip to the 34 mile Moose River Bow Trip, two of our group flipped their canoe in the middle of Holeb Pond. My friend John and I were nearby, and we quickly paddled over, tied a rope to the overturned canoe, and towed them to shore – an exhausting paddle that took nearly a half hour. My cousin Linwood, a Master Maine Guide, asked, "Why did you not rescue them?" My response was, "We did!"

Linwood then proceeded to tell us we should have righted the swamped canoe in the middle of the lake draining it of water, then getting the two paddlers back in the boat, and letting them paddle themselves back to shore. No need for an exhausting paddle towing an overturned canoe with two bodies hanging on.

At our next campsite, Linwood would teach us how to do this. The next day for nearly four hours, myself and six companions, under the tutelage of Linwood, learned and practiced two types of canoe rescue scenarios:

3) **Two or more canoes are paddling together and one flips over**. An upright canoe assists the capsized canoers by righting their boat, emptying it of water, retrieving their gear, and standing by while they re-enter their boat (even in deep water)

4) **Two paddlers, alone, flip their canoe and need to upright it without outside help.**

Interestingly - and here was my message to the youths about "practice makes perfect" - the next year myself with the same group of friends were paddling across Eagle Lake on the Allagash Wilderness Waterway. Suddenly, one of our canoes capsized in the middle of the one-mile wide lake.

By the time we reached them, the two occupants were swimming holding onto the canoe with their tents, food, and other camping gear drifting nearby (all protected by dry bags). With hardly a word said, this group, who had practiced the canoe rescue the prior year, immediately began their learned "two or more canoers paddling together" rescue technique. Within minutes, both paddlers were back in their righted and dry canoe with their gear intact, and we continued on to our next campsite.

The message to the youths is "practice makes perfect."

Camp OutdoorSteve Teaching "Practice Makes Perfect" Canoe Rescues

The next day after this fireside chat of our true rescue, my grandson and his friends asked if they could learn the canoe rescue. The below sequence of pictures and the following video is a wonderful afternoon of fun and learning. Most importantly, it demonstrated the value of practice and the resulting self-confidence if one day they face what might be a real canoe rescue situation.

Figure 192 - The Flip!

Figure 193 - Emptying the Canoe of Water

The two paddlers in the water get on one end of the overturned canoe and push down until the other end of the canoe releases its vacuum and rises out of the water. The canoe is then pulled onto the rescue boat and slid perpendicular across to its midpoint, resulting in no water in the canoe.

Figure 194 - Canoe Turned Over and Slid back into the Water

Figure 195 - Dry Canoe is brought parallel to rescue boat, braced by Rescuers, and the swimmers climb back in from the side.

Figure 196 - Away They Go!

Practice – Practice – Practice – Then the Actual Rescue is Easy.

Blog and Video Reference Practicing the Canoe Rescue at Perkins Pond http://youtu.be/gRFsWovoQ3g

Vermont Green River Reservoir Wilderness camping and paddling

"Everyone must do something. I believe I will go outdoors with family and friends."

Figure 197 - Super Swimming in an outdoors environment

In early July I did two days of paddling and one night of tenting in the Green River Reservoir of northern Vermont. My companions were my adult son Tim; my two teenage grandchildren; my friend Dundee and his adult son Paul; and Paul's two teenage boys and his ten year old daughter. Our transportation was three kayaks and three canoes.

The 5-minute video is better than words, but here is a summary:

- I used the Green River Reservoir website to identify our preferred camp site and make reservations.
- The nine of us in three cars had a two plus hour trip from Sunapee, NH
- Access to the Green River Reservoir is only through the Park Ranger Station
- All camp sites are only accessed via the water
- We had a half hour paddle to our chosen camp site #25
- We had intermittent rain throughout the first day, BUT rain in no way hindered our wonderful family and friends trip.
- Paul was our top notch menu planner and Chef as he did on a prior trip (Paddling the Waters of Quetico Provincial Park in Ontario, Canada). Paul made a marvelous macaroni, cheese, and hot dog supper – and a great McNestler egg-cheese-bacon-English muffin breakfast.
- We had three tents and a large camp tarp on site #25.
- We decided to see if we could start a fire with flint and steel – and each of us took a turn at this task. You will see this teaching moment in the videos.

Figure 198 - Flint and Steel Start our Dinner Fire

- This is a magnificent lake to swim in clear and deep water. The surrounding cliffs drop away into eight plus feet of water with no shoreline – so a person really must be a swimmer to dive and swim to shore. All nine of us are experienced swimmers.
- NEVER jump into water without first checking for rocks, depths, and dangerous obstacles. See the video for our cliff jumping fun.
- In the evening we went for a paddle around Big Island (we had stayed on site #33 in 2012 Peak Foliage Paddling and Camping in the Green River Reservoir of Northern Vermont)

Figure 199 - Cliff Jumping

- Wildlife is prominent in this area. We saw nesting loons, herons, beaver signs, and even moose scat. We were told eagles were there, but we saw none.

  No grandfather, father, or friend could have enjoyed a better time. Life is great!

For those interested in more details of our trip see a 25 minute video titled **Wilderness camping and paddling with family and friends: Green River Reservoir** (http://youtu.be/joTKzJI1r90).

About Green River Reservoir
Green River Reservoir became a state park in March 1999 when 5110 acres were purchased from the Morrisville Water and Light Department. This is not your typical Vermont State Park – Green River Reservoir provides camping and paddling experiences in a remote setting. All campsites can only be reached by paddling to them - some are a 1 to 2-mile paddle from the launch site.

The park will remain in its wild and undeveloped condition, with low-impact, compatible recreational use allowed on and around the Reservoir. Management activities will be only those necessary to maintain the property's character, protect the environment and critical resources, demonstrate sustainable forest and wildlife management, control excessive recreational use, and ensure high-quality outdoor experiences for visitors.

The 653-acre Reservoir includes about 19 miles of shoreline, one of the longest stretches of undeveloped shorelines in Vermont. Access to the park is in the southern part of the Reservoir off of Green River Dam Road. The Reservoir is designated as a "quiet" lake under Vermont "Use of Public Waters Rules." Boats powered by electric motors up to 5 mph and human-powered watercraft (canoes, kayaks, etc.) are only allowed.

There are 28 remote campsites at various locations around the Reservoir. Camping is allowed only at designated campsites and can only be reached by boat. Each remote site has a maximum site occupancy based on the characteristics of the site. There is one designated group campsite that can accommodate up to 12 people. Some campsites are closed each season and rehabilitated due to overuse through the years.

References
- **Green River Reservoir**
  http://www.vtstateparks.com/htm/grriver.htm
- **Paddling the Waters of Quetico Provincial Park in Ontario, Canada** http://tiny.cc/sfv26x
- **Peak Foliage Paddling and Camping in the Green River Reservoir of Northern Vermont** http://tiny.cc/xgv26x

Figure 200 - Green River Reservoir, Vermont

Fall

The roads are lovely, dark, and deep. But I have promises to keep, and miles to go before I sleep, and miles to go before I sleep. – Robert Frost

An Endurance Swim "Race for the Ages" Experience vs Youth.

Once a year, 74-year-old fitness enthusiast, Skip Hause, challenges a fellow swimmer to a half mile swim. Skip is a member of Outdoor Recreation for Seniors (ORFS). This year he invited 14-year-old, Vera Rivard.

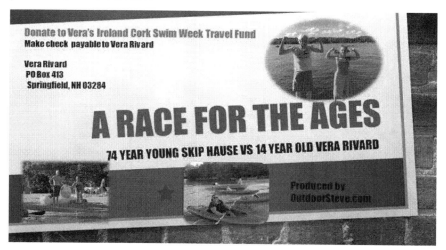

Figure 201 - A Race for the "Ages"

The race was held on September 7, 2018, at Lake Sunapee, from Skip's Sunapee harbor home across the Lake to Dewey Beach.

Skip will have a 14-minute head start.

Proceeds for this event go to Vera's invitation to travel to the Cork Swim Week Camp in July 2019 in Sandycove Island, Ireland, a tiny island off the south coast of Ireland. The Camp focuses on training the invited swimmers to swim the English Channel.

Skip's Bio. He is 74 years young and a lifetime Fitness Guru and Hogan Member at Coby-Sawyer College in New London, NH. He has five years of Mitt boxing training. He is an accomplished Open Water swimmer, years of pool swimming, a runner, and skier.

Vera's bio is equally impressive. She is 14 years old and a Hogan member. She swims for the Upper Valley Aquatic Club (UVAC) and is on the Kearsarge High School swim team. She has competed in many open water endurance events, and her accomplishments include a second place in the July 2018 25 miles (16 hours) Lake Memphremagog swim.

Outdoor Steve's Involvement
Skip called and asked if I would document and produce a video of this event. I clarified to Skip that my **Outdoor Enthusiast Blog** https://outdooradventurers.blogspot.com videos are created to motivate individuals and families to get outdoors. Skip had viewed many of my blog posts and assured me he wanted me to do a video with interviews to share the experience of this fun happening.

As an amateur triathlete, I certainly have some insights to endurance swimming and training, and I would bring this perspective for interviews with the two athletes in this challenge. I interviewed Skip, Vera, Darcie (Vera's Mom), and Kevin (Vera's Dad).

Will experience win the day? Will youth prevail?
The first video is 30 minutes and introduces you to Skip, Vera and Vera's family through interviews and learning of Vera's cold water endurance swims. Feel the friendly competition race as seen from my kayak. Learn of Vera's July 2019 "invitation only" to the Cork Distance Week camp fundraiser, and Vera's vision of swimming the English Channel.

The Second video is 7 minutes and is a summary of the swim with minimal detail. See both endurance swim videos at http://tiny.cc/omui1y

Cork Distance Week Camp
The Camp is advertised as the most stringent amateur marathon swim training in the world – with the fewest "frills". *By invitation only*...References below provide more insight into the Cork Distance Week Camp.

Support Vera in her **Never say, "I wish I had ... trained to swim the English Channel."**

References

- **Blog and Videos: An Endurance Swim for the "Ages"** http://tiny.cc/omui1y
- **Sandycove Island Web Book** https://sandycovewebbook.wordpress.com/cork-distance-week/
- **Dangerous When Wet: Learning to Survive Open Water Swimming** https://www.outsideonline.com/1916336/dangerous-when-wet-learning-survive-open-water-swimming?page=1
- **Documented Marathon Swims by Vera Rivard** https://db.marathonswimmers.org/p/vera-rivard/
- **List of successful English Channel Swimmers** https://en.wikipedia.org/wiki/List_of_successful_English_Channel_swimmers

Stinson Mountain Trail: White Mountain National Forest

On Monday three friends, my son Tim, and I hiked 2,900 foot Stinson Mountain located in Rumney, NH. The day before we hiked Mt Cardigan, a 3,155 footer in Orange, NH.

Figure 202 - Hike Stinson Mountain, Rumney, NH

Stinson Mountain Trail is the only maintained trail up to the summit. The trailhead is located off Doetown Road in Rumney, NH. The Trail is a low incline trail with no rock ledges or scrambles. The summit is all bare rock with 180 degree views and once home to a fire tower. Only the four footings remain of the tower... and as you will see in the video the footings make great tables and chairs for tired hikers and snowmobilers.

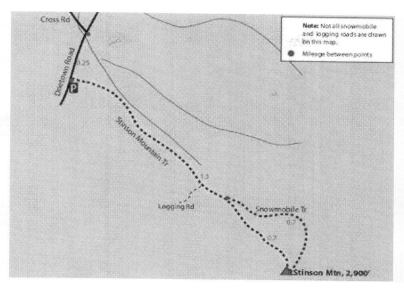

Figure 203 - Stinson Mountain Trail Map

From the trailhead, we hiked the Stinson Mountain Trail for 1.1 miles until we reached a vee (junction) with a snowmobile trail. We could continue left up the snowmobile trail to reach the summit, or veer right onto the "hiking trail" as signed. Each way is 0.7 miles to the summit... we went right on the hiking trail.

The trail does not have many direction markers, other than the trailhead sign and a hiking/snowmobile sign at the vee. We hiked in the fall season with leaves on the ground, and there were a few times we had to pause to locate the trail direction. For the novice hiker, leaves this time of year cover the trail and the trail sometimes blends into the forest and may be more challenging to follow. On the positive side, the trail is very well maintained as noted by new wooden planks for bridges used by snowmobilers and hikers.

We ascended the 1.8 mile trail to the summit in one hour and 37 minutes ... and came back to the trailhead more quickly via the snowmobile trail.

The snowmobile trail is wide and steep ... and slippery. It appeared to be groomed this summer, as the slope had boot-deep mud from fresh loam, fresh seeded green grass, and slivers of hoar frost

Figure 204 - Slivers of hoar frost

protruding from crystalline deposits of frozen water vapor formed over the new grass.

Over the Hill Hikers: 52 with a View

Stinson Mountain is on the **52 With a View** list (also known as the **Over the Hill Hikers**) of fifty-two mountains with elevations under 4,000 feet having incredible views.

The **52 With a View** list came about through a group of friends hiking in New Hampshire. The older members of the hiking group suggested a new hiking list (getting tired of only hiking the NH 4,000 Footers?) called 52 with a View. A list of mountains shorter than the NH48, but all with amazing views!

Now I never have to say, "I wish I had hiked the Stinson Mountain Trail".

References

- **Cold & Windy Fall Hike to Summit of Mt Cardigan, New Hampshire** http://tiny.cc/hl3o1y
- http://4000footers.com/stinson.shtml
- http://4000footers.com/list_52wav.shtml
- OutdoorSteve.com

+++++++++++++++++++++

Cold & Windy Fall Hike to Summit of Mt Cardigan, New Hampshire

Was it cold! What a surprise. Three friends and I decided to Hike Mt Cardigan. Mount Cardigan is a prominent stripped-rock summit in the towns of Orange and Alexandria in western New Hampshire. While its peak is only 3,155 feet above sea level, it has extensive areas of bare granite ledges and alpine scrub, giving it the feel to hikers of a much higher mountain. Most of the summit area was exposed by devastating forest fires in 1855 and did not revegetate. The fire tower on its summit quickly identifies Mt Cardigan throughout the area.

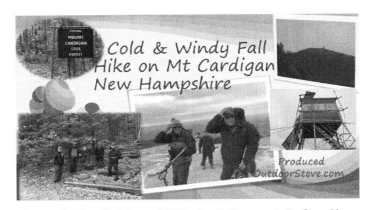

Figure 205 - Cold and Windy Hike on Mt Cardigan

We pulled into the Orange, NH parking lot from Cardigan Mountain Road. The weather was in the low 30's with high winds, and surprisingly we weren't the only ones willing to take on the elements ... the parking area already had a multitude of cars.

The first hour up the moderately difficult rock bound-West Ridge Trail was uneventful. However, once we reached bare granite ledges above treeline, things changed dramatically.

We faced below freezing temperatures, spitting snow, and extreme high and bone-chilling wind as we made our way over the baren ledges to the summit's firetower. We stopped twice in alpine scrub to block the wind, catch our balance, as our faces briefly enjoyed the warmth and shelter.

I removed my gloves each time I took a picture or video, and my right hand felt the frostbitten pain. The deafening noise in the videos you hear, once we entered the barren granite ledges, is the roaring of the summit's disrespectful winds.

The trip to the summit from the West Ridge Trail took an hour and 15 minutes. Due to the extensive freezing cold and dangerous 50 – 60 mph hour winds, we stayed on the summit less than ten minutes.

Our original plan was to hike to the summit via the 1.5-mile West Ridge Trail, and then return to the parking lot by the South Ridge Trail. This plan changed immediately once we reached the tree line of the summit and faced the treacherous winds and freezing temperatures.

West Ridge Trail (WRT) The WRT is marked with orange strips. These orange markers are assurance we are on the right trail.

Cairns

Figure 206 Cairns - Mt Cardigan

Cairns are vertical piles of rock. Cairns are another means of staying on the trail. It is against New Hampshire law to remove or change a cairn. I can tell you from personal experience, that they can be a life-saving indicator of the proper direction of travel in fog or low light conditions.

Directions

These are driving directions to the West Ridge Trail parking area. Take exit 17 from I-93 North to get on Route 4 West. Turn right onto Route 4 West / Hoit Road. Drive 1.2 miles and continue straight through the traffic circle to stay on Route 4 West. Drive 2.5 miles and turn slight left to stay on Route 4 West. Drive 15.2 miles and turn right to stay on Route 4 West. Drive 20.9 miles and turn sharply right onto Parker Street / Route 118. Drive 0.6 miles and turn right onto Cardigan Mountain Road. When you get the Burnt Hill Road, turn left to stay on Cardigan Mountain Road. (You will see a Cardigan Mountain State Forest sign here) Drive until you come to the parking lot.

If you have a GPS, you can put in Cardigan Mountain Road in Orange, NH and look for the parking area on the road.

References:
- **Blog and video: Cold & Windy Fall Hike to Summit of Mt Cardigan, New Hampshire** http://tiny.cc/es3o1y
- **Mt Cardigan** https://en.wikipedia.org/wiki/Mount_Cardigan.
- OutdoorSteve.com ++++++++++++++++++

Rowing in Peak Foliage Season on Perkins Pond, Sunapee, NH

Friends ask, "When is Peak Foliage Season in the Sunapee/Dartmouth region of New Hampshire?"

Yesterday, October 10th, I looked out my window in the early morning sunlight. The Pond was like clear ice, AND the trees around the Pond screamed of red, yellow, orange, and green fall colors. And these same rainbow colors reflected identical images on the window-glass-like water. I am enthralled with living here in New Hampshire.

Now was the perfect time to get my rowing scull moving ... picture-perfect calm water with Michelangelo painted views of the foliage, cloudless blue sky and Mount Sunapee rising in majesty above the Pond.

My rowing scull and I slowly entered the water, seeking a comfortable oar rowing rhythm around the Pond ... and relishing this magnificent sacred moment.

My usual early morning row is three times around the perimeter twice-a-week ... usually, these times are close to an hour. I go clock-wise one day and counter-clock-wise the next.

I passed my friend's dock and heard her call asking if she could take a video this gorgeous day. "Yes, thank you".

Her video is a "Wow" moment for me. See the peak rainbow colors on the mountains surrounding the pond. The reflections on the water are captivating and are equally spell binding.

And in the middle of this creation of mountains, forests, multicolored leaves, and water ... I blend as a rower.

I pass by my house and see the rewards of a life-time of saving.

Peak Foliage Season in the Sunapee/Dartmouth region of New Hampshire is NOW.

Figure 207 - Rowing Perkins Pond Fall Foliage

I never have to say, "I wish I had rowed in Perkins Pond in Peak Foliage Season"

Rowing Blog Posts by OutdoorSteve

- **Rowing through the eyes of a beginner**
  http://tiny.cc/s03o1y
- **Lake Sunapee Flag Pole Race** http://tiny.cc/1y3o1y
- **Book Review by OutdoorSteve for "Boys in the Boat"**
  http://tiny.cc/hq2o1y

++++++++++++++++++

Hiking Mt Kearsarge via Rollins Trail on a Wet Foggy Day

Mount Kearsarge is a 2,937 foot mountain located in the towns of Wilmot and Warner, New Hampshire. Mount Kearsarge has multiple trails and a bare rockbound summit with an observation fire tower and a cell phone tower. The summit can be reached by either Rollins State Park or Winslow State Park. Our ascent to the summit today starts at the Rollins State Park parking area.

From the summit on a clear day lies a spectacular view of the White Mountains and Mt. Cardigan in the north, the Green Mountains and Mt. Sunapee in the west and the Monadnock Region and the Merrimack Valley in the south. The summit with its towers are a distinctive landmark and is easily seen from its surrounding communities.

Figure 208 - Antenna's Top Mt Kearsarge, Warner, NH
As you will see here, and in the video referenced below, today's fog confined our views to less than a few hundred feet.

We chose to summit from Rollins State Park with the option of two trails. We chose the Rollins Trail beginning at the park's parking area. This trail is rock-bound and climbs for a 1/2 mile (1,100 vertical feet) and reaches the top over a bare granite ledge. The second trail, the Lincoln Trail, is more difficult than the Rollins Trail and we will keep this choice for another day.

The Rollins Trail, marked with white blazers, begins at the picnic area above the parking lot and follows what is described in the park's literature below as "follows the route of the old carriage road for 1/2 mile (300 feet) to the summit." Do not let the description fool you as this is a very rock-bound trail and climb. Sturdy walking shoes are needed along with drinking water and an extra jacket.

The rain, fog, and moss-covered rocks made today's Rollins Trail quite slippery, so caution was utmost in our mind.

Nevertheless, our challenging 40+ minute hike up, 1/2 hour on the summit, and 30 minute descent, was a fun day on Mt Kearsarge for Pops (John), Kaitlin (Mom), Riley (8 years), his brother Braydon (6 years), and yours truly.

A serendipitous encounter while hiking up was meeting a group of remote/radio control (RC) model truck enthusiasts and their battery-powered model trucks using specialized transmitters or remotes. This was my first experience seeing this type of sport. The club members enthusiastically answered our questions.

Figure 209 - Remote Control Model Trucks Climb Kearsarge

Never say, "I wished I had taken my family to climb Mt Kearsarge".

Directions to the Rollins Park:

From New London, New Hampshire, take Route 89 South to Exit 9, Right at end of exit ramp onto Rte. 103 east towards Warner for about 1 mile. Pass straight through a small roundabout on the way. Take a left onto Kearsarge Mountain Rd, marked by a sign for Rollins State Park and Indian museum. Go up 5 miles to the park entrance, then 3 ½ more miles to the parking lot to begin the hike. The moderate ½ mile trail goes to the summit, starting left of the portapotties. Take the same trail down. Trail involves some hiking on exposed rock and some steepness.

References

For a map and more information on Mt Kearsarge go to:

- **Blog and video: Hiking Mt Kearsarge from Winslow State Park in Central New Hampshire** http://tiny.cc/wd4o1y
- **Rollins State Park** http://tiny.cc/2f4o1y
- **Mt Kearsarge Hiking Map** http://tiny.cc/vh4o1y
- **OutdoorSteve.com** https://www/outdoorsteve.com

++++++++++++++++++++

McDaniel's Marsh Wildlife Management Area

Two friends and I picked a cloudy day in early November to kayak McDaniel's Marsh in Springfield, New Hampshire. We put in our kayaks at 9 am and took-out around noon. Indeed, there is a diversity of wildlife at McDaniel's Marsh.

Figure 210 - Kayakers and Eagles at McDaniel's Marsh

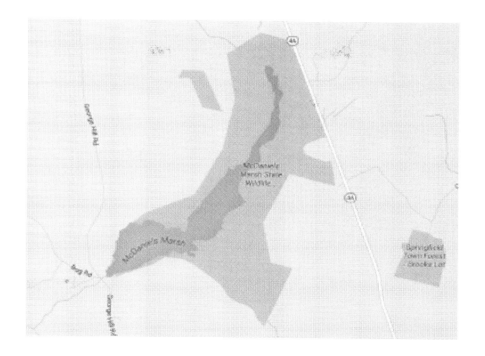

Figure 211 - Map of McDaniel's Marsh

We began our paddle close to the western shore. McDaniel's Marsh is generally shallow water with many floating islands of grass and muck. Its name "marsh" is very appropriate.

Two Bald Eagles

Within five minutes of our put-in, Mike spotted a bald eagle. We sat quietly bobbing in the water, watching our symbol of American freedom on her/his tall treetop perch. Mike whispered again, "Look, another eagle."

We watched both birds and listened to the second bird call from its perch. Then the first eagle flew to the tree of the second eagle. The birds sort of danced along the same branch in a "let's get to know each other better" fashion.

Figure 212 - 3.5-yr old female bald eagle

Figure 213 - 1.5 - 2.5-yr old male bald eagle

My bald eagle email inquiry to the NH Audubon Society was responded to by Chris Martin, Raptor Biologist. *"The bird on the top is a 3.5-yr old (hatched Spring 2012) based upon its whitish head and dark mask and some dark spots on tips of tail feathers. It is probably a female based on its slightly chunkier size. The mottled brown bird on the bottom is a 1.5 - 2.5-yr old (hatched Spring 2013) based on its yellowing beak, whitish crown, and overall mottled appearance. Possibly a male as it appears to be slimmer. It's pretty unlikely that they are related to each other, in fact, they are probably in transit, as most younger-aged eagles are during the Fall."*

Chris asked if I had any other pictures that might show if the eagles had leg identification bands. Upon receipt of my additional pictures, Chris emailed he could not see bands on either bird.

I shared with Chris the picture of the bald eagle I took last winter (Blog here) and he identified "the image clearly shows a silver band on the right leg and an orange band on the left leg, which signifies an eagle banded in Massachusetts, likely when it was a chick. Also shows a rather gutsy crow."

Figure 214 - Beaver Lodge in the left of the picture

Signs of beaver were everywhere – from floating beaver chews to lodges both close to shore and self-standing. The shorelines showed beaver paths into the woods where they were seeking trees and limbs for their winter food sources.

Figure 215 – Muskrat Pushup

Later we would see muskrat pushups – they somewhat resemble smaller beaver lodges neatly protruding two or three feet above the waterline.

We saw a greater or lesser yellowlegs, which are two rather similar-looking species.

Figure 216 – Yellowlegs

Statistics and References on McDaniel's Marsh Wild Management Area http://tiny.cc/1j4o1y

- **Approximately 2 miles in length and ¼ mile max width.**
- **Town:** Grafton, Springfield **County:** Grafton
- **Acres:**609

Bald Eagles http://tiny.cc/bl4o1y

Bald eagles are legally protected in New Hampshire. Possession (which includes harming, harassing, injuring and killing) are illegal.

Distribution: Bald eagles are present year-round in NH with pairs breeding and raising young in the spring/summer and many wintering in areas with open water such as Great Bay.

Description: 3' tall with a 6-8' wing span. Females weigh up to 14 lbs; males weigh 7-10 lbs. Immature bald eagles are mottled light brown, tan, and white until age 3 or 4. They have brown eyes, a black beak, and yellow feet. Adult bald eagles have a distinctive white head, white tail feathers, and a dark brown body and wings. Their eyes are pale yellow and the powerful beak and unfeathered feet are bright yellows.

Voice: Weak, high-pitched, chatters or whistles.

Habitat: Bald eagles breed in forested areas near bodies of water and winter near open water (i.e. coastal areas, rivers, and lakes with open water).

Nesting: Bald eagles can live up to 30 years of age and can begin breeding between 4-6 years of age. They build large nests in tall trees near the water's edge. Females lay 1-3 eggs in March - May. Both the male and female incubate the eggs and the young hatch after five weeks. Bald eagles often retain the same mate for many years and reuse the same nest from year to year.

Diet: Primarily fish; occasionally other birds, small to medium mammals, turtles and even carrion.

Muskrat Pushups
(https://en.wikipedia.org/wiki/Muskrat)

Muskrat families build nests, called pushups, to protect themselves and their young from cold and predators. When we first spotted from a distance these muskrat pushups, we thought they were beaver lodges as they are somewhat similar, but not as large. In marshes, push-ups are constructed from vegetation and mud. These muskrat push-ups are up to 3 ft in height.

References

- **Blog and video:** Kayaking McDaniel's Marsh Wildlife Management Area - Springfield, NH
  http://tiny.cc/9m4o1y

- http://www.wildlife.state.nh.us/maps/wma/mcdaniels-marsh.html

- http://www.wildlife.state.nh.us/wildlife/profiles/beaver.html

- http://www.wildlife.state.nh.us/wildlife/profiles/bald-eagle.html

- http://www.nhaudubon.org/about/centers/mclane/

- www.nhaudubon.org

- https://en.wikipedia.org/wiki/Muskrat

- https://www.allaboutbirds.org/search/?q=Greater%20 Yellowlegs

Welch-Dickey Loop Trail - A Training Hike for Mt Katahdin

In the fall, five friends and I would hike **Mt Katahdin** in Maine's **Baxter State Park**. Mt Katahdin is the northern terminus of the Appalachian Trail. One of the trails leading to the summit is known as **The Knife Edge**.

We expected this hike to be between nine (9) and eleven (11) hours over very rough terrain. We must be physically fit. As preparation for this trip, our group would do hikes of varying distances and difficulties. Each hike offers unique and beautiful scenery of New Hampshire. Our focus was on endurance and distance.

We carried day packs containing similar contents that we would carry on our Katahdin climb. We carried the same amount of water we would need for the Katahdin hike as well as other gear (e.g. at least 48 ounces of water, rain coat, winter hat, first aid pack, whistle, map, compass, camera, two light sources (flashlights and headlamps), duct tape, two 30 gal contractor for emergency shelter, bivy sack.)

We carry as a minimum what are known as the ten essentials for hiking http://www.outdoors.org/recreation/hiking/hiking-essentials.cfm.

Figure 217 - Welch-Dickey Overview

For five weeks my hiking partners and I did a variety of training hikes:

- Mt Sunapee's Rim Trail to Lake Solitude – 3.5 hours
- Mt Sunapee's ski lift trail with a return on the Access Road. I did this route twice on two different days - 3.5 hours
- The 7.5 mile round trip Pumpelly Trail of Mount Monadnock - 8 hours
- South Mountain of Uncanoonuc - 2.5 miles in 2.5 hours
- 4.5 mile Welch-Dickey Loop Trail - 4 .5 hours

Let me share the Welch-Dickey Loop Trail.

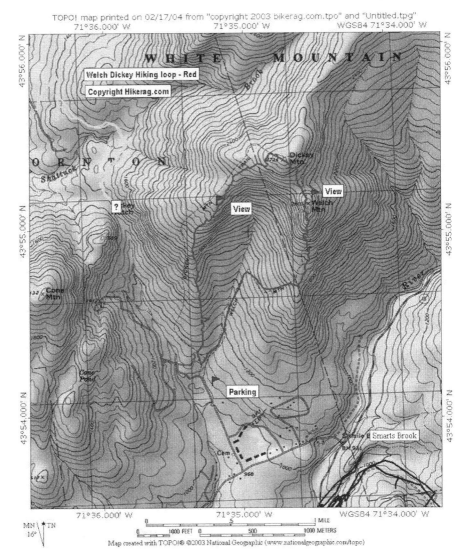

Figure 218 - Map of our Welch-Dickey Hike

I took the Welch-Dickey trail description from the **Hike New England** website:
http://www.hikenewengland.com/WelchDickey030719.html

    Mountains: Welch Mtn. (2605'), Dickey Mtn. (2734')
        Trail: Welch-Dickey Loop Trail

Region: NH - Central East
White Mountain National Forest, Waterville Valley
Location: Thornton, NH
Rating: Moderate/Difficult

Route Summary

This is a loop hike across the summits of Welch and Dickey Mountains, providing many views along the way as the trail winds its way across open ledges. It follows the yellow-blazed Welch-Dickey Loop Trail all the way. The different branches of the loop are commonly referred to as Welch Mountain Trail (the right-hand fork which leads most directly to Welch); and Dickey Mountain Trail (the left-hand fork which goes directly to Dickey Mountain.)

Figure 219 - Welch-Dickey Trail Sign

- Start on the Welch-Dickey Loop Trail, which will fork after just 15 yards.

- Take the right-hand branch to approach Welch Mountain first. (The return trip will be via the opposite leg.)
- After 1.3 miles on the Welch-Dickey Loop Trail, you will reach the open ledges and extensive views on the southern flank of Welch Mountain.
- Continue following Welch-Dickey Loop Trail and you will reach the summit of Welch Mountain 0.6 mile later where you will be treated to a 360-degree panorama.
- Descend the opposite side of the peak, continuing to follow the Welch-Dickey Loop Trail in a northerly direction.
- You will then need to do some uphill climbing before reaching the summit of Dickey Mountain 0.5 mile from Welch's peak. Dickey Mountain offers views of Franconia Ridge and Franconia Notch. Shortly before the summit, there will be a poorly marked 0.2-mile spur path on the right leading to an open ledge with an outlook to the north.
- Still, on Welch-Dickey Loop Trail, descend from Dickey's peak in the opposite direction from which you climbed it.
- After 2.1 miles, you are back at the fork near the beginning of the loop. Bear right to return to the parking lot.

Click the below 8 minute video as Dundee and I share our training for the Katahdin climb by hiking the Welch-Dickey Loop Trail.

References
- **Video and Blog: Welch-Dickey Loop Trail - A Training Hike for Mt Katahdin** http://tiny.cc/7o4o1y

Making Apple Cider in New Hampshire with Robert Frost's, "After Apple Picking"

On a recent fall Sunday in Elkins, NH, family and friends had the pleasure of making apple cider while enjoying apple donuts, caramel covered apples, apple bobbing, and apple slices with cheese - all topped off with a reading of Robert Frost's poem, "**After Apple Picking**".

We made Apple Cider the New Hampshire way:
  1) Pick the apples
  2) Wash the apples
  3) Cut apples into four quarters
  4) Put quartered apples through a masher
  5) Press the mash for the apple cider.
  6) Bottle the cider
  7) Sip and enjoy the cider

Figure 220 - Living Robert Frost's "After Apple Picking"

Below is a video of our family oriented day making apple cider. "Everyone must believe in something. I believe I'll go outdoors." – S. Priest

References

- **Blog and video: Making Apple Cider in New Hampshire with Robert Frost's, "After Apple Picking"** http://tiny.cc/hs4o1y

- **Bedford Community TV** Bedford Community TV (BCTV) is now playing **Making Apple Cider in New Hampshire with Robert Frost's, "After Apple Picking".** Check their Channel 16 schedule.

- Lea Newman, **"Robert Frost: The People, Places, and Stories Behind His New England Poetry"** Amazon.com at http://tiny.cc/927m4w

- OutdoorSteve.com http://www.outdoorsteve.com

- Download a streaming video from *Bedford Community TV* channel 16 of **Making Apple Cider in New Hampshire with Robert Frost's, *"After Apple Picking"*** http://tiny.cc/m3384x

Kayaking the Herring River Estuary and Popponesset Bay of Cape Cod

Figure 221 - Herring River Estuary

Day 1: Kayaking the Herring River Estuary of Wellfleet and Truro

John invited Dundee and me to Cape Cod for two days of kayaking. Day one was planned to be a full day paddling around Wellfleet Harbor. However, our plan was short-lived when we explored the Herring River Estuary, a tidal river with a history of bygone prominence.

We proceeded west along the shoreline from the kayak landing next to the Wellfleet pier. As we neared Chequessett Neck Road and the dike at the mouth of the Herring River, John recalled a recent newspaper article on this dike. When it was built in 1909, it significantly reduced tidal flow to the salt marsh on the other side of the Road. This dike transformed the estuary into one of the Cape's most degraded natural resources.

Figure 222 - Map of our paddling route

Development of a restoration plan for the Herring River

In 2007 the Towns of Wellfleet and Truro and the Cape Cod National Seashore signed a Memorandum of Understanding to cooperate on the development of a restoration plan for the Herring River.

In a November 2015 article by Mary Ann Bragg of the Cod Times: "As it stands now the dike under the road has three 6-foot-wide culverts that are open during the outgoing tide. Only one of them - at 2 feet high - is open for the incoming tide. Generally, kayakers and canoeists carry their vessels up and over the road to continue their trips up or downstream.

Currently, the tidal range in the area of the dike is about 2½ feet, but if the salt marsh restoration project is fully implemented the tidal range could ultimately reach about 6½ feet. The tidal range is the vertical difference between the high tide and the succeeding low tide.

If the salt marsh restoration project is fully implemented as planned, all tide gates in the new dike would be removed and floating vessels would be able to pass freely up and down.

The Cape Cod National Seashore expects to release a final environmental impact statement winter of 2016 for the salt marsh restoration project. The fully restored backwaters of the river would cover about 890 acres, according to the latest estimates.

The restoration is meant to reverse some of the negative environmental outcomes of a decision in 1909 to build the first dike at Chequessett Neck Road. Some of the issues are bad water quality and fish kills, according to the draft environmental impact statement.

According to Cape Cod National ecologist Tim Smith, "Construction of the new dike with nine tidal gates, measuring 165 feet wide and 10 feet high, could begin in 2018 if all goes as planned. Planners want to steer paddlers away from trying to pass through the gates until the implementation is complete. That could take anywhere from two years to 20."

It is expected that when the existing tidal gate structure at the mouth of the Herring is replaced, along with other upstream considerations, this significant change will restore and provide full tidal flow to the Herring River Estuary and a promise for shell-fishing and other community opportunities." (http://tiny.cc/iuqn6x)

If you are interested in more information, or to stay up-to-date on the Herring River Estuary, please visit Friends of Herring River. They have an email newsletter at http://tiny.cc/uz484x.

Paddling the Herring River Estuary

We decided it would be worth our effort to portage over Chequessett Neck Road and paddle up the Herring River. We had before us an opportunity to see a "before" peek of the Herring River Estuary - with an incentive for us to return for an "after" look of the restoration on the environmental vitality of the Herring River Estuary.

The Herring Run in Middleboro, MA

As we paddled along the Herring River I recalled to my friends how, as a youngster, I used to visit the Herring Run on the

Nemasket River in Middleboro, MA. Each spring, herring migrate from the ocean, up coastal rivers and into tributaries and lakes to spawn. The herring were so plentiful you felt you could walk across their backs on the river – and so hundreds of people would come to see them.

Figure 223 - The Take-out

Friends and I would go to the fish ladders and catch herring with our hands and sell them to people. I remember coming home soaked and with coins in my pocket from selling my herring catch to people for food and garden fertilizer. It was a marvelous memory – and my connection to the Herring River Estuary.

Our paddle up the Herring River was well worth the expedition of nearly seven miles in five hours up and back on the Herring River Estuary:

- We saw Swans, Great Blue Heron, Osprey, Red Wing Blackbirds, and other birds.
- Many times we thought we were at the end of the river and about to turn back, but we managed to find a path through the narrowing quagmire of brush, prickly bushes, and marsh weeds.
- We passed under old wooden plank bridges
- We went through culverts under tar and dirt roads
- At about the three hours mark we found a road sign that told us we were passing the intersection of Bound Brook Island Road and the Atwood Higgins House.

Figure 224 - Bound Brook Isle Road

Day 2: Paddling the Mashpee River and Popponesset Bay

Figure 225 - Map Popponesset Bay

Day two's paddlers were Tim, Rob, John, Dundee and I.

- We put-in at Pirates Cove in Popponesset Bay.

- Paddled up the tidal Mashpee River. After an hour or so, we were in marsh weed and decided to return to Popponesset Bay.
- Paddled around Popponesset Island. Beautiful homes and boats/yachts
- Lunch on the sandbar protecting Popponesset Bay
- Crossed Popponesset Bay to Pirates Cover in choppy water and wind
- Total paddling time about six hours

References:
- **Blogs and video: Kayaking the Herring River Estuary and Popponesset Bay of Cape Cod** http://tiny.cc/gy4o1y

- **Paddling in the Herring River Estuary: A nine-minute video.** http://tiny.cc/5f584x

- **Friends of Herring River** http://www.friendsofherringriver.org/
- **Project Management associate Position Opening** http://tiny.cc/6o584x
- **Wellfleet's Herring River Tide Heights and Salinity Study** http://tiny.cc/us584x
- **Middleboro, Lakeville monitor herring run at Nemasket River - Raynham, MA** http://tiny.cc/79484x
- **Design to aid kayakers, paddlers** http://tiny.cc/iuqn6x

Winter

There are three kinds of people in this world. Those that watch things happen. Those that make things happen. And those that wonder what happened. Which kind are you? – Author Unknown

Winter in New Hampshire is more than Downhill Skiing

New Hampshire is known for its marvelous downhill skiing. Yes, we are very proud of this, BUT, there are many other winter outdoor happenings. Let me share some of the activities where my family and friends were participants, such as a sleigh ride in the great north woods of northern NH, cross-country skiing, a moonlight snowshoe hike and more.

Other times we are observers enjoying the excitement of watching ice climbers scale a mountain side of ice near Crawford Notch with views of the snow-capped 4,000 footers of the White Mountains Presidential range.

Figure 226 - Winter in NH is more than downhill skiing

The below blog has two videos. The top video is 12 minutes and gives **a taste of 14 NH winter happenings – all seen in the above list**. The bottom video is 41 minutes and is being shown by **Bedford Community Television (BCTV)**. I created the top video (12 mins) from key elements from the BCTV video.

Grab your favorite wintertime beverage, relax, and enjoy as Outdoor Steve presents his first-hand and personal insights of a multitude of New Hampshire winter activities.

Never say, "**I wish I had enjoyed winter in New Hampshire**".

Figure 227 - Crawford Notch Route 302

Figure 228 - Ice Climbing School at Crawford Notch

Figure 229 - Mt Washington Resort & Presidential Mountains

References

- **Video and Blog**: Winter in New Hampshire is more than downhill skiing http://outdooradventurers.blogspot.com/2015/02/winter-in-new-hampshire-is-more-than.html
- **BCTV: Winter in New Hampshire is more than downhill skiing** http://www.outdoorsteve.com
- **OutdoorSteve.com Blog**: http://outdooradventurers.blogspot.com/
- **Monson NH Center Ski Trip -XC ski and snowshoeing for families** http://forestsocient.org/property/monson-center

Tai Chi Senior Capstone Project

Colby-Sawyer College (CSC) is a dynamic and innovative liberal arts and sciences college located in the scenic Lake Sunapee Region of central New Hampshire. (http://colby-sawyer.edu/).

I was a guest of a friend who was a community member of the Dan and Kathleen Hogan Sports Center. We were there for a physical workout of running, rowing machine, bicycle machine, weights, and one-on-one basketball.

On the reception desk, I saw the below sign by senior students seeking older adults to participate in a Tai Chi study. The students were looking for participants to engage in research looking at the effects of Tai Chi on the center of balance and fall confidence in senior adults. Given my mantra of, **Never say, "I wish I had ..."**, I provided my wife's and my email address to them. A week later we received an invite to participate in this six-week study.

Figure 230 - Sign for Senior Capstone Tai Chi Research

Figure 231 - Colby-Sawyer College Tai Chi Class

As the three students stated in the registration form, they were not Tai Chi certified.One of the students had taken Tai Chi lessons in the summer and prepared a proposal that would provide an opportunity for them to demonstrate to their faculty capstone committee, the application of their four years of academic study at CSC.

So, what is Tai Chi? *Originating in ancient China, Tai Chi is one of the most effective exercises for the health of mind and body. Although an art with great depth of knowledge and skill, it can be easy to learn and soon delivers its health benefits.*

During the first class, we were asked to demonstrate certain metrics for the students to measure (stand on one foot, rise from a chair, walk a circle), as well as complete a background form. The students stated at the end of the six weeks they were to again measure the metrics and do an analysis of change from week one to week six.

The below video was taken at the beginning of week three. The video is not for the student capstone, but the theme of this motivation blog, **Never say, "I wish I had …,"** will encourage this reader to try something they have never tried before. My wife and I, never have to say, "We wish we had experienced Tai Chi."

333

And yes, this video is at normal speed. Tai Chi moves are slow motion and low impact.

Oh, one more thing. I give my permission to the students to use this blog and video, and any follow-up post and video I do, in their capstone as they deem appropriate.

References

- **Blog and video: Colby-Sawyer College Tai Chi Senior Capstone Project** http://tiny.cc/la5o1y

Below are websites my wife and I researched to practice Tai Chi at home for days we did not participate at the college.

- **Tai Chi for Beginners Video |Dr. Paul Lam | Free Lesson and Introduction**
  https://www.youtube.com/watch?v=hIOHGrYCEJ4 35-minutes
- **Learn Tai Chi 8 forms for beginners (English version) - Hong Kong Jackysum - 5 minutes**
  https://www.youtube.com/watch?v=0ye2tnrow_I
- **What is Tai Chi**
  https://taichiforhealthinstitute.org/what-is-tai-chi/

- **The Harvard Medical School Guide to Tai Chi** by Peter W. Wayne, Ph.D. with Mark L. Fuerst,
  2013 by Harvard Health Publication

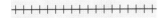

Four friends 60 + Winter Hike AMC Lonesome Hut

What does it feel like for four friends, all 60+years young in good physical condition to do a winter hike into Lonesome Lake Hut?

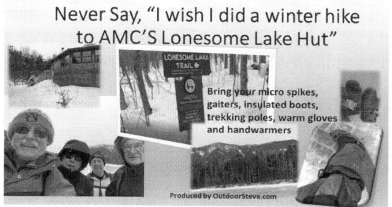

Figure 232 - Memories Lonesome Lake Hike

Grab your favorite beverage, relax, and enjoy the hike as Lennie, Joe, John and Steve hike from Lafayette Camp Ground uphill through woods to the Appalachian Mountain Club
(AMC) Lonesome Lake Hut. The temperature is in single digits, windy, and deep packed snow.

If you read about the Lonesome Lake Hut references you will see it is promoted as an easy hike for families. Well, I must admit it was a very challenging hike for us. The first hour was up – up – and up and we frequently paused to experience the Franconia Notch views, or as one of my companions suggested, "the views are an excuse to catch our breath". We added a stop to put hand-warmers in our gloves and mittens. The trail crisscrossed up the steep mountain through the trees and rocks, with the trampled trail sometime 1-foot in width embedded into the side of the hill. When you stepped off the trail, you could sink up to your thigh – and we quickly learned to stay on the snow packed trail.

How do we dress?

This winter weather demands we dress appropriately for very cold weather. We also need to decide, cross-country skis, snowshoes, or micro spikes? Given we are hiking uphill through the woods, that means XC skis are out. If we were the first hikers through 3 feet of snow, snowshoes would be our choice to keep us on top of the snow. However, we are not the first hikers on this trail, and the last week has resulted in hard-packed snow. Do we wear only insulated boots or micro spikes? Given rain last week on top of the snow, and we would be in single digit cold, we made micro spikes on our boots our choice.

Although Lonesome Lake Hut in the winter is self-service with sleeping accommodations, we planned only a day hike. Our uphill trip took just over one and a half hours to the hut. Our return downhill hike on the same trail was one and a quarter hours.

The below video is a celebration of Lennie's retirement.

About Lonesome Lake Hut

Lonesome Lake Hut's elevation is 2,760 feet with the 12 acre Lonesome Lake in its front yard. The hut is on the Appalachian Trail. The view from the hut provides spectacular views of the Franconia Ridge across pristine glacial Lonesome Lake and the nearby 4,000-foot peaks, including Cannon Mountain.

Lonesome Lake Hut is a 1.6 mile hike starting at Lafayette parking area ascending 950 feet. This is the westernmost hut of the eight AMC wilderness huts on the Appalachian Trail (AT) in the White Mountains of New Hampshire.

The below New Hampshire State Parks map is most interesting. You can see our trail in blue from Lafayette campground up to Lonesome Trail Hut (green). But this map has more ... you can identify the Franconia Ridge 4,000+ footers (Mt Layfayette, Mt Lincoln, Little Haystack, Mt Liberty) as you climb and descend Lonesome Lake Trail. Also, you can identify the

Cannon Balls and Cannon Mt mountains looking north from the porch of Lonesome Lake Hut

Figure 233 - View Lonesome Lake from AMC Hut

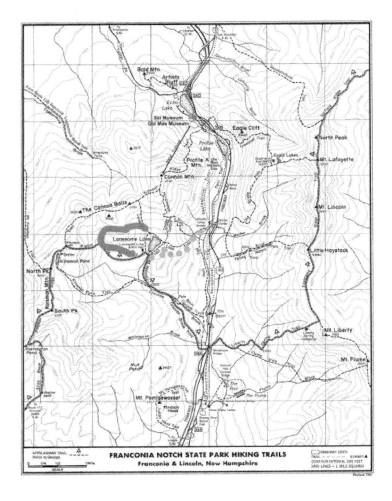

Figure 234 - Map AMC's Lonesome Lake Hut

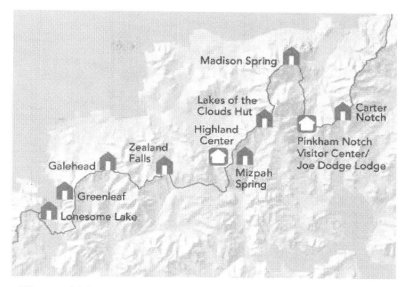

Figure 235 - Map of AMC Huts White Mountains, NH

References

- **Blog and video: Four friends 60 + Winter Hike AMC Lonesome Hut**
  http://tiny.cc/ok5o1y
- **Lonesome Lake Hut go to the AMC website**
  https://www.outdoors.org/lodging-camping/huts/lonesome

- **Franconia Notch State Park Hiking Trails**
  http://tiny.cc/np5o1y
- **New Hampshire State Parks** www.nhstateparks.org

++++++++++++++++++

" Everyone must do something. I believe I will go outdoors with family and friends."

A Winter Day on Perkins Pond

Figure 236 - Winter Day on Perkins Pond, Sunapee, NH
This video shares one winter day on Perkins Pond. On a snowy 10 degrees morning, we see the Isle of View. After a lazy breakfast, we walk through the woods on snowy trails. Later we clear a patch of ice near the island in preparation for a weekend of ice-skating.

On our legs, we wear gaiters for both hiking and working on the ice. The gaiters keep snow out of our boots and pants, provide a little extra warmth on a cold day, and keep the microspikes from snagging on our pants.

The red-colored microspikes we wear on our boots give us firm footing from slipping when both walking in the snow packed icy woods, and on the ice-covered pond.

A winter hike is educational with animal tracks in the snow bringing to life forest inhabitants that leave no trace in the summer. Later we snowmobile on the pond. Enjoy the **Reference** video.

Reference

- **Blog and video: A winter day on Perkins Pond**
  http://tiny.cc/0gbj1y

Ice Boating in New Hampshire

"Let's go ice boating!" It is a rare winter day in New Hampshire to have perfect ice boating conditions – meaning 2 inches or more of smooth ice with no snow coverage.

The temperature was 14 degrees. The ice had been frozen for the past month, and a few drilled holes showed the ice to be 8 – 10 inches thick – plenty of strength for ice boating – and smooth ice with no lingering snow.

Sailable ice is known in the sport as "hard water" versus sailing on liquid or "soft" water. Iceboats are strictly wind powered and need nearly snow-free smooth ice to sail.

The Homemade Iceboat

Dundee has many creative skills – and his iceboat reflects this.

Figure 237 - Dundee and His Handcrafted Iceboat

A Rare Opportunity

Ice boating can be a very unique experience. Once you get over the initial, "What am I doing here" feeling, you sense being one with the boat. You hear the wind in the sail and the rumble of the runners over the ice. Certainly, at 14 degrees, you must dress in layers for relative comfort.

Rare is the right ice boating conditions – sufficient ice – no snow – good wind – good weather – and not have to go to work! Smile.

Microspikes

Figure 238 - Microspikes – essential for walking on ice

The frequent crackling sound in the video is not the wind – it is the sound of microspikes as Steve walks on the ice. Microspikes offer serious traction on ice for walking and tasks such as pushing the iceboat.

See the below video and enjoy this unique experience – and even take an iceboat ride with Outdoor Steve.

Learn More About Dundee's Iceboat

Three 10" angle iron blades called "runners" support a triangular shaped wooden frame with a front steering tiller made from an old hockey stick. The blades are attached to the boat, one on each end of the rear cross plank and one at the fore end of the hull. The runner blade in the front is capable of rotation controlled by a tiller (the sawed off hockey stick). There is a backrest cushion seat in the middle for the driver.

Dundee drilled a sail posthole near the front of the boat. In the hole, he positioned the mast from his summer "Sunfish" sail boat. (A Force 5 or Laser sailboat mast will work just as well.) A rope is tied to the sail and used by the driver to control the sail.

The boat with sail weighs about 150 lbs.

Starting, Steering, and Stopping

The boat can be started by putting the boat sideways to the wind. You then pull onto the sail to capture the wind – and off you go.

The boat is steered with the hockey stick tiller to direct the front runner.

The driver pulls or releases the sail via the boom rope to angle the sail to catch the wind. The only seeming limitations to iceboat speed are windage, friction, the camber of the sail shape, strength of construction, quality of the ice surface, the level of skill, athleticism and fearlessness of the sailor. There are many styles of iceboats, but it is said, an iceboat of this style can go twice the speed of the wind, i.e., with a 20 knot breeze, your iceboat can reach a speed of nearly 40 MPH!

Tacking or coming about is a sailing maneuver by which a sailing vessel turns its bow into the wind through the 'no-go zone' so that the direction from which the wind blows changes from one side of the vessel to the other. The tacking method gets the iceboat up and down the pond. Catching the wind on an iceboat in the winter is exactly like sailing a sailboat in the summer.

Figure 239 - Ice Boating on Perkins Pond, Sunapee

References:

- **Video and Blog: Ice Boating on Perkins Pond**
  http://outdooradventurers.blogspot.com/2015/01/ice-boating-in-new-hampshire.html

- **Iceboat.org:** http://iceboat.org/faqiceboat.html
- **Tacking (sailing):**
  http://en.wikipedia.org/wiki/Tacking_%28sailing%29
- **Sailing:** http://en.wikipedia.org/wiki/Sailing
- **Ice Boating in New Hampshire - Bedford Community TV**
  http://tiny.cc/46y26x

Never say, "I wish I had visited the Ice Castle in Lincoln, New Hampshire

The Ice Castle is located on the west end of the Kancamagus Highway in the White Mountains of northern New Hampshire.

The Ice Castle website is http://icecastles.com/lincoln/. Below is a short video of our trip.

As I shared the above video among friends, I keep getting one inquisitive question on our Ice Castle visit. **"Will icicles fall on me?** Here is a picture I took looking up at hanging icicles as we roam in the Ice Castle:

Figure 240 - Inside of Ice Castle, Lincoln, NH

Below is the answer I copied from the Ice Castles website **Frequently Asked Questions**(http://icecastles.com/faqs/)

"There are several reasons why **Icicles at the Ice Castle** do not have these problems and do not fall like icicles attached to a roof:

- *Icicles at the Ice Castle are attached to ice. This means there is no weak point (i.e. a roof) limiting the strength of the structure.*

- *Connection points of icicles at the Ice Castle are proportional to the icicle. This means that the base of the icicle at the Ice Castle is the strongest because it is the largest in mass and diameter.*
- *There is no dark material at the base of all the icicles at the Ice Castle that will heat up and cause melting.*
- *When Icicles at the Ice Castle melt, they melt per the laws of nature. This means that the smallest parts of the icicle melt first and it will take more time for the ice in the center of the icicle to melt. On a warm day, the icicles will melt from the bottom up. The smallest parts of the icicles will drip and turn to slush. The slush at the end may fall in small pieces. Guests visiting on days where the temperature is sunny and above freezing will get dripped on, and occasionally small masses of slush will fall."*

We know icicles attached to roofs in New Hampshire may be dangerously heavy and knife shaped. You most assuredly do not want to be under a falling icicle. The FAQ explains roof attached icicles:
"Icicles attached to roofs almost always will fall. There are several reasons that Icicles attached to man-made structures will fall. Here are some of them:
The connection point of the icicles to the roof is inherently weak and it is usually not proportional to the icicle.

The connection point of the icicle (dark shingles) absorbs heat from the sun and causes that point to melt first.
The icicles usually fall when the weather warms up. The way it happens is that snow on the roof melts causing water to run past the small connection points of icicles causing melting at the base of icicles attached to roofs. The base of the icicle (which is usually smaller in mass, diameter, and width) melts faster than the large hanging portions of the icicles and the icicles fall."

Making Maintenance Ice

Figure 241 - Ice Castle Lincoln, NH

References

Blog and video: Never say, "I wish I had visited the Ice Castle in Lincoln, New Hampshire http://tiny.cc/et5o1y"

++++++++++++++++++

"Everyone must do something. I believe I will go outdoors with family and friends."

February and April Snowboarding and Downhill Skiing in NH and VT

Two Days at Mount Sunapee and One Day at Okemo Mountain

Figure 242 Mt Sunapee Trails
Blog and video: February and April Snowboarding and Downhill Skiing in New Hampshire and Vermont
http://tiny.cc/kc6o1y

Winter Hike - Carter Notch Hut on Appalachian Trail

My friend John called and asked me to join him on a winter hike into Carter Notch Hut. John's son Ryan would be hiking with a friend and John wanted to meet them at their overnight stay at the Appalachian Mountain Club hut located on the Appalachian Trail. John and I are life-long members of the AMC.

Mount Hedgehog – a warm-up hike

Figure 243 - Which Way to Mt Hedgehog?

To prepare for this 3.8 mile hike into the winter wilds of the snowy and icy White Mountains, John wanted to go to the White Mountain area a day earlier for a day hike.

On Friday morning we were at the Kancamagus Highway trailhead for the Mount Hedgehog (2520 ft.) loop trail.

The five mile loop trail was moderately difficult, meaning upward switchback trails, crossing small brooks, over and under a few downed trees across the trail, and a reasonable grade with only the final sections a bit steep and requiring climbing up and over granite ledges.

The AMC trail guidebook suggested this hike could be done in three hours. We did the loop in a respectable three and a half hours. We paced ourselves stopping every fifteen minutes or so to drink water and chew trail mix. As we approached the top, wind and cold caused me to don my winter gloves. We paused at the top for magnificent views of Mt. Passaconaway, the Presidential range and Mt Chocorua (see more on Mt Chocorua in the Summer section of this book).

Figure 244 - Can you see the Squalls of Snow Below Us?
Looking down from the peak over the tree-studded valley and north toward Mt Washington, we saw dark clouds blowing our way with squalls of snow beneath them – and we quickly picked up our pace, not wanting to be caught on the top of the mountain.

John took this picture from the top of Hedgehog and you can see the fast moving snow squall as a white-looking cloud spiraling to the ground in the valley and quickly heading our way.

The loop back to the trailhead was steep from the top and I could feel my quads aching. All in all, Mt Hedgehog was a good day hike and certainly helped prepare us for the next day's four mile hike into Carter Notch Hut.

Carter Notch Hut

Figure 245 - Carter Hut via Nineteen Mile Brook Trail

Carter Notch Hut, elevation 3,450 feet, is the most eastern of the eight AMC huts in NH. In winter the hut is self-service, meaning a caretaker stokes the wood stove at the hut from 5 pm until 9:30 pm (unless extreme cold dictates otherwise). Self-service includes self-cooking and hikers bring their own food and use the hut's utensils and gas stove for cooking.

Water Carried to Hut from Lake

Figure 246 - Drinking Water from Pond for Boiling

There is no running water inside Carter Notch hut in winter, but water is carried into the hut in five gallon jugs as needed for potable water (after boiling). Hikers share responsibility for getting the water through a hole in the ice from a lake near the hut.

Two bunk houses are separate from the hut and are unheated. The bunkhouses essentially provide bunk beds and protection from rain, snow, and wind. Temperatures may reach way below zero in the depth of winter, so a winter sleeping bag is advisable, if not mandatory, such as one rated to -20 degrees F and preferably even lower.

The Master Maine Guide I have often traveled with in summer adventures uses a bag rated for 35 degrees below zero whenever he ventures out into the North Maine Woods during the winter months on guided 5 day cross-country ski trips across Maine's Baxter State Park. Staying warm during the night makes your outing much more enjoyable. Being cold during the night not only saps your energy but leaves a bad taste in your mouth for ever getting out and enjoying those special scenic vistas and quiet solitudes that only a visit in winter can provide.

Figure 247 - Trekking Poles for balance and backpacks

John and I used trekking poles to reach the hut. Our poles were important for balance and saving our knees as we poled and stepped over and up on ice covered boulders. As we neared the Hut, the snow began to get deeper, maybe a foot or so in depth.

Figure 248 - John Crossed Over the Ice/Snow Plank Bridge

We crossed four wooden planked bridges of which one had obviously been washed out, most likely in last month's northern NH flood, and in its place was an eight inch ice covered plank. You will see our balancing acts in the video as we warily crisscross three to four feet above the waters of Nineteen Mile Brook and the mountain run-offs.

The Hut Experience

Very few people remain strangers at a wilderness hut. A winter hike to a hut offers a bond to each person there. We all got to the hut the same way, on foot.

Hut life offers a common denominator for camaraderie and a "Where are you from?" opener to sharing stories, asking strangers, now friends, to join a card game, and learning new games memorable to hut experience. Ryan taught us a game new to us, "Pass the Pigs" – and soon we had an exciting game going.

We shared conversation with hikers from Littleton, NH, Maine, and Canada. "He who passes through these doors are strangers no more".

For dinner that night at the Hut, John made a delicious entrée of chicken potpie. Ryan made an apple crisp that was to die for! The next morning's breakfast was at the hands of John with bacon and eggs enjoyed with hot coffee and chocolate to prepare us for the hike out.

Ryan and Peter decided to hike the Carter Dome and Mount Height trail back to the trailhead. This is a strenuous hike, but the rewards are magnificent views from the barren peaks of four-thousand footers. John and I returned via Nineteen Mile Brook Trail with a bit of regret for not bringing our crampons. John and I took the Nineteen Mile Brook Trail back to the Trailhead on Route 16.

Enjoy the video as John and I never have to say, "We wish we had spent a winter night at AMC's Carter Notch Hut."

Blog and Video of Hike to Carter Notch Hut

- **Blog: A Winter Hike to Carter Notch Hut**
  http://tiny.cc/co6o1y

- **Video of Visit to Carter Notch Hut via Nineteen-mile Trail** http://tiny.cc/qp6o1y

---

A New Hampshire Winter Sleigh Ride

One winter on a snowy February day at Dixville Notch, New Hampshire, I had the pleasure to interview sleigh ride owners Dennis and Tina Willey. The Willey's took Cathy and me " over the hill and dale" on a romantic sleigh ride at The Balsams Grand Resort wooded property.

Figure 249 - A Sleigh in the North Country of NH

Figure 250 - North Country Cross-Country Ski Trail

Video Reference A Winter Sleigh Ride and XC Ski

- **Blog and Video: A Unique New Hampshire Winter**
  http://tiny.cc/rv6o1y

Never say, "I wish I had enjoyed unique winter experiences in New Hampshire."

The Outdoors as a Daily Component of Life

Regret for the things we did can be tempered by time. It is the things we did not do that is inconsolable – Sydney J. Harris

Eclectic Sharing

Don't judge those who try and fail, judge those who fail to try. – Unknown

Community Emergency Response Team (CERT) Search and Rescue Training

Community Emergency Response Team (CERT) is your neighbors, friends, and co-workers - a collection of community volunteers that want themselves and their town to be prepared in the event of an emergency or disaster.

I am a member of Bedford, NH CERT and the Londonderry, NH ALERT (**A L**ondonderry **E**mergency **R**esponse **T**eam). Their missions are the same in maintaining a trained, dedicated group of volunteers:
1) Assist their communities and its public safety departments in times of need.
2) Serve as a community source for education on emergency preparedness and prevention.
3) Recruit and regularly train volunteer citizens.

Search and Rescue Training (SAR)
I have taken advantage of search and rescue training offered by both the Londonderry ALERT and Bedford CERT teams. The types of their search and rescue training I have been part of include:

- Wilderness line search to locate missing persons or objects (SAR).
- Orienteering – how to read and use a compass and/or map.
- Red Cross Advanced First Aid certification including CPR, splints, bandaging and moving patients.
- Amateur Radio (Ham Radio Operators)

Below are briefs of selected CERT and ALERT training exercises, which blend the above learned skills for SAR, map and compass, first aid, and ham radio communication.

Line Search and Rescue Training at Musquash Conservation Area, Londonderry, NH

Figure 251 - Searchers Prepare for a Winter Line Search

Under the general name of Line Search and Rescue training, the ALERT and CERT teams teach and practice four general steps:

1. **Locate the victim using Line Search Method:** Maintain a line of searchers arms-length apart. Walk straight ahead (as best in a wilderness environment). A person behind the line guides the line to maintain a straight line of search. Left and right end line searchers insure line is staying together. Move through assigned search area looking for signs of distress or hint of missing person or item. See **Figure 231 Searchers Prepared for a Winter Line Search**.
2. **Access the victim.**
3. **Stabilize the victim** by treating any life-threatening injuries.
4. **Transport the victim** to a safe area for professional assessment.

There is a safety dress inspection to be sure all line searchers have dressed appropriately for the condition of the environment. If someone is unequipped they cannot participate. For example, in winter weather a check is made to insure no cotton clothing is worn. No jeans are allowed. Best fabrics are polypropylene, silk or wicking fabrics on the skin layer. Then layers of wool and fleece. Proper footwear, hydration, and a snack are needed for an extensive excursion. No sneakers or sandals allowed.

For this exercise, a body (dummy) is placed within an area and the line search team assigned a section. When the dummy is found, the team proceeds to provide first aid and then transports the "person" to a safe area.

Figure 252 - First Aid Administered On-site

Training was at the Hickory Hill Road trailhead of the Musquash conservation area off High Range Rd. in Londonderry.

Map of Musquash Trails, Londonderry, NH
http://tiny.cc/iyd75x

Orienteering Training by Londonderry NH ALERT at Beaver Brook Association, Hollis, NH

Figure 253 - Getting a Compass Bearing

There is a Beaver Brook Orienteering Course laid out among the trails where we can apply map and compass skills and off trail navigation. Each attendee must bring their own compass and a GPS device (if they have a GPS), and print a copy of the trail maps and orienteering course. http://tiny.cc/zy8o1y
.

The Londonderry ALERT conducted the training. We combined hiking with a few hours of navigation training with map and compass. We practiced how to read a map, determine a compass bearing, and how to follow that bearing to 9 different points identified on the orienteering map.

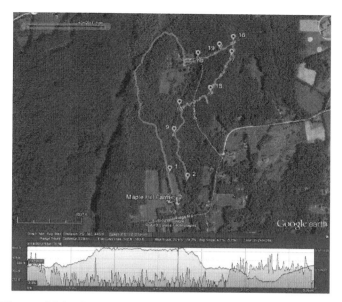

Figure 254 - Our Beaver Brook Association GPS Route

Amateur Radio – Ham Radio Operators

Both CERT and ALERT offer instruction in using hand operated radios. Members practice their radio skills in the SAR exercises. Ham operators have in common a basic knowledge of radio technology, operating principles and regulations, demonstrated by passing an examination for a license to

Figure 255 - Ham Radio

operate on radio frequencies known as the "Amateur Bands." These frequencies are allocated by the Federal Communications Commission for use by hams from just above the AM broadcast band all the way up into extremely high microwave frequencies.

Learn more about Amateur Radio at **New Hampshire American Radio Relay League Section WebSite** http://www.arrl-nh.org/

Map and Compass Training

The UNH Cooperative Extension provided a two hour class on the compass and topographical maps. The presenter emphasized Map, Compass, and Pacing, so, "you will know where you are."

Pacing: We began the class by going outdoors. The instructor used a measuring tape to lay out a 100 foot distance and had each member of the class count their normal paces back and forth to get the average number of steps. He wanted us to "memorize forever", that, in my case, 40 paces closely approximates 100 feet. *The Lesson: In the woods with a map, knowing distance can be critical.*

Maps: Here are a few map items discussed:
- Go to the Internet and you can get both a map and an aerial .photo (e.g. https://www.google.com/maps
- You can also get topographical maps on the Internet
    - http://topomaps.usgs.gov/
    - http://www.digital-topo-maps.com/
- Understand how to read topographical maps http://tiny.cc/49c75x

Compass tips:
- Declination – in New Hampshire, magnetic North is 16 degrees west from true North. Declination is zero degrees on the west side of the Great Lakes
- The compass arrow is ALWAYS correct!
- Box the arrow - aligning the compass needle north
- You can see about 100 feet in the woods of New Hampshire. Sight on a rock or a tree.
- Good to know measures:
    - 1 mile is 5,280 feet
    - 1 acre is 43,560 sq. ft. or approximately 208' x 208'

Compass and Map References (One Page Briefs from Appalachian Mountain Club):
- How to Choose a Compass http://tiny.cc/bwt75x

- **Don't Get Lost: Finding your way there and back**
  http://tiny.cc/put75x
- **How to read topographical maps**   http://tiny.cc/2xt75x

Figure 256 - SAR Bedford CERT & Londonderry ALERT

References:
- **Too learn more about Bedford CERT**
  http://www.bedfordnhcert.org/
- **To learn more about Londonderry ALERT**
  http://www.londonderryalert.org/
- http://www.extension.unh.edu
- **Map of Musquash Trails, Londonderry, NH**
  http://tiny.cc/iyd75x
- **Beaver Brook Association Orienteering Map**
  http://tiny.cc/s0c75x
- **Beaver Brook Association Trail Map**
  http://tiny.cc/g4c75x
- New Hampshire American Radio Relay League Section
  WebSite http://www.arrl-nh.org/

CERT Net Control Training on Search and Rescue (SAR)

The Bedford, New Hampshire Community Emergency Response Team (CERT) (http://www.bedfordnhcert.org) includes members trained as ham radio operators. To be a ham radio operator a person must pass an Amateur License exam conducted by the Federal Communications Commission Universal Licensing System. Upon passing the Operator Technician exam a person receives their unique call sign, such as KC1BJI.

Figure 257 - Hand Held Radio

An amateur radio net, or simply **ham net**, is an "on-the-air" gathering of amateur radio operators. Most nets convene on a regular schedule and specific frequency and are organized for a particular purpose, such as the Bedford CERT hams use a directed net to maintain and practice their radio communication skills. A formal, or *directed* net, has a single *net control station* (NCS) that manages its operation for a given session. The NCS operator calls the net to order at its designated start time, periodically calls for participants to join, listens for them to answer (or *check in*) keeps track of the roster of stations for that particular net session, and generally orchestrates the operation of the net.

I was the NCS person under the tutelage of Ric, Communications Officer of Bedford CERT.

Each week's agenda has a check-in with each person using their Federal Communication Commission assigned call sign. They also identify the type of power used (such as fixed station commercial power, fixed station emergency power, mobile or Handheld). Announcements and training education are part of this exercise. The announcements are items of interest to the CERT members (for example upcoming CERT training sessions and meetings).

Tonight's training session was conducted by Steve. The training focused on two related searches and rescue (SAR) topics of particular importance in rural New Hampshire:

- The Hiker Responsibility Code
- Ten Essentials of Hiking

The Hiker Responsibility Code was developed in 2003 as a joint program between the White Mountain National Forest (WMNF) and the New Hampshire Fish and Game Department (NHFG). The Hiker Responsibility Code was needed when the number of WMNF search and rescue occurrences were increasing because of negligence and ignorance on the part of wilderness hikers. The costs of air searches and rescues, along with the safety risk to SAR volunteers, were unacceptable.

The Hiker responsibility code is intended to ensure that hikers are equipped with the gear, knowledge, and experience they need to have a safe journey into the wilderness.

Knowing the **Hiker Responsibility Code** and the essential equipment and knowledge (**Ten Essentials of Hiking**) may save your life in the wilderness, it could also save you being charged thousands of dollars for YOUR search and rescue. The New Hampshire Fish and Game Department is authorized to sell voluntary Hike Safe Cards for $25 per person and $35 per family. People who obtain the cards are not liable to repay rescue costs if they need to be rescued due to negligence on their part in the wilderness. The card is valuable for anyone hiking, paddling, cross country skiing or engaging in other outdoor recreation. An individual may still be liable for response expenses if they are deemed to have recklessly or to have intentionally created a situation requiring an emergency response.

People who possess a current New Hampshire Fish and Game hunting or fishing license, or a current registration for an off-highway recreational vehicle, snowmobile or boat, are already exempt from repaying rescue costs due to negligence.

Follow the Hiker Responsibility Code
(http://hikesafe.com/)
You are responsible for yourself, so **be prepared:**

- **With knowledge and gear.** Become self-reliant by learning about the terrain, conditions, local weather, and your equipment before you start.
- **Leave your plans.** Tell someone where you are going, the trails you are hiking, when you will return and your emergency plans.
- **Stay together.** When you start as a group, hike as a group, end as a group. Pace your hike to the slowest person.

- **Don't hesitate to turn back.** Weather changes quickly in the mountains. Fatigue and unexpected conditions can also affect your hike. Know your limitations and when to postpone your hike. The mountains will be there another day.
- **For emergencies.** Even if you are headed out for just an hour, an injury, severe weather or a wrong turn could become life threatening. Don't assume you will be rescued; know how to rescue yourself.
- **Share the hiker code with others.**

Voluntary **Hike Safe cards** are available at http://www.wildlife.state.nh.us/safe/index.html.

Figure 258 - Hike Safe – It's Your Responsibility

Ten + 2 Essentials when Hiking
http://www.outdoors.org/recreation/hiking/hiking-gear.cfm
1. Map
2. Compass
3. Warm Clothing
4. Extra Food and Water
5. Flashlight or headlamp
6. Matches/fire starters
7. First aid kit/repair kit
8. Whistle
9. Rain/wind gear
10. Pocket knife
11. Contractor type 40- gallon trash bags
12. Duct tape

Notice the above **Ten + 2**. Most discussions deal with the ten essentials to carry, but personally, I also carry two trash bags and duct tape.

The below two White Mountain National Forest signs say it all when it comes to relating the **Hiker Responsibility Code** and the **Ten Essentials**.

Figure 259 - Signs to Hike Safe say it all

For those interested in more Search and Rescue information, see my Blog post **Community Emergency Response Team (CERT) Search and Rescue Training** http://tiny.cc/wa8e7x).

References

1. **For more information on Bedford NH CERT**
   http://www.bedfordnhcert.org
2. **Blog: Community Emergency Response Team (CERT) Search and Rescue Training** http://tiny.cc/wa8e7x
3. **Follow the Hiker Responsibility Code** (http://hikesafe.com/)
4. **Ten Essentials of Hiking**
   http://www.outdoors.org/recreation/hiking/hiking-gear.cfm
5. **New Hampshire Fish and Game Department (NHFG)**
   http://www.wildlife.state.nh.us/safe/index.html
6. **Federal Communications Commission Universal Licensing System**
   http://wireless.fcc.gov/uls/index.htm?job=home
7. **Amateur Radio Net**
   https://en.wikipedia.org/wiki/Amateur_radio_net

Places to Play in Northern New England

"Nothing preaches better than the act"
- Benjamin Franklin

For all sad words of tongue or pen, the saddest of all are these: "It might have been."
- Whittier, Maud Muller

The choice of outdoor sports in northern New England is nearly endless--ranging from hiking to biking to running to skiing to snowshoeing, etc. There are thousands of mountains, lakes, and rivers here. With its four-season weather, an outdoor enthusiast never runs out of a sport to "play".

The Internet is a significant tool for locating outdoor sporting events, organizations, instruction, and blogs. Searching on keywords such as, "Hiking in Vermont," "Cross-country skiing in New Hampshire", and "Paddling in Maine," reveals hundreds of websites. Enter "outdoor sports in northern New England" and you will see hundreds of sites to choose from and a variety of events in which to participate, learn, and never say, "I wish I had…".

Discussions with other outdoor enthusiasts will reveal personal sports of interest and places to visit and experience.

Outdoor enthusiasts with interest in triathlons can go to www.trifind.com, pick a state, and find a triathlon club, races, and coaches.

Most organizations, such as the Appalachian Mountain Club (AMC), Catamount Trail Organization, Peabody Mill Environmental Center (PMEC), and Audubon Society have websites with email lists and e-newsletters which routinely announce upcoming events.

Some organizations have diverse group activities. For example, the Appalachian Mountain Club (AMC) has an "Over 55 Club", a "Young Members Club", and "Singles Club. The Peabody Mill Environmental Center (PMEC) has daily wooded trail hikes and snowshoeing, and monthly "fireside chats" where experienced outdoor enthusiasts share their knowledge through presentations and demonstrations. The Catamount Trail Organization schedules group skis. The Granite State Wheelmen and the Green Mountain Bicycle Club offer group rides and workshops.

The New Hampshire website http://northeastmultisport.com/ offers a variety of triathlon oriented Clinics and Events for its members to improve performance as well as to encourage teammate camaraderie: bike time trials on summer evenings; winter fun runs for members to enjoy non-competitive group runs; transition clinics for tips and practice to minimize the time from swim to bike, and bike to run; and early morning open water group swims at local lakes.

Join organizations and clubs dedicated to encouraging and providing outdoor sports and recreation, to never have to say, **"I wish I had researched, investigated, and visited places to play in my community."**

Inter-State Opportunities for Outdoor Play

Northern New England has many scenic, relaxing, and exciting inter-state outdoor opportunities for all seasons. Certainly, waterways, forest trails, and mountains have no sense of state boundaries. Here are five non-profit organizations offering unique places to play in northern New England.

The **Northern Forest Canoe Trail**, **Appalachian Trail**, **Androscoggin River**, **Great North Woods**, and **Maine Island Trail** are highlighted.

The Northern Forest Canoe Trail (NFCT)

http://www.northernforestcanoetrail.org/ links the waterways of New York, Vermont, Québec, New Hampshire, and Maine.

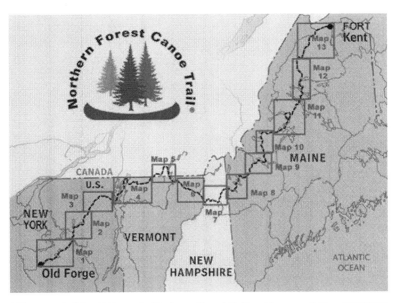

Figure 260 - Map defining the 13 Sections of the NFCT

The NFCT is a long-distance paddling trail connecting the major watersheds across the Adirondacks and Northern New England. The Trail links communities and wild places offering canoeists and kayakers a lifetime of paddling destinations within the 740-mile traverse across New York, Vermont, Quebec, New Hampshire, and Maine. The NFCT includes flat and whitewater paddling, poling, lining, and portaging (62 portages totaling 55 miles).

A visit to the NFCT can be a day-trip, an overnighter, weeks, or months. As hikers do sections of the Appalachian Trail, so do paddlers do the NFCT. You can put-in and take-out at any appropriate location. The NFCT organization is an excellent resource for your trip planning with web links and contact information.

Scheduled regional presentations by NFCT staff are on the NFCT website. See the **Plan a Trip** link at the site for guidebooks and maps. **https://www.northernforestcanoetrail.org/**

The sections to date of the NFCT that friends and I have paddled:

- The Allagash Wilderness Waterway, ME
- Lake Umbagog, Androscoggin River, NH/ME
- Lake Memphremagog, VT/ Quebec
- Connecticut River, NH/VT
- Moose River and Attean Pond on the historic "Moose River Bow Trip," ME
- Umbazooksus Stream, ME
- Clyde River – Island Pond to Pensioner Pond, VT
- Long Lake to Village of Saranac Lake, NY

Posts and videos on my blog for section travels on the NFCT are:

- **Paddling the Northern Forest Canoe Trail Section 2: Long Lake to Village of Saranac Lake**
  http://tiny.cc/ma9o1y
- **Three Generation Paddling in Saranac Lake**
  http://tiny.cc/pke01y
- **Paddling the Northern Forest Canoe Trail Section 6: The Clyde River - Island Pond to Pensioner Pond**
  http://tiny.cc/z88o1y

- **Four Days in Northern New Hampshire with Family and Friends Hiking, Paddling, Tenting, and Moose Sighting**. http://tiny.cc/zb9o1y
- **Exploring Lake Umbagog – a Gem in the Great North Woods** http://tiny.cc/xc9o1y
- **Paddling the Allagash Wilderness Waterway** http://tiny.cc/gd9o1y
- **Senior Hiker Magazine** https://www.seniorhikermagazine.com/

Appalachian Trail

The AT in northern New England passes through Vermont and New Hampshire and has its northern terminus at the summit of Mt Katahdin in Maine.

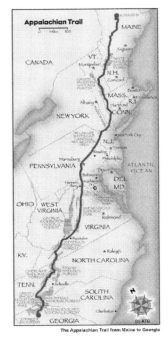

Figure 261 - Map of Appalachian Trail from Maine to Georgia

I recommend two references to get started with understanding the AT:

1) **The Appalachian Trail Conservancy**
   (http://www.appalachiantrail.org/)
2) **The Appalachian Mountain Club** (AMC)
   (http://www.outdoors.org/)

The Appalachian Trail Conservancy

(http://www.appalachiantrail.org/) preserves and manages the Appalachian Trail – ensuring that its vast natural beauty and priceless cultural heritage can be shared and enjoyed today, tomorrow, and for centuries to come.

The Appalachian Mountain Club (AMC)

(http://www.outdoors.org/) promotes the protection, enjoyment, and understanding of the mountains, forests, waters, and trails of the Appalachian region.

Paddling with the AMC

The New Hampshire Appalachian Mountain Club Paddlers website (http://www.nhamcpaddlers.org/) is an excellent resource for places to paddle in New Hampshire. The Paddlers welcome beginners, intermediate and experienced paddlers, 16 and older, who are interested in safely paddling and having a great time.

The Paddlers site has a free e-mail sign up for monthly notices of Paddler happenings. The emails include weekend and weekday trips, items for sale by members, such as canoes, kayaks, racks, and other paddling equipment and Paddler events.

The Paddlers website encourages you to join the Appalachian Mountain Club (http://www.outdoors.org).

The NH AMC Paddlers website "Places to Paddle" link (http://www.nhamcpaddlers.org/m_content/places.htm) has directions and descriptions to over twenty lakes, river, and marsh paddling trips, all in New Hampshire. Other links include, "Upcoming Trips" where you can join others for scheduled trips.

The NH AMC Paddlers have canoe and kayak paddles weekday evenings throughout the summer.

Four of my Blog posts on the AT:
- **Dreaming the Appalachian Trail** http://tiny.cc/rf9o1y
- **Springer Mountain, Georgia - Southern Terminus of the Appalachian Trail** http://tiny.cc/fg9o1y
- **A Mid-week Trek to Tuckerman Ravine** **http://tiny.cc/1g9o1y**
- **Hiking Mount Chocorua - White Mountain National Forest** http://tiny.cc/bi9o1y

Androscoggin River

The Androscoggin River is a major river in northern New England. The Androscoggin headwaters are in Errol, New Hampshire, where the Magalloway River joins the outlet of Umbagog Lake. It is 178 miles long and joins the Kennebec River at Merrymeeting Bay in Maine before its water empties into the Gulf of Maine on the Atlantic Ocean. Its drainage basin is 3,530 square miles (9,100 km2) in the area.

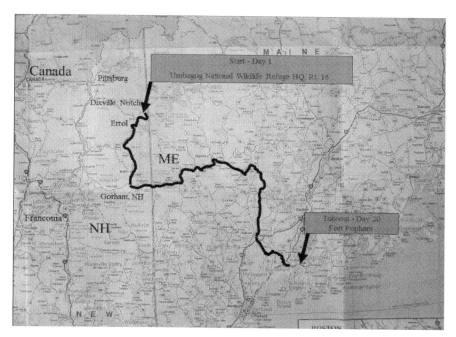

Figure 262 - Map - The Androscoggin River Source to the Sea

The Androscoggin River Water Shed Council
http://arwc.camp7.org/ offers protection, history and paddling
groups on the Androscoggin River. The ARWC sponsors the
Source to the Sea Trek http://arwc.camp7.org/trek.

Outdoor Steve has paddled twelve sections of this Trek and you
can find numerous descriptions of this fabulous paddle at
http://www.outdoorsteve.com/. For articles and other stories such
as **Androscoggin River Source to the Sea Canoe and Kayak
Trek** visit http://tiny.cc/tk9o1y

Interestingly, 19 miles of the Androscoggin River headwaters are
also part of the Northern Forest Canoe Trail (NFCT)!

Great North Woods

Northern New Hampshire, also known as the Great North Woods
Region, is the official state tourist region located in Coos County.
This area includes Northern New Hampshire, bordering Northeast

Kingdom Vermont, and unincorporated townships in the northern and northwestern part of Maine

Ten Things to do in the Great North Woods of New Hampshire
http://tiny.cc/4l9o1y

Great North Woods Online
(http://greatnorthwoodsonline.com/)

Enjoy the Great North Woods
http://www.outdoorsteve.com/_pdffiles/23_21Jun08_Great_No
rth_Woods_NewHampshire.com.pdf

A Hike to Table Rock, Dixville, New Hampshire
http://outdooradventurers.blogspot.com/2010/07/hike-to-table-
rock-dixville-new.html

Maine Island Trail (MIT)
http://www.mita.org/

The MIT begins at Maine's coastal border with New Hampshire and ends in Machias, Maine, with an additional collection of two islands in Passamaquoddy Bay and the New Brunswick region of Canada.

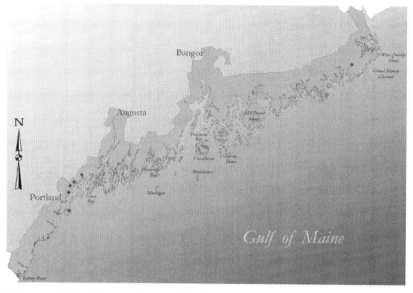

Figure 263 - Overview of Maine Island Trail

The Maine Island Trail is a 375-mile-long waterway along the coast of <u>Maine</u> that connects approximately 200 islands and mainland sites available for day visits or overnight camping. The trail is maintained by the <u>Maine Island Trail Association (MITA)</u>.

Through partnerships with the State of Maine, as well as land trusts, non-profit organizations, and generous private property owners, MITA ensures access to these sites for visitors in kayaks, sailboats, motorboats, and other watercraft. In exchange for access, MITA members agree to visitation guidelines set by the island owners and provide a wide range of stewardship services including island monitoring and management by trained volunteers with organized regional island cleanups each year.

The FAQ on Site Reservations

The only sites (public or private) on the **Maine Island Trail** that take reservations are Warren Island, Swan Island (Kennebec), Cobscook Bay State Park, and Butter and Burnt Islands. All others are first-come-first-served (FCFS). Details are in the member Trail Guide. The MITA advises people to have a backup in mind and arrive with time to spare. However, the fact is that except for peak weekends on smaller most favored islands, people typically do not report difficulties. There are a lot of islands to go around!

See the **Outdoor Enthusiast** blog post on Steve's Maine Island Trail trek.

- **Blog and video: Places to Play in Northern New England** http://tiny.cc/jn9o1y
- **Blog: Sea Kayaking and Camping on the Maine Island Trail** http://tiny.cc/qo9o1y

New Hampshire

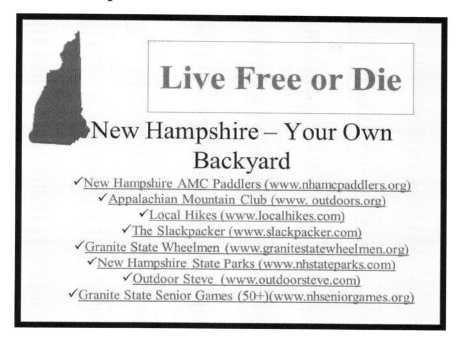

Live Free or Die

New Hampshire – Your Own Backyard

✓New Hampshire AMC Paddlers (www.nhamcpaddlers.org)
✓Appalachian Mountain Club (www. outdoors.org)
✓Local Hikes (www.localhikes.com)
✓The Slackpacker (www.slackpacker.com)
✓Granite State Wheelmen (www.granitestatewheelmen.org)
✓New Hampshire State Parks (www.nhstateparks.com)
✓Outdoor Steve (www.outdoorsteve.com)
✓Granite State Senior Games (50+)(www.nhseniorgames.org)

Figure 264 - Places to Play in New Hampshire

Below is but a small sample of paddling opportunities in southern New Hampshire.

- Veterans Park on Naticook Lake in Merrimack NH http://bluetoad.com/display_article.php?id=1127713

- Nashua River. A good put-in behind Stellos Stadium.

- Great Turkey Pond, west of Concord NH.

- Lake Massabesic, East of Manchester NH in Auburn. Many put-ins. Try the Auburn Town Beach.

- Hopkinton Lake west of Concord NH. Exit 5 Rte 89 west of Concord NH

- Hoit Road Marsh north of Concord NH

- Glen Lake in Goffstown, NH

- Dubes Pond, in Hooksett, NH. GPS has it at 270 Whitehall Road, Hooksett, NH

- McDaniel's Marsh. Exit 13 from I89 to East Grantham. Route 114 to West Springfield. North on George's Hill Road. At the intersection of Bog Road and Georges Hill Road. The Marsh put-in is directly across from Bog Road.

- Merrimack River. Many put-ins and take-outs. One put-in is the boat ramp behind Franklin High School. Paddle 10.5 miles to Boscawen ball fields takes about 4-5 hrs.

Hiking Year Round

- **Welch-Dickey Mountain Trail**
  A unique scenic loop over and around the summits of two mountains. Great view of the Mad River in Waterville Valley. A 4.5-mile scenic loop. In wet weather, the bare rock may be slippery, so this is a summer hike. Located I-93 via Exit 28.
  http://tiny.cc/9yoruw

Figure 265 - Welch-Dickey Trail

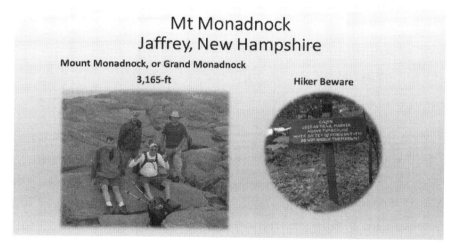

Mt Monadnock
Jaffrey, New Hampshire

Mount Monadnock, or Grand Monadnock
3,165-ft

Hiker Beware

Figure 266 - Relaxing Atop Mt Monadnock

- ○ Mount Monadnock Southwestern, NH
  3,165-ft. Mt. 40 miles of maintained foot trails. 100-mile
  views into all six New England states. Second most
  frequently climbed mountain in the world, after Mount Fuji
  in Japan. http://tiny.cc/xr9m5x

- o **Mount Willard Trail**, White Mountains, NH
  The Mount Willard Trail leads from the AMC Crawford Notch Visitor Center to scenic ledges overlooking Crawford Notch. Two hour round trip hike. Just fine for a family day hike. http://tiny.cc/kqoruw

- **Cohos Trail**
  The Cohos Trail is New England's newest long-distance hiking route, extending 162 miles through the woods and mountains of northern New Hampshire. Most likely, you will have a day of absolute solitude. http://www.cohostrail.org/

- o **Mount Kearsarge**
  Directions: Wilmot and Warner, New Hampshire. From Route 89 take Route 11. 2,937-foot summit, length: 2.2 miles http://tiny.cc/naan5x.

Figure 267 - The Peak of Mt Kearsarge

Local References with Nearby City Trails & Maps

- Where best to look for "places to play" than in your backyard. I entered keywords, "Bedford New Hampshire hiking trails" into my browser, and saw http://www.traillink.com/city/bedford-nh-trails.aspx. The site easily identified:

  - Bedford Biking Trails

  - Bedford Running Trails

  - Bedford Walking Trails

  - Nearby City Trails & Maps

- Entering keywords, "Sunapee New Hampshire hiking Trails" I found: http://www.lakesunapeenh.org/discover/hiking-lake-sunapee-region/. This reference includes New London, NH and a list of organizations and town conservation commissions which offer trail maps that include hiking opportunities within the Mt. Kearsarge/Lake Sunapee region:

Maine

Maine – Your Own Backyard

✓Maine Island Trail (www.mita.org)
✓Maine Outdoors (www.maineoutdoors.com)
✓Local Hikes (www.localhikes.com)
✓The Slackpacker (www.slackpacker.com)
✓The Loonsnest (www.loonsnest.biz)
✓Outdoor Steve (www.outdoorsteve.com)
✓Maine Senior Games (50+) (www.mainesrgames.org)
✓Granite State Senior Games (50+)(www.nhseniorgames.org)

Figure 268 - Places to Play in Maine

Hiking

- **Hiking in Maine** is a favorite reference for hiking trails. Maine has a variety of hiking options available. Paths can be above tree line, trails meander through cool pine forests, and trails run along Maine's rugged coast.
  http://www.maineoutdoors.com/hiking/hike_info_trails.shtml

- **Slackpacker.com** provides access to informative Maine hiking websites. Hikers post comments on their personal hiking experiences, thus making research easier to get "an upfront and personal" sense of the trails difficulties.
  http://www.slackpacker.com

- **The Local Hikes** provides information on local hiking opportunities in all areas of the United States. You can find a preferred trail by selecting your metro area, browse the available hikes, or by using the search feature to find the paths closest to your home or office. Volunteer hikers contribute reviews on this site. http://www.localhikes.com

Canoeing and Kayaking

- **The Loon's Nest** specializes in wilderness river canoe trips. The site has all forms of outdoor wilderness recreation and is a wealth of information about animals; (hear the four major loon calls); has a fantastic photo gallery of outstanding outdoor pictures taken in all seasons from summer canoeing, sailing, and hiking to winter xc skiing and snowshoeing; as well as many beautiful photographs of Maine's wildlife caught in their natural habitat.
http://www.loonsnest.biz

The Maine Island Trail
http://www.mita.org

See the narrative earlier in this section for Maine Island Trail with over 200 islands to "play" on.

Northern Forest Canoe Trail
http://www.northernforestcanoetrail.org/

The NFCT has over 345 miles traversing some of the most scenic, remote, and rugged landscapes that Maine has to offer.

Vermont

Freedom and Unity

Vermont – Your Own Backyard

✓Vermont Living (www.vtliving.com)
✓Green Mountain Club(www.greenmountainclub.org)
✓Local Hikes (www.localhikes.com)
✓The Slackpacker (www.slackpacker.com)
✓Catamount Trail(www.catamounttrail.org)
✓Frozen Bullet(www.frozenbullet.com)
✓Vermont Senior Games(50+)
(www.seniorgames.org/stategames.htm)

Figure 269 - Places to Play in Vermont

Hiking

- **Vermont Living** and **Trails.com** websites have trails and backpacking areas
http://www.vtliving.com/hiking/
http://www.trails.com/toptrails.aspx?area=10012

- The **Long Trail** was built by the **Green Mountain Club** between 1910 and 1930. The Long Trail is the oldest long-distance trail in the United States. The Long Trail follows the main ridge of the Green Mountains from the Massachusetts-Vermont line to the Canadian border as it crosses Vermont's highest peaks.
http://www.greenmountainclub.org/

Canoeing and Kayaking

- **Vermont Living** is an excellent site to locate places in VT for canoeing and kayaking. Some of Vermont's most notable canoeing and kayaking waterways include the Connecticut River that serves as the border between VT and NH, the Batten Kill in southeastern VT, the Lamoille which crosses Vermont's northern region, the Missisquoi in the northwest corner, and the Winooski and White Rivers in north central Vermont http://www.vtliving.com/canoeing/index.shtml.

- **Northern Forest Canoe Trail** has over 170 miles in Vermont and Quebec http://www.northernforestcanoetrail.org/

- **Outdoor Enthusiast: Never say, "I wish I had…":** 2009, 2014, and 2016 hard copies and e-books have more Vermont "places to play".

XC Skiing

- **The Catamount Trail (CAT)**

  The CAT traverses approximately 130 miles of public land including the Green Mountain National Forest, Vermont state land, and town-owned parcels. The CAT divides into 31 sections. The CAT is appropriate for a broad range of skiing and snowshoeing abilities. http://www.catamounttrail.org

Biathlon
- The United States Biathlon site is an excellent reference to biathlon events and places for instruction and training. http://www.teamusa.org/US-Biathlon.aspx

- Go to **How Stuff Works** to learn more about the rules and basics of the biathlon. http://tiny.cc/vp9o1y

Senior Games

Encouragement of healthy lifestyles certainly includes outdoor activities for senior athletes. **The National Senior Games Association (NSGA)** is a not-for-profit member of the United States Olympic Committee dedicated to motivating senior men and women to lead a healthy lifestyle through athletics.

NSGA is an umbrella for state organizations across the United States that host State Senior Games or Senior Olympics. States have both winter and summer athletic games for female and male athletes over 50 years young. Games may include triathlons, cycling, race walking, track and field events, swimming, road races, pistol shooting, archery, and golf. Some states do paddling, downhill skiing, and cross-country skiing.

New Hampshire, Maine, and Vermont are very active both within their states and in national competitions.

- o **National Senior Games Association**
  http://www.nsga.com/
- o **Granite State Senior Games**
  http://www.nhseniorgames.org/
- o **Maine Senior Games**
- o https://www.smaaa.org/maineseniorgames/
- o **Vermont Senior Games**
  http://www.vermontseniorgames.org/

So What Do You Do Now?

This Northern New England section is but the tip of the iceberg to locate areas of opportunity, clubs, organizations and fellow outdoor enthusiasts. Local activities are often in our backyards, and are found by looking in newspaper sections for Outdoor Activities or simply by Internet searching for events in your city or town.

Use Google keywords (such as orienteering, biathlon, bicycle clubs, snowshoe, etc) to search for locations and sports of interest near you.

Conditioning

The beginning of this book offers **How to be an Outdoor Enthusiast.** It describes a process of physical fitness and how it directly relates to mental preparation and health. Knowing one is not in shape makes it very easy to rationalize postponing an adventure. Moreover, without proper conditioning, we make our companions and ourselves susceptible to injury and failure. Physical fitness complements mental fitness.

The Commitment

A significant part of adventure commitment is preparation. The weeks and months before an event are critical. Preparation starts with a mental walk-through of the happening itself and working backward to create a check-off list of things to do and when they are done. Do you need campsite reservations? Must you register for the event?

Registration is part of the commitment. When there is a delay, the promise is not there. A registration commitment can include hotel, campsite or airline reservations.

There must be a plan to reach the required level of physical conditioning. Physical conditioning for a triathlon is much different from white water rafting. Most adventures need stamina, endurance, and quick recovery from cardio exertion. A daily running routine - four to five days a week - provides a baseline conditioning level from which specific conditioning exercises, such as upper body weight training, can support an adventure, such as kayaking and canoeing.

We need to know the extremes of weather we may encounter and plan accordingly. The expected weather conditions may mean gathering specific weather-related clothing, food, and medical supplies.

Other preparations, such as for hiking, may include developing skills for map and compass reading. If we work backward from the event, this should provide us with a checklist upon which to plan our preparations (i.e. scheduling our time, equipment needs, and training). If you are going winter camping, you might practice by sleeping in your backyard to learn what you need for comfort. It is far better to know your sleeping bag does not support cold weather camping when you are in your backyard rather than to discover this when you are in the middle of the mountains miles away from your car!

Let's continue to play. To enjoy "play", one must be physically ready. Hence, exercise is a key enabler of "play." Knowing I have tried, for me, is as important as winning. Regardless of success or failure, my participation provides a never-ending sense of achievement. To me, partaking at any level is more rewarding than observation of the highest level.

We need to commit never to say, "I wish I had". Once we have done that - and this could be a financial commitment such as membership in the YMCA outdoor club or the Appalachian Mountain Club. Then we need to commit to a training program.

We also must recognize it is OK to finish 485th out of 501 entered in a race. It is also OK to finish last! After all, someone has to, why not me! We need to realize that we do not need to go to the other side of the world to achieve a dream. If we merely look around we can see roads for running, lakes for paddling, and woods and mountains for hiking. Even our backyards can supply the opportunity for the "snow-cave" you might want to build.

A nice thing about being an outdoor enthusiast is that most activities cost only our time. A small investment in a canoe, running shoes, bicycle, or cross-country skis will be enough to give us a lifetime of adventure. We often need to look no further than magazines and newspapers to see these opportunities.

If I have shared my story appropriately, I have both encouraged and supported your enthusiasm for a daily outdoors commitment, made you crave your own "beginnings", and have given insights into new outdoor activities and places to go.

I will thus have achieved my goal of helping others become an "Outdoor Enthusiast" and forever make "Outdoor Play" a component of their daily life.

Never say, "I wish I could find an outdoor activity close to my home."

The Beginning

- *In the long run one hits only what they aim at. Therefore, though they should fail immediately, they had better aim at something high.*– Henry David Thoreau, Walden
- *Give yourself permission to dream - Randy Pausch*
- *The journey of a thousand miles begins with one step. - Miryamoto Musashi*

Introduction

This last section of the book is my beginning. I add it here to encourage individuals and family to make the outdoors a part of their daily lives. And here is my start.

Have you ever thought about sleeping overnight in a snow cave, built by yourself, in the middle of the wilderness? How about running a marathon? What about canoeing through white water, visiting a Shaker museum, or attending a lecture on alternative medicine therapies?

Some folks call these outdoor experiences 'play'. If "play" is defined as the choice made to take a course of action based on the rewards of participation and getting a perspective that can only come from 'doing', outdoor adventures are indeed "play". Many folks, both adults and children, do not play enough. "Play" is personal and winning is of no importance. Outdoor play should be a daily component of life.

"I wish I had..." is an expression people often mutter as they rationalize their regret for not having done something. Is it better to have tried and failed than never to have tried at all? Absolutely! Indeed, physical limitations may relate to achievement, but sometimes we erect personal barriers of embarrassment, reluctance, and other self-administered hurdles.

Try an outdoor trek. Take a chance and peek into a side of outdoor life observed by only the few that do take the opportunity. How do you describe how beautiful Allagash Falls is at dawn? You can view a thousand pictures, but until you exit your tent at first light, you will never honestly know what it is like to experience the sun popping into the sky.

The Opportunity: The Torn Achilles Tendon

Any enthusiast needs to start somewhere. My outdoor emergence began while in an injured state: I had been a couch potato absorbed with the pressures and problems of work and felt no commitment to outdoor activities other than mowing the lawn. Taking time to 'smell the roses' was not a scheduled event, and surely visiting museums was not a part of my lifestyle.

Maybe the outdoor enthusiasm all started with the "good fortune" of tearing my Achilles tendon. Coincidentally, this injury came two years after I had completed my Master's dissertation in Management Engineering with a thesis entitled, The Achilles Tendon as an Indication of Thyroid Function. Years later the anatomy studies required to understand the function of the Achilles tendon helped me to accept my injury.

My injury came as I was playing basketball in a pick-up game. I had positioned myself for a clear outside shot and was in the process of shooting the ball. Suddenly I felt as if someone had hit me in the back of my ankle. I dropped to the floor and turned around expecting to see who had taken my legs out from under me. Nobody was there. The damage is done – my Achilles tendon had ruptured.

The healing process progressed erratically. A noticeable indentation appeared where the tear had taken place. The medical opinion was that surgical treatment would not necessarily help. Medical professionals told me there was a fifty-fifty chance that the tendon would tear again. I was determined to prove them wrong.

The First Mile

One day, about a year after my injury, I decided to do something about my twenty-five-pound weight gain, a perpetual "tired feeling", and a general lack of exercise. I went down to my cellar and rummaged through old boxes of shoes. I found my ten-year-old ankle-high Army combat boots and reminisced to myself about boot camp and its daily mandate to hit the road running.

Figure 270 - The Army Combat Boots

The boots were intact, though the leather was a bit stiff and needed a softener. I ignored the tautness and proceeded to lace them tightly in the hopes of ensuring protection for my "healed" Achilles tendon. Now was the time to determine if exercise would free me from my couch.

I went outside and ran - maybe limped is a better word - a distance of two telephone poles. Even though I was breathing heavily and sweating profusely, it felt good, despite the sensitivity of a now sore tendon.

The next evening, I climbed back into my combat boots — this time with a determination to exceed the previous day's run of two telephone poles. I lumbered, limped, and puffed to achieve the distance of three telephone poles. My quest had begun.

Figure 271 - Walk-Run Between Two Telephone Poles

Daily, after work, I continued extending my distances one pole at a time. My Achilles tendon threat to tear again concerned me, but I fervently decided against returning to inactivity.

Initially, my running goals are measured in those ever-present telephone poles. However, after two weeks, I abandoned this strategy, and I reset my goals to reach the end of my street without stopping - about a third of a mile. By the end of the third week, not only had I achieved my objective, but I also turned around and began running back home.

I now had a dream that one day - maybe, just maybe - I could jog around my neighborhood block. I measured the distance with my car and determined the loop was exactly a mile. Each evening I came close to completing the neighborhood loop, but exhaustion resulted in walking before I died. Five weeks had elapsed since my emergence from the couch. Each day at work, I would picture myself accomplishing the mile. Every evening I would start, determined to run the one-mile route, only to end up walking.

During week six, I had a feeling that this was to be my time, my day. I saw my house in the distance and was having no difficulty breathing. I had no thoughts about my Achilles, and until this moment, I was merely concentrating on an issue at work. I suddenly realized I was less than four telephone poles from my quest. With extreme joy shared with no one but myself, in what seemed to be mere seconds, my goal was now history. Sucking air with sheer exhaustion, I stumbled into my backyard overjoyed with the thrill of victory.

I ran this one-mile loop - usually six days a week - for nearly two years with no thought of extending my distance. Indeed, other outdoor challenges, such as biking, canoeing, hiking, and kayaking, were not even a consideration.

One day I read in the local newspaper about a seven-mile running race. The race was four weeks away. I dared to think that perhaps I could finish this distance. I began extending my daily run, and in one week I was able to make my one-mile loop twice! I had doubled my distance in only one week. I set my next goal at four miles and accomplished it within two weeks. It was now time for me to assess myself against other athletes. I submitted my entry form.

The appropriately named Freedom Trail race was a seven-miler at the University of Massachusetts campus at Dartmouth. My pre-race jitters were compounded by second-guessing myself as to whether I should even be here. I had never participated in any official running race before, and I had visions of being elbowed and trampled by a pack of passionate runners.

I overcame this distress by positioning myself at the back of the mass of lightly clad runners who were stretching, jumping up and down, trying to relieve their nerves while waiting for the start of the race.

I had anticipated all participants to be thin, athletic, and young. Instead, I encountered all types, men and women, young and old, and people in various degrees of physical shape - thin, fat, short, tall, and plump. Naively, I thought that I surely would finish in front of the older and overweight athletes.

I got a quick education when the race official fired the starter's gun. Not only was I holding up the rear, I was yards behind the last runner. I began to have thoughts of not finishing, and worse, becoming lost as the runners in front of me continued to get further ahead. At the second mile marker, a few runners were still in sight. I resigned myself to complete the race.

At the five-mile marker, I was running side by side with a young woman who appeared to be in her late twenties. We were the last two racers. I was sure she had slowed down to let me catch up because I knew I was in no condition to speed up. We talked about our jobs and our families - anything to help forget the pain we were both experiencing.

With about a mile to go to the finish line, she suggested we pick up our speed. Unfortunately, I was already at my maximum speed. Off she went, with my blessings, and I was the last runner to cross the finish line. There were only two people at the finish line - my encouraging and excited mother and the timer. My mother would not let the timer leave until I had finished!

The immediate aftermath of this seven-mile "triumph" was that I could not sit down! Every time I tried to bend my legs and lower myself to the ground, my hamstrings would begin to cramp. Indeed, I was a "winner", but I now had to pay the price of my personal best distance.

The outcome of this story was that I had run seven miles! Little did I know this experience would be the beginning of a lifetime enjoyment of outdoor challenges.

Yes, a benefit of physical conditioning was my weight loss of nearly forty pounds. I felt different both physically and mentally. The seat of my pants was floppy and my face lost its fullness. Friends began to ask if I was "sick". I had to buy new suits. I felt great being asked all these personal questions!

A Family Revelation

My outdoor enthusiasm carried forth to my family as we began to participate together in outdoor fun and exercise. My wife and I regularly walk and run together. A summer night can find us kayaking or canoeing on the lakes of New Hampshire.
My two sons and my grandchildren are essential components of my daily outdoor life. As a family, our activities include hiking, canoeing, kayaking, running, and morning and evening moose sightings.
Let me relate a father-son-revelation that occurred while hiking with my son Timothy when he was a teenager. Hiking provides an opportunity to share experiences on an adult level and leave behind the typical parent/child relationship of the home environment.
Hiking in the mountains requires reliance upon your partner that breaks down parent/child barriers that develop from the routine of daily life. At home, the parent sets an example and provides the child with an opportunity to learn. This pattern is adjusted in the wilderness.
Tim and I lumbered along the Appalachian Trail planning to spend the night at the Mizpah Spring hut, one of the eight White

Mountain huts maintained by the New Hampshire Chapter of the Appalachian Mountain Club. Just as we reached the peak of Mt. Franklin, the weather quickly changed and it began to rain. The rain became heavy, the sky grew darker, and suddenly we were engulfed in a torrent of rain. Driving rain pelted us, and thunder and lightning roared and crackled all around. It was only three o'clock in the afternoon and yet it was nearly pitch dark. It was a strange and awesome sensation. The top of Mt Franklin is entirely ledge and rock, and we knew we were in a dangerous position - on top of a mountain and without shelter. It was a bizarre and scary feeling as we stood there in our rain suits, rain pouring off our faces and our features illuminated sporadically by flashes of light. An unbelievable sensation of excitement and strength came over me. I felt I united with the earth and the elements and had all their power at my command. At the same time, I feared that this angry and violent deluge would overcome us, and we might not survive this encounter. I suddenly knew before Tim or I died - and it could have happened at any moment - I wanted Tim to know how much a part of me he was. I had an unbelievable urge to hug Tim, kiss him, and tell him how much I loved and admired him - and so I did! It was a moment I still remember today - hugging my teenage son with all my strength and telling him how much he meant to me.

Meanwhile, thunder cracked, and lightning illuminated the darkness, filling the surrounding countryside with shadows and ghostly sensations. We were in the middle of an enormous storm, terrifying, yet beautiful at the same time.

Tim responded to my hug and kissed with the same embracing closeness and finality that I did. I could feel his strength and our oneness as he embraced me for what could be the last time.

Then, just as suddenly as the storm had come, it was gone. The sun came out as if to say, "Together you have seen the light and felt your courage and unity." We were wet and shivering, but thankfully we were without injury. We continued our journey.

Tim had avoided my invitations to learn in the past - that is what it seemed to me. Our stay at Mizpah Spring showed I was wrong. The volunteer naturalist at the hut led an evening tour to learn about the birds, animals, shrubs, and trees native to this high altitude habitat. With obvious interest, Tim asked many questions of the naturalist.

A sunrise tour for a different aspect of the habitat was scheduled. Given the previous day's tiring adventures, I never expected to see Tim. We went to bed that night, exhausted.

At 4:45 AM, my watch alarm went off. I quietly whispered to Tim I was getting up for the tour. I left the bunkroom pleased at Tim's delight with the previous evening. To my surprise and much pleasure, who should appear at the morning walk-about but Tim! On that hike, Tim and I experienced a bonding we still discuss today. We depended on each other in a death-defying situation. I saw that he is caring, self-reliant, and levelheaded under pressure. He has a thirst to learn. I have come to recognize these qualities and more as we have shared the joys, challenges, and revelations provided by hiking trips along the Appalachian Trail and many other "Outdoor Play" adventures.
If the facts are known, the awakening and growth in maturity was solely mine.

So, What Do You Do Now?

If tearing my tendon made me recognize the limits of my knowledge and appreciation, the pain and struggle of recuperation were worth it.

This book shares short stories of outdoors and wilderness knowledge gained through personal involvement. It can be a guidebook of places and events to play. It is not a traditional how-to or you-should kind of book, but life stories for individuals and families to motivate them to make the outdoors a daily part of life.

These stories are meant to stimulate the reader to enjoy the outdoor world and the people around them. The message is, "It is okay to listen to your inner calling." You will never regret that you did not experience the renewal and fulfillment venturing into the outdoors may provide. Simply being in an audience as others perform and share their views cannot satisfy an eager human being. The motivation is to "get off the couch," and not let others dictate what you know or do.

I do not want to pretend I am a philosopher of what life is about, or a preacher of outdoor activities, nor a non-conformist in life. Henry David Thoreau appears to express my approach to outdoor living. In Walden he said, "I went to the woods because I wished to live deliberately, to front only the essential facts of life, and to see if I could not learn what it had to teach, and not, when I came to die, discover that I had not lived. I wanted to live deep and suck out all the marrow of life…"

My Achilles tendon has never completely regenerated to its former strength. I sometimes have a noticeable limp at the end of a long day on my feet, but the tendon has no pain and does not hinder any of my outdoor activities.

I mention my past injury because some people use self-imposed physical and mental barriers, and say, "I wish I could do physical exercise and outdoor adventures similar to yours, but I tore my Achilles tendon" (or whatever physical ailment they have). Other "wish I could" reasons I hear are, "I am too old", "I am way out of shape," and "I do not know where to start." Hmm, guess they did not read the section in this book, **How to be an Outdoor Enthusiast.**

Be aware - outdoor enthusiasm includes family revelations. As I learned more about myself when hiking with Timothy and Shaun, so did I see my sons become mature and responsible adults. My sons and I have done numerous canoeing and kayaking trips and have sat beside campfires talking about life, ambitions, and family issues.

My wife Cathy and I regularly walk, hike, camp, and paddle together. Most important are the conversations we have on our family, finances, and other life issues.
Never say, "I wish I had made the outdoors a part of my daily life."

Figure 272 - "Everyone must believe in something. I believe I'll go outdoors with my family." – S. Priest

Table of Figures

Books by Stephen L. Priest

- • **Outdoor Play "Fun 4 4 Seasons" Volume II**
  Amazon.com e-book and Hard Copy
- • https://www.amazon.com/dp/B0190XCFWI/

 ISBN 978-0-9850384-3-4

- • **Outdoor Play "Fun 4 4 Seasons" Volume I**
  Amazon.com hard copy and Kindle e-book
- • https://www.amazon.com/Outdoor-Play-Seasons-Stephen-Priest-ebook/dp/B00C2G20HQ/

 ISBN **978-0-985-03840-3**

- • **Outdoor Enthusiast: Never say, "I wish I had …"**
  Amazon.com Hardcopy and Kindle e-book
  https://www.amazon.com/Outdoor-Enthusiast-Never-say-wish-ebook/dp/B004S7EZLQ/

 ISBN 1440438404

- **Avoiding Injuries: Great Tips From Master Outdoorsman Steve Priest**
  Hard Copy Amazon http://tiny.cc/v10j1y

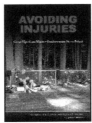 ISBN 9781440438455

Community Television Outdoor Documentaries by OutdoorSteve

Steve's below **Community Television Outdoor Documentaries** are available for community and non-profit organizations by **Bedford Community Television (BCTV)** at **603-472-8288** and http://www.bedfordtv.com/:

√ **Three Generation Paddling in Saranac Lake** http://tiny.cc/h8wm1y
√ **ROWING through the eyes of a beginner** http://tiny.cc/c9ow6x
√ **Winter in New Hampshire is More Than Downhill Skiing** http://tiny.cc/t9ow6x
√ **Knife Edge Trail to Baxter Peak, Maine** http://tiny.cc/oapw6x
√ **Ice Boating in New Hampshire** http://tiny.cc/zapw6x
√ **Robert Frost's Apple Picking Time in New Hampshire** http://tiny.cc/0bpw6x

√ **Ocean Kayaking in the Deer Isle Region of the Maine Coast – Stonington to Isle au Haut** http://tiny.cc/6cpw6x

√ **Northern Forest Canoe Trail, Section 2, New York** http://tiny.cc/fdpw6x

√ **Northern Forest Canoe Trail, Section 6 Clyde River, Vermont** http://tiny.cc/4dpw6x

√ **Making an Ottertail Paddle** http://tiny.cc/pepw6x

√ **Four Days in Northern New Hampshire Paddling and Moose Sighting** http://tiny.cc/kfpw6x

√ **Goffstown Pumpkin Weigh-in and Regatta** http://tiny.cc/jgpw6x

√ **Re-using Outdoor Hand warmers** http://tiny.cc/8apw6x

Online access to the documentaries can be found at http://www.OutdoorSteve.com and http://outdooradventurers.blogspot.com/

"Everyone must believe in something. I believe I'll go outdoors with my family and friends." – S. Priest

About the Author

Stephen L. Priest lives in Sunapee, New Hampshire with his wife Catherine, his partner outdoor enthusiast. He has two adult sons, Shaun and Timothy, who also serve as his outdoor playmates. His grandchildren, Madison and Carson, and daughter-in-law Christine, are in many of Steve's short stories.

Steve has a B.S. in Engineering from the University of Massachusetts (Amherst, MA), and a master's degree in Operations Research from the University of Rhode of Island (Wakefield, RI). He has served as a healthcare administrator specializing in information systems, and authored two healthcare management information systems textbooks. He has been an assistant professor of information systems at Daniel Webster College (Nashua, NH) and an adjunct professor at Saint Joseph's College of Maine. Steve is the author of six outdoor guidebooks, and is a producer of community television outdoor documentaries. Steve has served in the U.S. Army.

Visit **OutdoorSteve.com** and **Outdooradventurers.blogspot.com** for more of Steve's outdoor guidebooks and documentary videos.

Notes

Outdoor Play "Fun 4 Seniors" Volume III

Made in the USA
Middletown, DE
13 November 2022